D0544914

SANDWELL LIBRARIES

I 1825549

Collected memories of a bygone era

Best Loved Tales
of the Countryside

David & Charles

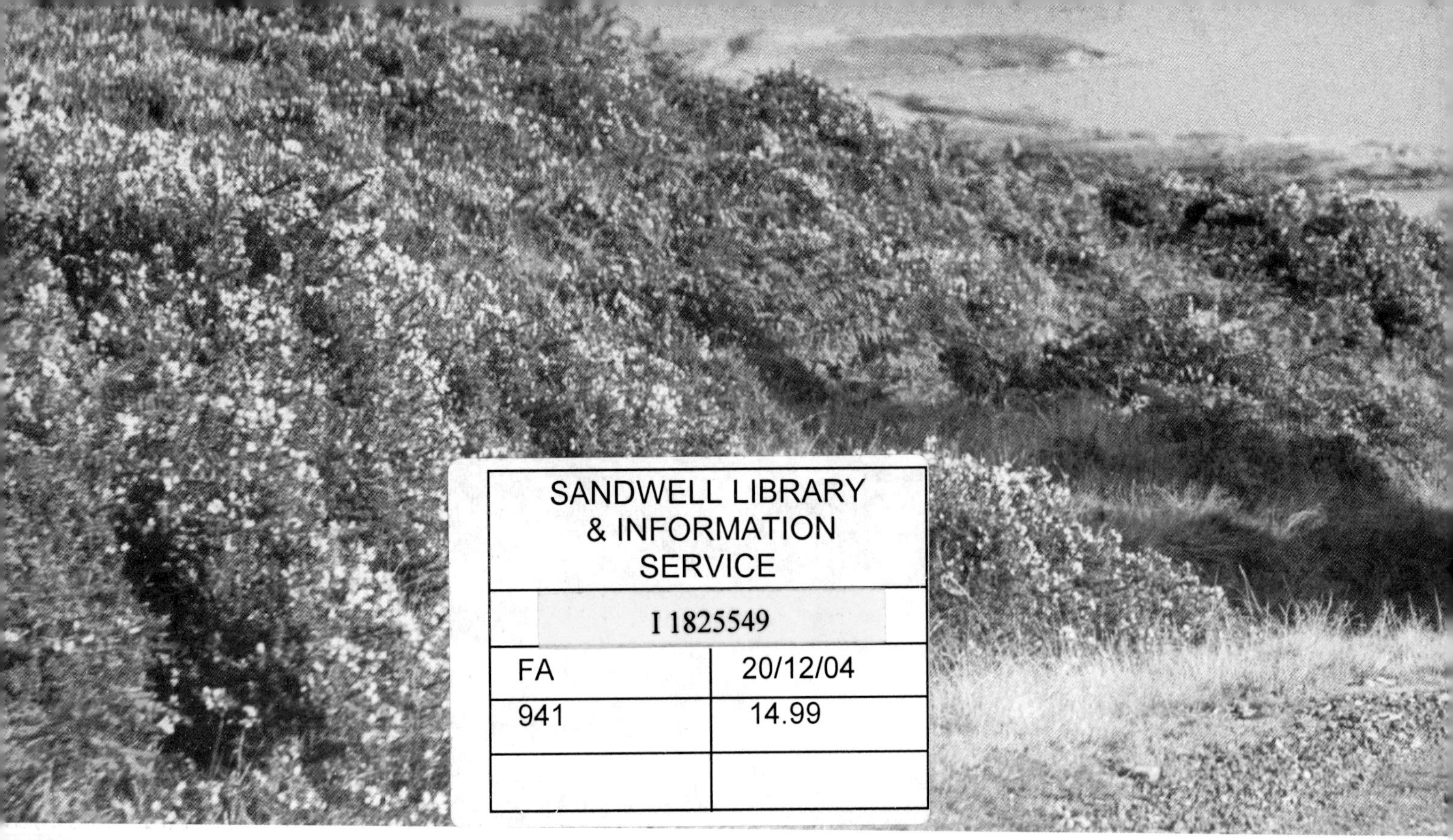

SANDWELL LIBRARY
& INFORMATION
SERVICE

I 1825549

FA	20/12/04
941	14.99

A DAVID & CHARLES BOOK

First published in the UK in 2002
First paperback edition 2004

Copyright © John Humphreys, Tom Quinn, Brian P.
Martin, Euan Corrie, Jennifer Davies, Lousie Brodie,
Jean Stone, John Bailey, Valerie Porter 2002, 2004

Distributed in North America
by F&W Publications, Inc.
4700 E. Galbraith Rd., Cincinnati, OH 45236
1-800-289-0963

The authors have asserted their right to be identified as
authors of this work in accordance with the Copyright,
Designs and Patents Act, 1988.

All rights reserved. No part of this publication may be
reproduced, stored in a retrieval system, or transmitted,
in any form or by any means, electronic or mechanical,
by photocopying, recording or otherwise, without prior
permission in writing from the publisher.

A catalogue record for this book is available from the
British Library.

ISBN 0 7153 1458 0 hardback
ISBN 0 7153 1732 6 paperback

Printed in China by SNP Leefung
for David & Charles
Brunel House Newton Abbot Devon

Visit our website at www.davidandcharles.co.uk

CONTENTS

INTRODUCTION

The countryside holds memories for us all, some drawn from visits to relatives or from family holidays taken in childhood, some are the recollections of a life lived in a rural area. Our encounters with country ways and our meetings with the people who worked the land and served in its communities, provide a sense of the colourful tapestry that makes up life in the British countryside.

The nature of daily life far from the city – its gentler pace, its close-knit villages, and even the sometimes tough conditions – has produced a wealth of characters with a rich store of tales to tell. The gamekeeper, the pub landlord, the thatcher and the local vet all have stories that offer an insight into their lives and those of their families and friends. This compilation gathers the very best of these tales from a wide range of countryside characters.

For all its diversity and interest, the world described in these pages is on the brink of disappearing forever. Country life has been altered almost beyond recognition by the introduction of mechanisation and improved communications. The gatherers of the tales in this book made it their goal to seek out the true country people, those that could give first hand recollections of a way of life that is all but gone, and as such these stories stand as an important record of a bye gone age. There is no better way to immerse ourselves in the richness of the countryside's past than to share these recollections.

King of the Norfolk Poachers

East Anglia

KING OF THE NORFOLK POACHERS

The biography I Walked by Night written by Lilias Rider Haggard uses the words and the curious spelling of an old Norfolk poacher to tell of an eventful life recalled in lonely old age. Lilias Rider Haggard was the daughter of the creator of Allan Quartermain, the great African hunter, hero of King Solomon's Mines. Her imagination was fired by the ancient poacher, now in his old age, who had lived a lawless life in the woods and fields of old Norfolk. Wisely she used his words and guessed at his spelling to give us an authentic record.

Sent to Norwich prison when twelve years old, convicted of taking a rabbit with the evidence against him suitably embroidered, loathed by keeper and landowner alike, the 'King' was able still to carry on his calling, suffering uncomplainingly some fearful beatings but not incapable of dealing out the same medicine.

This poacher's tale tale is a charming, moving and sometimes amusing record of hard and bygone times.

The Seed is Sown

I stayed at school till I was thirteen years of age, but duren that time wen I was a boy about nine year old some thing hapened. I was with father in the garden, it was winter time, and snow on the ground. Well without a thought he shewed me were a hare had been eaten his plants off. I made up my mind wen I saw that that I would get her.

There was a big trap hangen up in the shed, it had hung there as long as I remembered. I got it down wen father was gone, and sit the trap in the snow. Wen I come home from school the next morning of cors the first place I went to was to look at the trap, and you bet I was something pleased to find the hare there. I verry sone beat the life out of her and carried it to Mother. She near had a fit at what I had done, and carried it upstairs and put it under the bed.

As soon as father came home I went to tell him, I had not got far with my tale before he caught me by the coller and gave me the soundest floggen a boy ever received. He thought to stop me from playen those tricks in futur, but it seem that the seed was sowen by that hare, and it did not take long to germate.

Not long after I rember well me and another Boy was goen up a hedge and we found some snars. Of cors I had to make shure how they were put and then we took them up, and not many days after that I tried my hand at that game. I rember well the next morning taken two hares.

Stitched Up

In the village there was large amount of comon land, of corse it was enclosed as there were plenty of rabbitts there and I sone got to work snaren them. Some kind frend gave me away and wen I went one morning there was a Police man and a Keeper there waiten for me. They did give me a chance of getten away with [getting rid of] the rabbitts in my hands, but they swore I had some in a bag. As a matter of fact I never saw any in the bag till they shewed me some.

Well of corse they sumoned me and to make the case as bad as they could they told a lot of lies as well. Wen it came to it the Justice of the Piece sentenced me to a Months hard Labour wich I did at Norwich Castle.

In those days if a lad did a bit rong it was Prison for him, now he is given a chance as a first ofender. Dear Reader, it was hard lines to send a Boy to Prison for killing a rabbitt. No doubt the Maderstrates thought to cure me with a lesson, especially as the Police had painted me so black to them. Be that as it may, I know they soured me to the Laws of the Land by that treatment, though there is no telling if any man would go a diffrent way to what he has in the end. I always was a belever in Fate.

Keeper Bested

There was a verry clever keeper come to the next village about this time, and he used to boast that he had forty hen pheasants under wire. He knew all about my Job, and he used to tell People he would get me befor the year was out. Of corse I sone got to know that he had the birds there. He used to talk a lot and tell People that no one could get at them as he had a dog tied up and an alarm gun set.

It was not long before I had hatched a plan. I got a chap to go to him and ask if he had any ferrits to sell and told him to keep his eyes open and look round to se were the gun was fixed. He did and brought me back word of the exact tree the gun was screwed to.

Well first of all I set to work to find a market as I had made up my mind to get them birds and sone I found one about four miles away. The next thing to do was to get a bitch in use wich I did and took with me and let her run wich is an old trick and verry useful wen you have a dog to deal with, I soon found the gun and put that right and then cut a hole in the wire and got evry one of them birds. I did not do that job alone but two of us did – we got safe away to the road and the birds were at there new home befor they were missed.

Of course the rout was out and a lot of enquiries were made and they came and serched my Place but as there were neither Birds nor Feathers they were lost to know what to do. I got just five pounds for them Birds that trip.

A Bag of Rabbitts

There were a Clever Chap and he got thorns and all the Busshes he could colect, and made Burrers for Rabbitts on a medaw. Then he boght a lot of tame rabbits and got some wild ones to run with them – in fact they Bread verry fast. Well he was goen to have all the Publicans and Shop keepers down on Boxing day to turn the place over and he stood to make a bit out of it. He watched this place and the Rabbitts verry carefully, but a day or so befor Christmas we got

bussy and went and put the nets round that field and scooped the lot. Of corse they all come as arranged and turned the Place over but the game was gone, and that chap had a good bit to say.

I got the creddit for it as I did for evry other Job at that time, wether I was in on it or not but as the Rabbitts were at Lynn, that fell through.

A Bad Beating

I was in a wood one night and had had a few shots wen I walked into four Keepers. Of corse I knew I was beat that time. I had not a chance, and was willing to give in but they knocked me about with sticks and kicked me most onmercifull. Then they got a cart from the farm nearby and took me to the lock up and left me.

The next morning I was nearly Dead, so bad that the Police had to send for the Doctor and wen he had looked at me he ordered me to be taken to Lynn Ospitall. I had a verry bad cut head and Brused Boddy. I stayed there for a fortnight

and wen I was able to get about and got my Discharge, a Policeman was waiting for me. Well wen it came to it the Keepers swore that I had put up a terrible fight – thretned to shoot them and all that. The Judge did not beleve them, but as I was Poaching I had to get it, but he let me off with twenty one days and told the keepers that they had behaved verry cruele to me. I was sent back to Norwich – to the new Prison on Mousehold this time but they gave me no task there as I was still verry sore. I think the judge had some thing to do with that.

Well the Head Keeper got the sack … he should not have allowed the other ones to have knocked me about as they did, I supose they thought they were getten some of there own back on me for all the tricks I had played them, but that never stopped me.

Revenge

The 'King' is returning with his friends from a live pigeon shooting match where he had won the double breech loading section. On the way cycling home, they spotted a pheasant roosting in a tree.

No sooner seen than it was dead, and that started us off. I suppose we all had a merry time and were verry well pleased with ourselves, anyways we soon got bussy in the wood.

That was all right but things bein what they were we were not as careful as we should have been and I expect we made a bit of a racket. Two keepers must have heard us and they come along and was on us befor we knew. One of my mates sone laid one of them out and I had the pleasure of stoppin the other one. He hapened to be the man as had treated me so bad befor, and as by that time we was well in, I did not stop to think or lose the chance of payen some of the score back that I owed.

Well the Game was up for me then, and I knew I must get away as quick as I could or they would be on to me as I was thinking we had hurt both them keepers verry badly and were in for a lot of trubble soon as they was found. So I got to the nearest town and into the train for the North of England before many hours were past.

Nightsight

Years ago we used to use a sight of this kind. Cut a pair of ears out of a stuff piece of leather and use it on the muzzle of a gun – so it look like rabbitts

ears on the end.
Wen the Poacher could see the bird between the ears he was shure of his kill but since then the Eleumintaed sight is much more used and the four point ten gun. I have tried it with a lot of success. The gun in the old days was a muzle loader with the Barrells cut off to eighteen inches and as small a bore as we could get, mostly sixteen bore.

Lamb Stew

I had lerned how to make my owen nets, and I sone had plenty of them and a pair of lurchers and I knew well how to use both. I rember one night I was out and set a net at a gate and sent my dogs to hunt the field. It turned out that there was lots of lambs in it which I did not know, and the dogs scattered them in all directions. One, I am sorry to say ran at the gate and Broke its neck, which was unfortunate – but me being done, me and my chum was rather pussled to know what to do with it so he suggested we should take it to his house which we did. We sckined it and Burried the skin the same night a mile from home. Strange to say that lamb was never missed, at least if it was we never herd of it.

A Haul of Partridge

The rearin season soon came round again and I got to know that they had reared a large number of tame partridges not far from my place. There was a chance for me, and with a little spyen and some enquirs, I sone made out were they were feeden. The night before they came into season, my mate and me took the net and dragged a large medaw and caught one hundred and sixty, I believe it was, Of corse they were missed and they came to me stright away, but the birds were in Norwich by that time, so I had the laugh of them again.

Hieding

I have hid and seen the Keepers go past me many a time. On one ocation I was in a wood at Whaton and three keepers were looking for me.

I had killed a bird within a few yards of them. While they were looking for me I got out of the wood and shot all the way home. Of corse it is a useless job looking for one man in a wood wen it is dark, he have only to lay down or stand still and let those that are looken pass him.

In a genrall way the keepers are a lot more excited than the Poacher. I have often smiled to myself wen I have got away to think what a stew they were in, wen they found me gone. If I have had a gun I have often fired it to let them know that I was gone – and wich way. It is a rum job for the Keepers to catch a lone Poacher wen it is dark.

One time I rember I was surrounded by keepers, I could hear them talking while I was layen there quite still and as sone as I could I drew away from them and they never heard me or knew I was there.

Dogs

I had one old dog so perfectly trained if he walked to a field gate he knew well enough if there was a hare on that field. He would just whine and stand still till the net was ready and the hare would be quickly dead. Me and that dog killed hundreds of hares and rabbits. I kept him till like me he could not work any longer. If there was a keeper or Policeman about he knew and would let me know as plain as if he could speak.

I had another small retrever bitch I trained for the gun at night. She could find a phesant up a tree as well as I could all I had to do was to watch her and she would find them. As sone as the bird was killed I had it in my hand but like a lot of useful things she died before she was very old. I well rember going to a wood not far from Bungay. I shot a bird from a tree and the bitch brought it to me growling. There were two keepers within twenty yards of me, but I simply crawled in the wood and laid down and they passed me by.

The Norfolk Hingle

A snare is used were the Phesants creep through the hedges, a how stick being put round the hingle to make the bird drop his head. Another way is to make a hole in the ground three inch deep and two inch across the top. The hingle is laid round the hole that have already been partly filled with white peas. He come along and put his head in the hole, bring the hingle up on his neck and is verry sone dead. The hingle is also used in the hare and rabbitt runs in the long grass in a wood with a bender over the hingle to keep his head down to the level of the snare.

The hingle for phesants is made of four strands of plible copper wire, as sone as he pull the wire tight he is dead.

A Fishy Tale

There was a big hall with a sort of ornamental fish Pond beside it, with some very fine trout in it. The water was quite shallow not more than a foot deep. Those fish were talked about quite a lot so the two of us went there one moonlight night and captured the lot of them. We had a good haul and there was one, a fine fish of the Rainbow class, weighed Just over nine pound.

We got the fish to Lynn befor they were missed but a few days after I saw in the paper that a gentleman had caught a fine trout wich he was haven stuffed – I knew the fisherman verry well.

I went and asked the dealer who he had sold the fish we cought to, and it was the same Gentleman that had caught the fish – so much for his Catchen it.

Epitaph for a Poacher

My memry often goes back to them days wen I played the game all out and made a good thing out of it for many years. Well. I think to myself, I have had my share of pleasure and my share of trubbles and now I am alone and my work nearly done, and I make myself content until the finish. I have rote these lines and told what I know not to lern the young man of today the art of taken game but Just to show how one man can dupe a lot of others. I am now seventy five, and if I had my time to come over again I would still be what I have been – A Poacher.

From Fireman to Foreman

Ray Beeson: Driver on the
Southern Railway

FROM FIREMAN TO FOREMAN

Ray Beeson, now a decidedly youthful-looking sixty-three, started his working life as an engine cleaner at Guildford station in Surrey in 1950. 'It was just a job,' he says with a smile, 'and there was certainly no family interest in the railways; but once you'd joined you knew you were part of something a bit special.'

Ray's father was a policeman who didn't want his son to follow him into the force: 'I suppose that, apart from being steered away from the police, it was just luck or fate that took me to trains,' he says now. He grew up at Chilworth, in Surrey, and trains ran past the end of the family garden so the sound of the railway may well have worked its way into his subconscious; this idea he finds faintly amusing, but can't quite bring himself to reject outright.

'I left school in 1950 and the railway seemed a good, secure job. I started as a cleaner because that was the first rung of the ladder, but it was an important job. In those days trains had to be spotless before they went out, and nationally, I should think thousands of us were employed in this way since it was a job done almost completely by hand; we did it all with paraffin and oily cloths, and no part of an engine was left untouched. When you first started you had to clean up under what we called the motions – the wheels, pistons and so on – and it was absolutely filthy work; but if the driver came along and saw that some part of the engine wasn't clean he'd make you go back and do it again. No driver wanted to take out a dirty engine. You had to do

---

FIREMAN'S DUTIES

'The fire was always lit by the time the firemen arrived, but it wasn't the sort of fire that you could use to get the train going; it was really just a little bundle of flame right inside the door that just kept the thing warm and gave you a start. I always used to begin by opening the door and simply spreading around what little fire there was; that was the first step on the way to building up your steam. It used to take about an hour to get up sufficient steam to move the engine, but during this time there were lots of other things to do: it was a routine of checks and procedures. You'd get oil for the driver, and you'd check the smokebox, making sure it was nice and tight – if it was loose you'd hear a sort of suction noise and it would be difficult to make steam. You'd watch the pressure gauge until it reached somewhere between 120lb and 220lb per square inch, though on engines for the big Channel packets you might have to get up 240lb or more. If I remember right, it was 180lb on the U-class and about 220lb on the Q-class. Q-class engines were used for goods work where, typically, you might be working with sixty-five wagons behind you. Keeping an eye on your steam was vital because you were on a booked time – if your steam wasn't sufficient to get you going at the right time, then all the other trains behind you could be disrupted.'

An M7 tank
engine at
Guildford station;
the driver lived
in one of the houses
on the skyline

the outside as well, of course. The length of time it took to clean each engine would obviously depend on the sort you were dealing with – the biggest at Guildford in those days was the U-class, and the smallest was the M7 tank engine. We had C3s, too – we called them Charlies, and they went from one to forty. Qs were really just wartime engines, and weren't meant to be used once we'd stopped fighting the Germans; but they were actually kept in regular service for another twenty years after the war ended. They were very powerful because they'd been made to pull tank trains. On average we reckoned to clean two locos in an eight-hour shift; that would be a team of half a dozen of us, so you can see, it was a thorough business.'

For a man who joined the railways with no real enthusiasm for trains, Ray has developed something of a passion for them, and there's nothing he enjoys more than a long chat about the ins and outs of steam working. He also has a great memory for odd details – like the resident tube cleaner at Guildford who jealously guarded his own special iron rod with a brush on the end. Though it is now long gone, the Guildford shed once housed something like thirty locomotives, used both for freight and passenger work. Ray quickly realised that here, as elsewhere, seniority was the only route to promotion, although he was quite happy to bide his time.

'It took me ten years to progress to being a fireman, but that was pretty standard in those days. You started by getting just a few turns as a fireman, and then when you'd done enough turns, they made you a passed cleaner, which in my case meant I was working roughly 50 per cent of the time as a fireman and 50 per cent as a cleaner.

'Firemen signed on at the same time as their drivers, and we always did eight-hour shifts, with a start at 2am, or 4am, or the early shift which was one minute past midnight.'

Passed cleaners were frequently expected to change back and forth from cleaning to firing from day to day, but once they'd reached a stage where they were no longer doing any cleaning – in other words, by the time they were fully-fledged firemen – they were treated with more consistency, particularly when it came to shift working, as Ray explains: 'A fireman could expect to start at the same time each day for at least a week, unless he had to cover a rest day or something.'

Ray believes there are many misconceptions about the role of the fireman, particularly the idea that the job meant hours of unrelenting shovelling on the footplate. He argues that in fact there was nearly always time to stop and think when you were firing: 'If you knew what you were doing, I suppose you could describe the

job as keeping the fire topped up, once you were underway, and how frequently you had to top up would depend on the weight of the load and the quality of the coal. There were times, though they weren't too frequent, when you were pretty nearly shovelling for all you were worth – the Waterloo to Basingstoke, Bournemouth and Salisbury run with ten coaches is a good example; on that run you were pushed to get the odd minute between bouts of firing.'

The fireman at Guildford, as elsewhere, had a wide range of duties, but they were all concentrated on enabling the driver to do his work; it was very much a team effort, as Ray explains: 'I don't know what people did in other areas, but teamwork was definitely the key word on my patch. When it was foggy, for example, and you couldn't see the semaphore signals, you'd both of

you, driver and fireman, be desperately keeping a lookout. It was all right on the mainline, or at least it was better, because they had coloured lights, but on the less important lines – say, Woking to Basingstoke – it was all semaphore which was a nightmare when visibility was poor.'

For Ray, one of the great pleasures of the footplate was simply the sense of speed, the warmth on hot days, and the exhilaration of firing on crisp, frosty mornings: 'On a bright winter morning it was wonderful when you had time to look about a bit as you steamed along – though of course that was only true when you were going engine first; if you were the other way round – that is, tender first – you'd be so cold that I can assure you there was no pleasure in it at all!'

In summer the footplate could be unbearably hot until the train had picked up sufficient speed to pull a breeze through; but winter or summer, Ray was always astonished, particularly in his early firing days, by how well the drivers knew every inch of the road: 'They always knew exactly where to start braking on every gradient.' Mind you, the process of bringing the train to a halt was also a big part of the fireman's job; with loose-coupled freight wagons, which had no brakes of their own, Ray would start braking using the turned handbrake on the tender. 'That would bring the wagons together, so you'd have captured the whole weight of the train ready for the driver to put the engine brake on.'

Ray's own memory of the area he worked is still detailed and thorough despite the fact that he has now been retired for a number of years; but of course it is the difficult parts that he recollects most clearly: 'One or two bits of our area

Overleaf:
A typical 1950s scene with a Brighton to Cardiff express, which would have passed through Ray's domain in Salisbury en route; (inset) a Q1 locomotive and wagon at Cranleigh station, which no longer exists

were notorious – Virginia Water Bank between Reading and Feltham was really extremely difficult, and there was a very steep section between Reading and Redhill known as Dorking Bank. It was places like those two that made it absolutely essential that you knew the road and your engine; if you didn't, you would almost certainly get stuck on that Reading to Redhill section, with all the timetable consequences that that would entail for your passengers and all the passengers in the trains behind you.

'There were different skills, too, with passenger as opposed to freight working: with freight you had to start braking a lot earlier because of all those loose-coupled wagons with no brakes, whereas passenger trains all had continuous brakes on all carriages. The guard at the back of the train would know all the gradients, too, and his brake van would come into operation.'

The area Ray covered was Guildford to Salisbury via Waterloo, but it also included Southampton, Redhill and Bournemouth; it was the heart of the Southern Region. After a number of years firing – he can't remember quite how many – Ray became a passed fireman, to all intents and purposes a driver. A few years later he took over as relief foreman at Guildford locomotive shed. 'That meant that one day I would be working as foreman and the next I'd be back driving.' As it turned out, Ray was the last foreman at Guildford loco shed before it closed for good.

'People at Guildford didn't like change, and it was particularly unsettling when Guildford closed as a depot and we all went to Woking. Southern Region was unusual in that we'd had some electric trains since as early as the 1930s; they were clean and efficient, but they didn't have the character of steam. I drove some of these early electric trains – you just had to push a button and that was it. With steam it was more unpredictable even though we knew what we were doing; it relied more on intuition and judgement, and of course things did go wrong occasionally, however good you were. Sometimes you just ran out of

The Brighton terriers were one of the best loved types on the Southern Railway

Ray in the early 1960s

steam, and you'd then have to stop, build up your steam again and then off you'd go.'

During his time as a driver Ray worked passenger and freight trains, and he recalls the working practices of the past as if this was all still a central part of his life. 'Well, it all became so much a part of your life that you knew it without thinking about it. We were in rostered links, twelve pairs of men in each link, and each week your link would do a different shift and work on a different line. The top link did all the best shifts, and you only got into the top link through seniority; thus the longer you were around, the better your chance of moving up – but it was very much a question of dead men's shoes because you only moved up when someone else died or retired. But at least it was the same for everyone, so there were few complaints. The only alternative was to try to get promotion by going to another depot. People didn't get made redundant in those days and some people were happy to stay where they were; others wanted to move and get on, and you certainly got the chances if you did that.

'Some men were desperate to work the electric trains, but not me! I was more than happy with steam. Kids were always coming up to the cab and asking for a ride, and we used to let them come with us – and unless you've travelled on the footplate as a child it's impossible to imagine the excitement of it. It was all more relaxed in those days – you wouldn't dream of giving a kid a ride in the cab today, you'd be sacked. We had some lovely runs, too – I always enjoyed Redhill to Reading because it was such beautiful country.'

The latter part of Ray's career included stints as a relief train crew supervisor, and station supervisor at Woking where he was responsible for platform safety and for looking after the platform staff. He then became a train crew supervisor looking after crews, finding engines for them, organising special trains, and finding cover if a driver went sick. 'I enjoyed that because I was back working with the blokes who actually drove the trains. My last job was as relief stationmaster: I covered Woking, Surbiton, Basingstoke, Guildford and Haslemere whenever the regular stationmaster was ill or on holiday.'

Ray spent the last few years of his career helping with the rebuilding of Guildford Station, a job which he knew would make him surplus to requirements once it was completed. 'I'd taken on the job of assistant stationmaster, but the new station didn't need an assistant, so I suppose I built myself out of a job! I had a few other jobs

SAFETY FEATURES

Ray is annoyed by the commonly held belief that steam locomotives were completely lacking in fail-safe systems, and he goes to great pains to explain how at least one of these systems worked: 'If your steam pressure got too low the brakes came on automatically, and if your water got too low a lead plug would be melted by the heat of the fire and whatever water was left would crash down on your fire, put it out and the whole thing would shut down, thus avoiding an explosion. This was very rare though – it never happened to me, and I was never involved in a crash, either!

before I finally retired; I was what was called a 'task force manager', supervising men who cleaned the stations in my area.'

Like many railwaymen, Ray has particularly strong memories of the fuss the imminent arrival of the royal train in the area would cause. Usually these trains were on their way to Southampton, with a specially appointed driver and top security all along the route, as Ray explains: 'There would be armed police on every bridge under which the train had to pass, and absolutely everything else moved out of the way long before the train got anywhere near us –

nothing was booked to move in the area. We also always had a standby engine waiting along the route in case the royal train broke down. Sometimes a spare engine would follow the royal train all the way.

'But my happiest memories are of firing and driving steam engines; they gave you a real sense of achievement, and if you wanted to get home at night it was up to you and your skill. You couldn't just press a button. Mind you, when I was depot foreman I also enjoyed that. We used to wear a trilby and a blue smock – but that's now gone the way of steam, too!'

Brideshead Revisited

Stanley Ware: Gamekeeper, Castle Howard, Yorkshire

BRIDESHEAD REVISITED

In the 1980s, independent television made its blockbusting series 'Brideshead Revisited' at Castle Howard, and the headkeeper then had to help keep adoring spectators off estate roads so that filming could continue. But at least the commotion did not appear to affect the pheasants, so Lord Howard, ironically Chairman of the BBC, could continue with his celebrated sport. Castle Howard's rise to shooting prominence was largely due to the loyalty and skill of this one man: headkeeper Stanley Ware, who has spent most of his working life nurturing the gamebirds of Yorkshire.

Stanley Ware outside his Castle Howard cottage in 1988, with his old anti-poacher truncheon

Stanley was born on 5 May 1918 in the tiny village of Gillamoor near Kirbymoorside, Yorkshire. His father was a rabbit catcher for much of the year, mostly September to April; otherwise he would break up stones in the quarries and dig trenches for water pipes at 3d a yard.

Most of the rabbits were ferreted or caught in gin traps and snares; only a few were shot because a couple of good, 'clean' rabbits would fetch 1/6d whereas a couple of shot ones made only between 8d and 10d. 'But father didn't get all that', said Stanley. 'He was employed by Colonel Holt and his estate paid him 3d for each rabbit caught. Most rabbits were crated and put on the train for the London markets. But there were a lot of rabbits then and a lot people were worse off than us. And in the Great War, when father was rejected by the Army on account of his feet, the Government sent him all over the place to keep the rabbits down on many estates.'

When he was still at school at Gillamoor, Stanley started to become interested in keepering through his grandfather, who was a beatkeeper for Lord Feversham at Nawton Towers. But Stanley had to walk the eight miles to visit him.

At the age of twelve, Stanley had his first experience as a beater, for Colonel Holt on the Ravenswick estate, near Kirbymoorside. The pay was 2s a day, but beaters had to take their own lunch, with cold tea in a bottle (no flasks in those days!). Stanley was often given an easy job as a stop because he knew the ground well through going there with his father to catch rabbits.

Stanley was pleased to leave school at the age of fourteen, to get out into the fresh air and help his father with his work. He did not have to set the ginns because he was particularly good at snaring – 'The best place to snare was where the rabbits ran across a grass field to feed in a field of roots. It was quite easy to spot their runs in the long grass, especially after frost.' In return for this work, Stanley received free board and lodging with his parents, but no pay.

Four years later the headkeeper at Castle Howard asked Stanley's father, who caught rabbits there, if he knew of a lad who wanted to take up keepering. Not surprisingly, he suggested his own son, and thus in 1936 began an association which has lasted to this day.

His employer was the late Lord Grimthorpe, who then leased about half of the Castle Howard estate and had a brood mare farm there; he was also a Master of the Middleton Foxhounds, Headkeeper was Joe Durno, 'a damn good man', and Stanley was paid about 10s a week, of which 5s went to his aunt for lodging with her at the appropriately named Gunthorpe village on Castle Howard estate.

He started at the end of February and one of his main tasks was killing vermin, especially crows, magpies, jays and jackdaws. The main method of catching crows was to place eggs on a tree stump to entice the birds down and lure them into a trap. 'But foxes were taboo. Being an MFH, Lord Grimthorpe would have sacked us if he had seen us shoot one. So generally they were left alone, and if one became a real nuisance it had to be a three o'clock in the morning job!'

In the late thirties farming was more sympathetic towards game and wildlife. There were many more hedgerows and no spraying so the partridges could usually be left to fend for themselves. The keeper's main work was concerned with rearing large numbers of pheasants, and that really got underway in April when rabbit catching was finished with. 'At home we rarely ate rabbit and mother always had to disguise it in the cooking pot. But father always knew it was there. You can hardly blame him for turning his nose up at it, having had to gut them all day long.

'Our broody hens were bought from farms and local people – everybody kept a few hens – for 2s 6d each, and put into sitting boxes with six compartments. The hen's quota of eggs depended on her size and varied from eighteen to twenty.

'Every morning the hens were taken out of their boxes and tethered by one leg to a stick, and each hen had to be put back onto her own nest; after a few days they got used to this. When a hen was taken off the nest, the keeper had to put his hands under the bird and move her back slightly to lift her feet from the eggs so that she would not drag them forward and break them on the board. Then the hen was passed to another man, who put her on her tether.

'Before and during sitting the hens were dusted with louse powder to kill any fleas they might be carrying. Infested birds would shift about relentlessly on the eggs and break quite a few.

'During the first part of incubation the hens were allowed only a short time off the eggs, but as time went on they were allowed longer spells off duty. When they were finally put back on the eggs we went round with shovel and hose to clean up any mess they had made or food not

Before they were protected, sparrowhawks and kestrels were commonly shot by keepers, including Stanley Ware at Castle Howard

Stanley Ware and
headkeeper Joe
Durno at Castle
Howard in the
days when
pheasants were
reared under
broody hens

Opposite: The
rearing field hut
at Castle Howard

covered several acres of land, which was rented from one of the tenant farmers.

'When the coops were first put out they were turned upside down and limewashed inside. Small runs were placed in front of the coops for the first few days. Then along came the rearing hut complete with pans, buckets and feeding bowls. And as soon as possible we had to find lots of dry wood to store under the hut in case of wet weather as all the food was boiled.

'By this time all the chicks were hatching out. When they had dried off under their broody they were taken to the rearing field in boxes, the hen in a sack. In each coop a hen had about eighteen chicks.

'Then we started boiling the food. Eggs were cooked forty at a time and put through a fine sieve. Rice, kibbled maize, linseed and wheat were boiled too. This was all mixed up in the feeding bowl with scalded fine biscuit meal and finally dried off with

eaten. And we always turned the drinking bowls upside down to keep vermin away.

'The siting of the sitting boxes was very important. Too much direct sun would make the hens shift about on the nest, and even sometimes rise from the eggs, which would then be chilled. They had to be placed a few inches above ground level in case of heavy rain, ideally on a ridge of sandy soil which was well drained. At the same time this made it a little bit easier for the keeper to remove the birds.

'This done, the nests were shaped with a rounded stone and lined with hay or dried grass into which hot eggs were placed. These were left with the hens for a couple of days to discover which were the best sitters. Some of the hens never took to the boxes as they had gotten used to running around free on the farms. And we had to put a wire fence around the boxes to keep out dogs and foxes.

'While the hens were still sitting the rearing field had to be prepared, first by putting tunnel traps all around the hedgerows. Then we cut rides about a yard wide across the field to stand the coops in, twenty yards between the rows and twenty yards between each coop. All this

barley meal and dusted with a tiny amount of Pheasant-tina spice to make the food taste better.

'After each feed the bowls were immediately put into boiling water as soft food soon went sour. The coops were moved onto fresh ground every day or two.

'Often the chicks became infested with gapes: these are little, pink worms which get into the windpipe and lungs, and if they are not treated up to half the birds could die. We would block up most of the air vents in the coop and use bellows to blow in some powder call Kamlin, which the birds breathed in for a few minutes.

'At this time of year you were on the rearing field from six in the morning till the birds were shut up at night, and as the birds got older this became later: on very mild nights it could be eleven o'clock.

'With three keepers on this shoot, two were on the rearing field while the other went around the woods cutting rides with a scythe ready to receive the coops and in preparation for the birds release.

'At four to five weeks old the birds were moved to cover. The night before they would be fastened in; we would place a sack under the coop and lift the thing bodily onto a cart, and as we had a horse to pull it we could reach wherever we wanted to go. The coops were placed out on the ride as on the rearing field, but the hens were facing in all directions so that they could give us warning when any vermin came in sight.

'The hens stayed in the wood for several weeks before being taken home. By this time they were in laying condition and sold as laying hens for the same price as we gave for them.

'The keeper still had to boil the food and see the birds had plenty of water. His last job before going home for the night was to boil the food ready for the morning feed. At the same time he would see the birds had some grit and light the hurricane lamps to keep the foxes away.

'From twelve weeks old the birds started to stray away from the coverts so then we used a dog to drive them back home.

'Lord Grimthorpe was a real gent, but Colonel Deacon took charge of the shooting for him as he was away hunting several days a week. The other Guns were mostly ex-military. We had about four partridge days of 50–70 brace each and ten or so covert shoots with bags of 140–150 pheasants.

SPRATT'S KEEPERS' REQUISITES

Spratt's Portable Food Boilers

Fig. 1. – Strong Cast Iron Boiler with Cast Iron Pan.

Firebrick Linings to Fire Box.

Fig. 1 — Prices :—		£	s.	d.
No. 6, to hold 6 galls. ..		2	17	6
No. 8 „ 8 „ ...		3	4	6
No. 10 „ 10 „ ...		3	13	3
No. 12 „ 12 „ ...		4	0	0
No. 15 „ 15 „ ...		4	8	0

Prices of larger Sizes on application.

Fig. 2. — Complete with the following extras.

Galvanised Iron Steamer and Cover ... ...
Galvanised Cover only ...
Mounted on Wheels ... ...
Black Wrought Iron Flue Pipe
Raincap ... ...
Brass draw-off Tap ... ...

Prices on application.

Write for complete list to :—
SPRATT'S PATENT LTD.,
APPLIANCE DEPT.,
24/5, Fenchurch Street, London, E.C.3

Fig. 1.

Fig. 2.

'Our beaters were paid 2s 6d a day and given a bottle of beer each. The lucky ones were given a cartridge bag to carry and for this they might get an extra half crown each. One gentleman used to give a pound so everybody rushed for him.

'The poachers then were all local people as there was very little transport. But we had to be nightwatching from the start as they could still take a lot of birds. We used to take turns with neighbouring keepers to watch for these trouble-makers – one man in the Territorial Army used to knock off birds with his .303.

Young Stanley Ware (centre) and keeper Fox (right) at Castle Howard

'When the shooting season was over we had hen pheasants to catch for the laying pens, about seven hens to each cock. This done, we started on the rabbit population as in those days there were so many of them. After some time at them with ginns, snares, ferrets and guns, a lot of them would take to sitting out on top. These were dealt with by a few farm tenants and others who helped during the nesting season. The keeper drove the rabbits forward with dogs and hopefully they were shot by the people standing forward. But we still left snares and traps going until April.

'Then we started on carrion crows and magpies, which were sitting by this time. Tunnel traps were kept going for ground vermin.

'Early pheasants started to lay in April and English partridges early in May. We found as many of these as possible so we could put Renardine around the nests in cartridge cases to take away the scent of the birds, which otherwise might attract predators. On wet days we went to the shed to creosote the coops and sitting boxes.

'By the middle of May it was time to start all over again with the broody hens.'

This regime continued until January 1940 when Stanley was called up to join the Royal Artillery; he hoped to 'give 'em what for from a long distance'.

After the war Lord Grimthorpe lost his lease at Castle Howard so Stanley worked single-handed for three doctors on another part of the

A GAMEKEEPER GOES TO WAR

'At first I was stationed all over England, but in March 1942 I was sent to Ceylon and then to India for three or four years.'

The worst incident Stanley saw in service was at the Filton aircraft factory near Bristol when he was on ack-ack defence. 'We couldn't reach the bombers with those peashooters and one Wednesday they dropped a stick of bombs right across the countryside because they were not sure where the factory was. One fell directly onto an air-raid shelter and killed a hundred people.

'Next day our boys sent in a squadron of Hurricanes. Jerry came again on Friday, our lads took off and we thought that's the last we'll see of them. Then suddenly they reappeared out of the cloud, came right down on Jerry and knocked out eleven bombers in as many minutes.'

estate, having been highly recommended by both Durno and Deacon. Part of the land encompassed Stanley's old beat so he knew the ground well. Rowntrees of York boss Dickinson ran the shoot on behalf of the medical men – a gynaecologist, a GP and a radiologist – and started Stanley on £2 a week, but he did also get a good income from the sale of rabbits.

Boxing Day was 'the big one', when wives and families always turned out to beat 'and I had a job to keep 'em all in line. And it was a good job I had a few Christmas boxes, as tips were few then. The most you would ever receive was £1 but I would say I never really had a good tip in my life. They don't realise what a keeper has to do to put a few shots over them.'

During his eighteen years with the doctors, Stanley lived in a rented house at nearby Welburn, having married during the war.

Then came a telephone call from Mr (later Lord) George Howard of Castle Howard, asking him to go for interview with a view to replacing the headkeeper Joe Durno, who had unexpectedly taken a job as a milkman at Malton. Stanley was the obvious choice as he had been on the estate the longest.

Mr Howard interviewed Stanley in his office at the Castle in January 1964, prior to starting the job in February – traditionally the beginning of the keepering year. Stanley told him he had been on the estate since 1936. 'Good Lord', said Mr Howard, 'and I hardly know you'. The truth was that he had never even spoken to Stanley before. In fact he hardly ever spoke to anyone on a shoot day and, in Stanley's words, 'could be rather odd at times. He was a fairly good shot with his Purdeys and loader, but he was away from home a lot with his BBC commitments (he was a governor from 1972, becoming Chairman between 1980–83) and everything to do with the shooting parties had to be organised for him by his wife, Lady Cecilia, the daughter of the Duke of Grafton. When he came home at the weekend all he had to do was pick up a gun.'

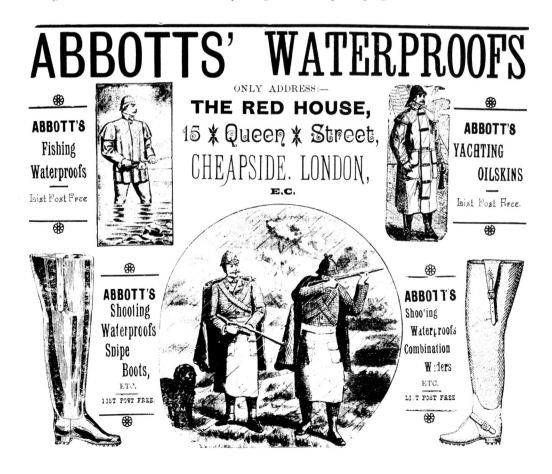

ABBOTTS' WATERPROOFS

ONLY ADDRESS:—
THE RED HOUSE,
15 ✠ Queen ✠ Street,
CHEAPSIDE. LONDON,
E.C.

ABBOTT'S
Fishing
Waterproofs
List Post Free

ABBOTT'S
YACHTING
OILSKINS
List Post Free.

ABBOTT'S
Shooting
Waterproofs
Snipe
Boots,
ETC.
LIST POST FREE.

ABBOTT'S
Shoo'ing
Waterproofs
Combination
Waders
ETC.
LIST POST FREE

Nothing would come between the enthusiastic shot and his sport. This advertisement from 1895 offers sturdy protection from the elements

Stanley started on £12 a week in 1964, payable fortnightly in arrears, but there was also a dog allowance of 10s a week and the cottage was rent and rates free. He had the help of five other keepers as the idea was to build the shoot up; Mr Howard had started to take land back, at the same time injecting a considerable amount of cash. Thus bags rose from around 120 in 1964 to over 400, Stanley's highest being 700 for one day.

There has been a steady stream of interesting guests on the mostly two-day shoots. Lord Whitelaw has been a regular – 'a grand chap, not an outstanding Shot but he killed a hundred birds here one day and he was very pleased with that. Anglia Television chairman Lord Buxton, the Survival wildlife film maker and conservationist, has been quite a bit, too.'

But like all headkeepers, Stanley did not actually see much of the Guns on shoot days: he was too busy organising his retinue. 'Sometimes I did not see them at all until after the last drive. One of my biggest problems was getting 'em back out after lunch at the Castle. This usually went on from about 1 to 2.30pm or 2.45pm, and of course, there wasn't much light left then in December – perhaps time for only one short drive. And you hadn't to strike a match when you passed those merry Guns! It was entirely Lord Howard's fault.'

Yet Stanley obviously had great respect for his master. 'Lord Howard once shot a pheasant which fell through the ice on a pond near the house. A keeper's spaniel was sent to retrieve it, but fell through and couldn't get out. Without hesitation, Lord Howard plunged into the icy water up to his neck, with stick in hand to smash his way through to the struggling dog.

'Eventually he succeeded and the dog scrambled out, but it took about seven of us to free Lord Howard as it was very muddy and he was a very big chap.

'It was a wonderful effort on his behalf and I decided to write to the RSPCA about it as I thought they should give him one of their awards. But do you know they threw it out because it happened on a shoot day, despite the fact it certainly saved the dog's life. I was furious, and when I told her ladyship about it she said: "Well, I've patronised the RSPCA for years, but I'm afraid this will have to be the end of it."'

Another guest from the world of television was one-time BBC director-general Alisdair Milne who certainly made an impression on Stanley, but for all the wrong reasons. 'Judging by what he left me at night, I don't think he was a shooting man: he never left me a penny!'

The 'undesirables' also included the then boss of Comet discount shops, Mr Hollingbury. His syndicate bought five days one year and eight the next and he complained about everything. On his last day we guaranteed a bag of 200 and they shot 232, yet he still moaned to me. When I told Lord Howard he said: "Right, he's out". Mind you, Hollingbury didn't winge when we shot 400!'

Stanley has worked on the estate under five agents, one of whom was Lord Morpeth (now Viscount Morpeth). But when Lord Howard became ill, and since his death, the third of his four sons, the Honourable Simon, took over the

THE DANGER OF NOVICE GUNS

Lady Cecilia was involved in another shooting incident which remains clear in Stanley's mind, though she never used a gun herself. 'We were driving partridges, hares and rabbits with the tenant farmers and there were three Guns each side of a fence when we came to a potentially dangerous spot where I had placed a blue plastic bag in the fence, to warn people not to shoot towards it.

'At the end of the drive a hare came forward and one of the Guns swung through it and towards the bag. I cried out 'No, No', but he still fired and immediately there was a yell from the other side. The silly ... had put a few pellets into the legs of both another Gun and her ladyship, who was standing with him.

'We used to have up to fifty volunteers on hare shoots as the agent used to write to the tenant farmers saying 'Bring a friend'. I never knew who would turn up and many of them would be very inexperienced.'

running of the estate – but there is no lord of the manor now, as Simon's father had been a life peer.

Many of the traditions continue, even though most shoot days are sold now. They still hold a Christmas party at the Castle for all the staff and everyone receives a present – in the old days only the heads of staff were invited. 'Young' Simon Howard still takes Stanley a brace of pheasants at Christmas – though the keeper admits to not liking pheasant too much and prefers it cold.

Stanley retired from full-time keepering in 1983, but did a further three years part-time. He received his CLA long-service award for forty-seven years in 1988, and now lives in a delightful divided cottage on the estate, where he and his wife tend a very traditional garden bursting with flowers and magnificent vegetables. But he stresses that 'the pheasant is not the gardener's friend', and he now views them differently as they parade along his wall.

Mrs Gertrude Ware is an excellent cook ('she was my underkeeper, you know – strong as I was'), but a low-sugar diet means that she has to resist most of the fine fare she puts on for Stanley. Despite their remoteness, they are well served by visiting traders – the butcher, fishmonger and baker all still call regularly, a luxury rare in much of England today.

Typically spartan, but with mementoes of old country life, the Ware cottage is extremely quiet – when I was there the only sounds were the tick of the clock and, appropriately, the occasional kok-kok of a pheasant. It is a fitting place to recall the highlights of a successful partnership. For Mrs Ware there is the cherished memory of being given a small role, with other locals, when Paul Newman, Sophia Loren and David Niven came to film at Castle Howard; and for Stanley there is immense pride in a lifetime devoted to sporting duty, throughout which 'everyone called me Stan – even his lordship'.

Stanley Ware (centre, sitting) received his long-service award at the 1988 CLA Game Fair at Floors Castle. Also pictured are the other award-winning keepers (front), the Duke of Roxburghe (centre, standing) and the Duke of Atholl (standing, third from left)

Boating 'til the Last

Sam & Gladys Horne: on the Grand Union Canal narrowboats

BOATING 'TIL THE LAST

During World War II the Grand Union Canal Carrying Company was desperately short of crews for its long distance carrying narrowboats. Various outsiders were recruited, including a number of young middle-class women who formed all-female crews, initially under the guidance of instructors. Several of these women, including trainer Kitty Gayford, were profoundly affected by the life of the waterways and have subsequently written accounts of their experiences which have been published elsewhere. To those born and bred on the boats they remained something of a curiosity and are still referred to as the 'trainees'.

Previous page: Hunter's Bridge, Kings Langley, on the Grand Union Canal, as it was during Gladys' childhood in the 1930s

When I first met Sam and Gladys Horne at their canalside home in Berkhamsted, Gladys quickly made me aware of Sam's inexperience on the cut after a mere half century: ''Course, he's only a trainee, you know. He didn't come on the boats till he was seventeen. He wasn't born to it.' Thus Sam is condemned never to *really* know how to steer a boat! Sitting in their kitchen with the sound of boat engines and the rattle of lock paddles coming through the window, I set out to discover if Gladys was qualified to appear in these pages since Sam would apparently not be able to tell much of canal life!

'I was born on the boats, in Birnigum [Birmingham], on 13 December 1931. My mum and dad was on the boats and all the families

---

BORN ALL OVER THE PLACE

'I remember as I got a bit older that my mum had a baby at Cosgrove, on the Grand Union Canal. As you come round to New Bradwell from Wolverton, there's a long straight across the valley to Cosgrove Lock. I remember my dad got off at that first bridge and biked ahead and got the midwife on the lockside for when we got there! My mum had the baby while the lock was filling! That was one of me brothers. Then I had a brother and a sister born in Northampton. Another at Kingswood, at the junction where the Stratford Canal goes off just before you go into Birnigum. Me second oldest sister was borned at Wolverhampton and my oldest sister at Leicester. We were born all over the place. The older kids used to have to help.

'We stopped at Cosgrove just that one night for the midwife to come back. I remember that midwife telling my mum, "You can move off tomorrow, you'll be all right because you've got the kids to help you!" She was telling my mother that she went to a gypsy camp and borned a baby. She said to the woman there, you must stop in bed today and I'll come back tonight. Well, she went back that night and this woman was chasing her old man round the van with a frying pan!

before them, right back, they'd always been boat people. They was working for Fellows Morton & Clayton when I was born. I was born on the butty *Fazeley*, that's still about on the canal. When I was small we had a motor which was a boat built new, at Uxbridge, for my dad, the *Elder*, a wooden boat.

'People working for Fellows Mortons had quite a lot born in Birnigum where they loaded and unloaded. I was born at the first of their wharfs you come to; coming from London, it's called Warwick Wharf, close to the HP sauce factory. We used to carry a lot of HP sauce and the stuff that went to make it.

'My own dad was Ted Price, but he died and my mum married again, when I was eight, to Philip Ward. There was no way a woman could work a pair of boats, not with a Bolinder engine. You need a man to start it, you see! Not like when we used to have the Nationals and Petters. There was no press button or winding handle to start.

You had to pull that pin out of the flywheel, put you foot on it and then kick it over to start.

'I never did that. I started a Petter once, and I nearly went mad! It was after I'd left home. We was at Braunston and we'd to take an extra boat round to Sutton's Stop [Hawkesbury Junction, near Coventry]. You used to have warm the top of the engine up with a blow lamp before they'd start – well, Jack [Skinner] said to me, "Go and get the lamp on. I'll have a cup of tea and then we'll start it and get going."

'Well, those Petters aren't like a Bolinder; you don't have to lift the floor plate up to get to the pin in the flywheel, you can just swing them over with your hand. So whilst it was warming up I was just stood there playing with the flywheel, swinging it back and forward and singing to myself and she started! Oh, I was going mad, shouting, "She's going, she's going!" I did go mad, hopping about all over. I'd be about sixteen then. Then we had to take that boat round

Sam Horne and his 'steerer' Gladys, during the period when they unofficially operated a pair of Samuel Barlow Coal Co boats together. This now battered photograph was taken at Sutton Stop, officially known as Hawkesbury Junction, at the northern end of the Oxford Canal

to Sutton's for a bloke working round the Moiry Cut because something had happened to his. [The Ashby Canal is often known as the Moiry or Miry Cut because it was never completed beyond Moira to Ashby de la Zouch.] That was the *Wasp*. I'll never forget it.

'As far as I can tell my mum's maiden name was Payton, Elizabeth Payton. I stuck with them about five years after she was remarried but my stepfather got worse and worse. When he wanted you to wake up to get the locks ready and that he would never say, "Come on" – no, he'd go in the cabin and hit you with a belt or smack you round the face and say "Get up". He got so violent with us, and I can't understand why

me mum never done nothing about it. I said I'd had enough, but my oldest sister had went first, then my second oldest sister went. It came on to me worse when they'd gone. He was a sod, he was.

'When he died, ten years or more ago now, my sisters and brothers, they said, "He's died, are you going up to his funeral?" My oldest sister was alive then, living down at the next lock below here, and she said, "If we go it'll only be to kick him down the hole!"

'So I left home a bit after my mum married again and went to work with Jack and Rose Skinner. There was just them and me grown up, but they had two children. Sam had worked with them before. He was bred and borned on a

Following the ice-boat: Cairo, Malta and other Samuel Barlow boats lead a train to assist one another through the thick ice of the Coventry Canal at Griff Lane in the winter of 1947. Several of these craft were on the short-haul power station coal traffic on which the Skinners and Sam Horne, with his 'steerer' Gladys, were working. At least fifteen boats are visible on the original print

farm. He had a job for a little while, and then he decided to go onto the canal and he went with them. They learned you how to boat, didn't they?' Gladys glanced over at Sam.

'Yes, that was in that big frost – what was it?.…1947. My family lived on a farm at Kidlington, near Thrupp, a little farm just across the field from the cut, and of course we used to see the boats coming down there. I got talking to one or two of them and to one of the girls, you know. That's how I got interested in the boats. I used to go with the gas boats [which collected the tar or waste gas water to take up to Birmingham] to Banbury and then come back home. Then Jack come along one day and asked me if I'd like to go with him. He had the Barlows then. [The Samuel Barlow Coal Co of Birmingham ran a fleet of boatsand a boatyard at Braunston which delivered fuel as far as Oxford and London.] So when I left school I went with Jack until I was just over army age. If I'd have stopped with him I'd have never went in the army, but I didn't, and as soon as I got back home of course they got me for the National Service.

'When I came back home I couldn't settle and I went Barlowing again. I had a pair of my own with a young chap from Leicester. He didn't know nothing, a trainee. We worked up and down the Moiry Cut then for a long while together. He left in the finish. Then I went and worked with Jack Skinner, the two pairs of boats together, and Gladys steered the butty for me for a while.'

'If it had been now I'd have went and lived with Sam. But you couldn't do that then! That wasn't allowed on boats. No, you'd got to be married and that was it. It was an instant dismissal otherwise! I was just steering the butty for him. That's how it was put into the bosses, "steering". We was just on short journeys, down the Moiry

Gladys uses the mast line to slow the progress of her Willow Wren butty Wagtail as it enters Baddesley Lock on the Atherstone flight of the Coventry Canal. Motor boat Warbler waits behind; it was usually quicker to send the butty down a flight of locks where it has to be bowhauled first with the motor steerer refilling the locks for the second boat. Sam and Gladys were on their way to load coal either at Baddesley Colliery basin just below this lock or Pooley Hall a few miles and five locks further on

Cut to the Longford Light Works [Hawkesbury Power Station, on the outskirts of Coventry].'

Gladys recalls that the Skinners had left Barlow's by the time she went to work with them. 'Jack and Rose had British Waterways boats when I went to them. Rose was born and bred on the boats, they used to have two-horse boats on the Oxford Cut. But for some reason after she had the kids she hated the boats and she kept harping him and harping him to go and live at Banbury in a house which he didn't like. Well, I thought I'd go with them and I think I was there

Warbler and Wagtail awaiting orders to load from the coalfield traffic office at Sutton Stop near Coventry. Sutton Stop, where the Coventry and Oxford canals join, is so-called after a family who kept the office where the boats stopped to pay their tolls there for several generations

about six months, which is when I met Sam. As soon as he got to know they was at Banbury he came up to see 'em and that's where we met.

'Jack, he tried his hardest to settle down there, he went to work in a brewery. But he just couldn't settle away from the water. So we decided to go back on the boats and he went and had another pair of Barlows again. Sam had his own pair of Barlows, too, and during the time that happened the Willer Wren's [Willow Wren Canal Carrying Co] started up and we were the first captains for them.'

Sam: 'One day, whilst Gladys was working with me as "steerer", the Whitlocks was tied up at Heyford Bridge. They must have just stopped a moment for something because the boats were only tied up by the mast line, which is only thin, you know. Well, his string broke and he said we was going too hard. Well, we couldn't have been going that hard because I was right up behind Jack and so I had to pull out of gear so as not to catch his butty. I happened to run into Bill Whitlock in Barlow's Yard just after and he was carrying on

about this so I threatened him. Because it was on the premises, like, I was sacked for that.'

Gladys: 'A bit before that Barlow's had given Sam a roll of lino for the motor's cabin, a thick green lino. So when they told him he'd got to get out of the boats, he rolled the lino up, it was thick stuff, and opened the office door and threw it in.'

Sam: 'I said, "You'd better have that back then." And it sprung open and everything flew everywhere, papers all over the floor, everything off the desk! Then the Willow Wren job came up and we had the *Warbler* and *Wagtail*.'

Gladys: 'There was a painter at Braunston that was very thick with Jack Skinner and knew Morton, who was Willow Wren's boss. Well, we was round the Blisworth Pound in a frost, Linford it was, and he knew that Sam had had the sack for hitting old Bill, and he come over and seen him and told us that there was this new firm starting up, and give Sam the address. He wrote off and we got the job straightaway.'

Sam: 'We got married to go to that, at Oxford, and Leslie Morton came over and picked us up.'

Gladys still remembers the optimism of the start of her new life on new boats with a new carrying company: 'Ooh, yes. We'd got a boat at Rickmansworth, because the dock there was going then, Walker's. And the motor, *Warbler*, was at the dock at Leighton Buzzard. Just before we got to Leighton, they'd varnished all the cabin out in the motor. We stuck everywhere! Well, we were lucky that there was another pair of Barlows laid there because her husband wasn't very well. We knew them quite well and she said, "Come and sleep on our motor tonight. You can't lay on there!"

Sam recalls that not all was right with the world: 'Next morning, when we come to start the engine, we found the big ends had gone. Nobody had told Morton – they'd brought it down and just tied it up. Leslie Morton had to come over again. He came from Paddington, they had a caravan in the basin there as an office when they first started. He had to come over and fetch us, and some of our things, and take us to the butty boat at Walker's. But, you know, we had a lovely welcome there. They'd even got a fire in it for us, the dock people.

'Then me and John Hemylrick, who had that *Peacock*, we had to come back to Leighton and tow *Warbler* back down to Uxbridge. They took the National out and put a Bolinder in it, and we laid there whilst they done it. Len Hough, the fitter at Uxbridge, he was a good bloke for them engines; he took it out of one of the old Fellows Mortons and put it in *Warbler*.

'Then we went down to Limehouse for our first load. That butty had been empty so long it had all dried out, and the seams between the planks open up when they're like that, you know. So when we loaded, the water poured in everywhere! It was a good job there was a lot of boat people there. They helped us pumping and chucking ashes round it.'

The caulking between the planks of a wooden boat dries and the planks themselves shrink with exposure to wind and sun if they are not regularly soaked by immersion in the canal when the boat is deep laden. A well placed shovelful of ashes or sawdust will often be drawn into the worst of the cracks by the water movement and this helps to form a seal until the timbers swell again. But, as Sam described, this was an anxious time in the deep water of the Regent's Canal's ship dock.

'You see, when you had a load off a ship like that, the last boats loaded had to stop and get the customs clearance papers for all the lot. Sometimes you could be stopped there three or four weeks or more. You could never tell how long it would be. Well, we should have stopped,

but old Sam Beechy, he said, "You get out of this dock. If you go down here you'll be out of sight! I'll stop in your place." Well, that was good of him because he didn't know how long he'd have to wait and not be earning any money.

'Well, once we'd got out into the canal, it hardly leaked a drop. You see once the planks got soaking up the water they swelled up and the gaps closed and then it was in canal water which is full of mud instead of clean so that went in any cracks and helped to seal it up.'

Gladys remembered being an onlooker on a similar occasion: 'There was one chap, Charlie Atkins – that's old chocolate Charlie's son – he used to like those old wooden boats. Well, when

Gladys poses on the running planks over Wagtail's coal-filled hold as she is towed along the Oxford Canal in 1954 by Warbler which is visible in the background

he was on British Waterways he went mad for one that was lying empty. But it hadn't had a load in it for ages and we was at Longford, by Coventry, loading coal, and they all betted him that he'd have to call the men out to it from the dock at Hillmorton. He said, "I bet you I don't", and they all said, "We bet you you do!" Well, we knew what Charlie was like. He sat in the deck locker at the fore end because he knew that's where she'd leak first, they always do. You could see through between those planks! He had three packs of his missus' sanitary towels with him, and as soon as the water started to come through he was furiously hammering them into the cracks!

FOLLOWING IN THE FAMILY FOOTSTEPS

Gladys recalled that whilst working for Willow Wren, the first of their family put in an appearance.

'I had my first son, Barry, born on the boat at Tusses Bridge, just as you get to Sutton Stop, near Coventry. 1955 that was. The midwife still came out to you in them days. The second one, Roy, I had in the hospital at Bull's Bridge [the former Grand Union Canal Carrying Co fleet depot near Southall which had been operated by British Waterways since nationalisation at the beginning of 1948] because British Waterways used to have five beds to be kept for boat women to have their babies. You used to have to register when you was pregnant so that they could have the bed ready for you at the right time. They used to let you tie up for the last three months by those days. See, with Fellows Morton's, like my mother, they used to get pregnant and they used to carry on and carry on until it was time to have it. In them days you could guarantee there would be a midwife to come out more or less wherever you were. Then they used to have the baby and off the next day. Now look at it these days. Tablets and injections and I don't know what! The kids were better in them days than what they are now. Stronger.

'When I was expecting my oldest one I used to carry on as normal, jumping down off the lockside onto the cabin top of the boats. We were tied up for about six weeks with him. Leslie Morton, our boss then, used to be called 'Whip and Windlass' because he wouldn't let you stop too long! I was lucky to have a little bit longer off because it was in the winter and we got froze up so we couldn't move. I had my third one, Robert, here, after we moved into the house.'

'Those wooden boats, you know they'll tighten up with keeping the planks wet. I remember we was going down to Talbot's Lock one time when we had that *Kingfisher*. That was an old Fellows Morton, but Willow Wren used to name all their boats after birds. We had Jack Skinner's dad along with us. He used to look after his boats like they were glass. Sam went in the lock so fast, and I jumped off to stop the butty with the checking strap and it broke! Oh it did hit the gate, bang! and I thought, now I'm for it for knocking boats about. But he didn't moan, he just said, "That does a wooden butty good, it tightens up the planks!" They do say that would tighten up the joints between the planks. I didn't much care about that, it broke a lot of my pots, that did!'

'Sam later asked Mr Wood, at Bull's Bridge, if we could have a pair of Waterways [British Waterways' boats]. I always wanted to get back down there because that's where my friends was. I didn't like the Barlows because they didn't get down to Bull's Bridge a lot; they only used to go to the jam factory and empty and go straight back up. You never got a night at Bull's Bridge.'

Despite Gladys' enthusiasm: 'That didn't start too well because the first run we had was with a little Woolwich motor, *Virgo*, up to Rose's at Boxmoor with lime juice, and when we got there that run a big end out. That was a National and I used to like them better than Bolinders. But there was no worries with Waterways because all you'd to do was get on the phone and their van could come anywhere.'

Sam found life changed in the bigger carrying fleet, with a greater variety of trips. 'At Bull's Bridge you generally wouldn't get any choice in the orders. You had a ticket given you for what you'd to load and where. If there was a steel ship, then they was all the same and there was such a scratch. They'd all come running along the lay-by from the office to try and get going the first. Lime juice wouldn't necessarily be a very good order because it was low pay. And then sometimes you had to go on up to the coalfields for coal so you wouldn't get back for another quick order. Nobody would want that. Also there used to be maize to Fenny [Stratford] to the brewery which was very low pay.' Gladys remembered that 'There used to be a buffer depot up here at the Cowroast, and maize to there was low pay. My dad would never have a short journey if he could help it. Birmingham was always the best paid. People used to break their necks to get that. Wheat at Whitworth's mill at Wellingborough wasn't too bad.'

Sam recalled that there was also extra work required: 'Only a lot of work cleaning up your boat afterwards. You had to turn all your floors up after emptying to try to sweep it all out. You had cloths like sacking under the wheat to keep it off the floors and sides of the boats, but it still got between and under the floors. When you got to the mill and they started to empty it, it used to stink – like stale wine – as you got down into the load. Then you used to have to try and sweep it all out. But even so after a couple of days it would start sprouting everywhere. If you got just a little bit of moisture in the boat it would sprout green shoots two or three inches long in a couple of days. We used to hate that.'

Gladys: 'We would never come back to Bull's Bridge from that far away, we used to go for coal then, except when the coalfields had their regular ten days' holiday at the pits. At one time of day you could stop up there for ten days to wait for a load, but later on they made you come back down to Bull's Bridge. They wouldn't pay you to stop up there. Then just before the Waterways finished they come up with the idea that the quicker you done your trip the more you got.'

Sam: 'One time I tried to go through a bridge that had no water in it. That was at Cannock Chase, wasn't it? Just before you got to the loading basin at Anglesey. There was a turn to the left and a side bridge on the right of the canal, and a lock through it. Well, this lock and

Sam steers Warbler out of Black Jack's Lock, near Harefield on the Grand Union Canal, while Gladys shares the butty with her brother Jake who had been riding ahead on the bicycle preparing locks until meeting a pair coming uphill which had left the next few ready for the Hornes' boats. They were loaded with cocoa waste which went from Cadbury's, at Bourneville, to the Thames for export

Gladys and Barry Horne pose with their British Waterways butty Ayr at Sutton Stop before carrying another coal cargo southwards

Right: A young Barry Horne on the wharf at Brentford; with little space for toys on the boats a wheat grab might come in handy

the canal beyond had been shut up years ago. It was dark and you couldn't see where you was going, so I thought I had to go straight in there and of course there was no water. Well, we stopped a bit quick!'

Gladys: 'We'd been sitting in the cabin when he went on in there, and we wondered what the heck he'd done. We had a struggle to get the motor out of the mud.

'When we got into the basin there for loading they poked the boats about just like they did the joey boats there. They'd get the point of a shaft and poke it in your cabin side to move the boats about when they wanted them for loading.

'Dickinson's used to pay for a full load of coal but I don't think they ever got one. You should have seen our load in 1963 when we was frozen in all that time – there was a blooming great hole in the starn end. Thirteen weeks we was frozen up. It was weighed in and they gave us a ticket but it was never weighed out at the other end. Sam stopped me burning coal from the butty cargo in the end. British Waterways took

all the boatmen out hedge cutting and he started to bring bags of wood back. Otherwise there'd have been nothing left!

'At Bull's Bridge you'd all be in the lay-by maybe thirty boats in a row. The mums all used to be standing in the door holes chatting while they did the washing and cleaning. There was a loudspeaker there and I remember the chap in the office saying, "Calling all steerers, boat numbers so and so"!'

Sam would be looking after the engine or the boats' equipment. Gladys recalls: 'Every night at about four o'clock they used to call you up for your orders. You listened for your number. If it came up, the first thing my mum used to do – and I must admit I used to do it too, later – was to get all the water cans and get them all filled up. Because Sam'd come back and he'd start straightaway, tonight, and not wait for morning. A lot of them would come out of the lay-by and go down to the next bridge, to the pub, the Grand Junction, instead of stopping in the lay-by. What they used to come out for, you see, was so that they didn't wake anybody on the other boats by setting off early in the morning.'

Sam is more concerned with the boating: 'You could be so tight in the lay-by in that line that you'd got a job to get out sometimes. We nearly always used to go down to Brentford and leave the beer. You could go steady down the locks without having all the others on top of you breathing down your neck, see. That was better with being two-handed.'

Gladys recalls: 'Those locks wasn't too bad because there used to be a lock keeper to help you at every lock. But two-handed at the Northampton Arm with a pair of loaded boats, and two or three pair behind you with three crew on each, it was hell down there, trying to keep ahead of them. I used to have to bowhaul our butty boat by myself, like a horse! I had nobody to steer it whilst I did that, so sometimes it would get stemmed up on the bank. I had nobody old enough to steer. Then you'd got them behind you, flushing all their water down – it could fill up your cabin if you weren't careful.

'I could stop that if I was crafty. You see, they could get their boat into the lock behind, above mine, before I'd got my butty into the next lock because there was more of them and so they'd got a steerer. Then they'd draw the paddles up, and the water would come over the top gate at my lock and might get in my cabin. So what I

used to do was wait and not empty the lock. Then when their lock was empty and all the water had gone, I'd wind my paddles up and get down, and they'd just have to wait.

'I did that one particular time on one of my step-uncles, and when we got to Wellingborough his missus was going to do this to me and that to me for keeping them waiting. Well, we weren't

---

GETTING THEIR OWN BACK

Sam: 'We done a quick load back from Birmingham one time. It was just 19 ton of dog spikes for the railway – they were going on a ship abroad somewhere. Anyway, most times when you got a back load like that at Birmingham it was urgent to catch the ship, you see. So we worked day and night to get it back, but then when we got it there they put it in the warehouse, didn't they! They said 'Well, nobody told you to go mad, rushing down with it!' I'd had me own back anyway, because at Tyseley they said, "There's only 19 ton, so you can leave the butty here and work single motor." Well, we lived mostly on the butty, you see, so I said, "I ain't leaving that here – it won't make that much more work." He said, 'Oh well, please yourself.' The loaders at the works put a bit in each boat. So then we got paid for 40 ton. That was the minimum for carrying in two boats; it was meant to compensate if you got a very lightweight cargo that took up all the space. If we'd have had it all on the one boat we'd only have got paid for the 19 ton!'

Gladys: 'I remember going for that because Sam had never been along there, Black Country way, so he said, "You've been there with your dad, haven't you? Tell me when we get to it." Well, I'd been, but only when I was young, about ten, and then it was all a new galvanised building and lovely. Well, I looked and I thought, "It's got to be here somewhere"; but I never said anything to him, I just let him keep going. There was this rusty old shed all hanging down in the canal, and I thought "This looks a bit like it". So I said to Sam, "I think that's it, back there." "Nah," he says and kept going; but it was! By that time he was well gone by it! There's an awful lot of turns and arms in Birmingham there, and I had only been about those parts when I was small.'

*Awaiting orders
at Sutton Stop,
time was easily
filled with domestic
chores – Gladys
busy aboard Ayr
in the late 1950s*

unloaded when they got down to Wellingborough Mill with the grain. Down there there used to be a little raft because the mill was built straight down into the water. So you tied up against this little raft and the bloke from the mill got down onto it to look after the elevator in your boats. Well, she came running on there to give me a good hiding, but I went and jumped onto the raft – and she couldn't run back up that ladder fast enough! She didn't think I'd get off the boats to her!'

I wondered why Sam and Gladys hadn't thought of taking on a mate to ease the work-load and speed up their trips, but naturally they had. Gladys well remembered the days when life was easier for the womenfolk.

'The like of us, there was fifteen of us kids, they wasn't all old enough to work; but I was ten when I was getting the locks ready and that. Fellows & Morton's used to have plenty of mates

so we always used to have a mate along. We would never have gone two-handed with a pair of boats like Sam and I did. One of my sisters was nineteen and the other was eighteen so they used to help a good bit, but you never used to see a Fellows & Morton's with just two people on. If they hadn't got nobody of their own they used to pay a bloke to come with them, a mate. We did when we was Willer Wrenning, we used to have one of my brothers with us, especially when we had the first child. But you used to have to pay 'em so that made you short of money, then.

'If we had a mate on and did a load both ways in the late fifties – say we brought coal down and then went to Brentford and loaded to Birmingham – he'd get £3; but if we took a load of coal down to Croxley and had to go back empty with nothing, they'd get thirty shilling. When I worked with the Skinners they used to give me £3 whatever we did. So I was all right with them and I used to save a lot of money. You used to get treats off them, as well — like they took you to the pictures, and if you went in the pub they'd buy you drinks. Every young girl that was a mate on the boats, they was envious of me because I always had money when they hadn't because I'd such a good skipper.'

Gladys continues: 'I think that before the war Fellows Morton's was on their last legs. But during the war it was all nationalised, well, under the government, and there was so much stuff to move, it made them. There wasn't one boat stopped in the war, they was always on the go. We took it all over the place. After the war a lot of places kept their work on the canals, like Tate & Lyle's and all them, they proved it could be done on the canal so things was better for a while after the war. That was until the M1 was built — as soon as that was built, places like Croxley [John Dickinson's paper mills] they didn't want the boats, they wanted the lorries. I think that's what did it. You see, there could be a string of boats waiting there at Croxley, with a pair emptying, and if a lorry came in they'd just leave you and go off and empty the lorry. The motorways did it.'

Sam, too, was frustrated by the way boats were kept waiting: 'All they saw the boats as were store warehouses. Those lorries could do about two trips a day. We used to be two-and-a-half days from Suttons to Croxley. See, I had this argument once with one of those lorry drivers. I said, "I've been waiting here to be emptied fourteen days. Now *you* get in that queue and then we'll see who's the quickest in terms of delivering the bulk!" He shut his mouth and never said no more. You see we brought 52 or 53 tons each trip.

'I went down there a bit before I retired, taking a boat to Bull's Bridge — well, when I went round the turn to Croxley there was nothing there, just a grass hill! I said, "Where's the factory?" There's just nothing left.'

'It's the roads that's done it,' affirmed Gladys.

'Then at the finish, about 1963, Gladys and I got called up to go carrying the piles from Marsworth. Me and Sam Brooks, that was. They more or less sold all the other boats up and put everybody off. I didn't want to take the job on. I said to the boss, "There's older captains here than me, it's not fair." He said, "That doesn't matter, we can trust you when we wouldn't trust some of them. We know that you'll go and do your job, and not be tying up here, there and everywhere for half a day or a day."

Gladys was pleased to get the pile-carrying job: 'They wanted us and Sam Brooks for piles and Ernie Humphries, Tom Humphries and Fred Powell because they kept the contract on for lime juice to Rose's at Boxmoor. I didn't want to do the lime juice. You could always tell when you'd got that on in the summer because you'd

There could be waits for loading orders at the southern end of the Grand Union too. Here Gladys stands on Aynho's counter deck whilst tied stern on to the wall with numerous other boats in the lay-by at Bull's Bridge depot. Here orders for loading in the London Docks and at Brentford were issued

got a cloud of wasps following you everywhere!'

Sam: 'We was mostly carrying them piles out from Marsworth, but sometimes, if they had none to go out, we had to go out and work on the length, on maintenance.'

Gladys: 'That was OK, because if they had none to go out for a while Sam went working on the length and the headmaster would let our kids go in the village school there. My first two

by Old Ford Lock. There's a very low railway bridge there, and if the water's high you go round that turn and by the time you realise you can't get under that bridge it's too late! You used to meet those big lighters coming with a tug, as well; they never used to steer them when they were empty. The last one used to trail all along the bank.'

Sam: 'Then, the agreement was that if a house came empty I could have it. Well, this one

Barry in the butty cabin doorway and Roy out in the hatches learning to write numbers by looking at the large numerals that were clearly painted on the locks of the river Nene. Gladys, here looking after the motor boat in the background, recalls that 'when they were young the children used to be tied. You know round that coaming in the hatches in the butty they made me a rail at Bull's Bridge and they threaded a steel ring onto it and fastened the rail to the woodwork. Well, then you used to be able to buy a harness for the kids and you just clipped that to the ring and they could walk about but they couldn't climb to get over the side'

boys went there, and then when we'd got a load and we was ready for going away, we'd go in and tell him and he would give the kids enough to do to keep them going till we got back. So the two boys could read and write before I could.

'We didn't go round on the Lee at all before we started on the piles. Sam was ever so scared!'

'No, I didn't want to go round on that big wide river. I was scared stiff!'

'It was Charlie, the store keeper at Bull's Bridge depot, as persuaded Sam to go on the Lee. He'd been before. He said, "You come down to the depot and we'll fix you up with a horn and whatever else you want. You'll be all right round there." This was the first place he got frightened, because there's a huge turn there, at Lee Bridge, it's a bad bridge. That's as soon as you got on the river, just after you turn out of the Ducketts Cut,

came empty and I applied for it and they let me have it. Then there began to get less work for carrying the pilings, so towards the end there was really only just enough for one pair of boats. We come in this house in 1966 after three years on the pilings. That was with the same boats all through, *Aynho* and *Ayr*.'

Sam was thereafter employed on general maintenance work, involving little actual boating. The in-house manufacture of concrete pilings was phased out by British Waterways in favour of the use of galvanised steel trench sheeting for bank protection. Sam spent over 25 years looking after the banks and towpaths, in between assisting at stoppages for lock gate replacement and other work in the area supervised from the Marsworth maintenance yard. He made the headlines in British Waterways' house

The prolonged freeze at the beginning of 1963 confirmed the British Waterways Board's decision to withdraw the nationalised narrowboat carrying fleet. Here Sam Brooks stands on the Oxford Canal towpath at Sutton stop chatting to Gladys, aboard Aynho. Sam's boats lie across the canal where they froze in with several other pairs beyond

journals, with three successes in the lock and bridge competition for keeping his house frontage and lockside immaculate.

'I had three cups for the lock and bridge competition. I wasn't really no gardener, the only experience I'd had was with the farm when I was young.'

In 1970 the last long regular distance trading narrowboats passed through his lock en route to Croxley Mills and the Kearly & Tonge jam factory at Southall. Then for over twenty more years Sam presided over the passage of pleasure craft.

Gladys: 'Our son, Roy, died in the February, and then British Waterways put Sam off work in the April; two years early, that was.

'That was when I was having my left hip done, before I'd even had any trouble with the right one at all. It really annoyed me, that,

because there was no way anybody knew whether I'd work again. I hadn't had any trouble with my right hip then. It broke my heart that did really, because there was still plenty of jobs I could have done full time, even if I wasn't really allowed to lift. After 35½ years that was, you know.'

Gladys remains unsure of the advantages of life in a town-centre house with all its conveniences: 'We haven't really got any good friends in Berkhamsted except on the boatyard just up here. We still miss that after the boats, because when you were on them it didn't matter where you were, you knew you'd always got friends nearby. You never used to go a day without speaking to somebody. Round here, people just don't seem to want to be friendly.

'I'm proud of being a boat person, I am. But it was difficult when we first come on the land,

From 1963–66 the Hornes were based at Marsworth maintenance yard from which concrete piles were despatched to bank repair sites on several of the southern waterways. Barry (left) and Roy spent much time with Sam Brooks' children (whose parents also boated piles away from the yard) playing along the towpath at the head of the branch canal to Aylesbury

In an attempt to reduce the amount of unproductive waiting time they paid boatmen for, BW employed a number (including the two Sams) cutting overhanging trees along the Oxford Canal, which was easily carried out from the ice. Sam Horne photographed George Wain, Sam Brooks, Bert Wallington, Ronnie Hough and Les Lapworth standing on the canal near Hillmorton

with not having been to school and all. But since then I've been to night school. When you was all on the boats you were nearly all of you the same so you never used to take no notice. The lock keepers used to write letters or anything for you. You see when I first met Sam he used to write letters to me and send them to the toll offices and when I got one I used to open it and the toll keeper would read it to me. Then if there was any answers they would write a letter back. They

A small mobile crane and stacks of new concrete piles form the backdrop to this photo of Gladys and Roy encouraging their dog to pose for the camera

Right: A favourite game at Marsworth was always Cowboys with occasional ambushes from the deck of motorboat Aynho

always used to do that, the lock keepers or toll keepers did.'

Sam received many such letters written for Gladys. She recalls: 'The one at Cut End [Autherley Junction, where the Shropshire Union joined the Staffordshire & Worcestershire Canal] was the best one at that, Sam Lomas. And him that was at the top of the Marsworth Locks never used to be too bad. But the letters Sam used to send to me used to be like a writing pad. So I used to say to the lock keeper, "Just tell me the interesting bits and skip the rest!" But, you see, when I did come into the house here I found

it difficult not being able to read and write because of mixing with other people. When Robert was five I took him down the infant school and the headmaster said, "You'll have to fill this form in," I said, "Oh, I can't do that, I can't read and write." He said "Would you like to?" I said, "Yes, I would!" So he got me in with his colleague.

'I wasn't sure about it at all, because I didn't want to be the only one who couldn't read and write. But when I saw her, she had quite a lot to teach, all adults. She said, "It's better with you, because we can start from scratch; a lot of these have been to school but have learned nothing of it." She said, "Let me take you into the Dacorum College at Hemel Hempsted. We'll get a coachload up and go, and you'll see how many people can't read or write." I was amazed at all those people who couldn't read and write. I got in with a bloke who used to live just up here and he was with the post office putting telephone poles in the ground.

On seeing this shot of the Dinkum dredger being used to ease the work of delivering the Horne's cargo to the latest bank re-enforcement job Sam recalls that, 'You wasn't supposed to unload them with the Dinkum'. Health & safety regulations only reached canal maintenance work in fairly recent years (Sam Horne)

Overleaf: After leaving the boats and becoming lock keeper at Berkhamsted, Sam still had regular contact with former Willow Wren colleagues. Here he is (in white shirt) assisting the skipper of Ascot who was towing the broken down motor boat Stirling on 27 August 1967

He and I used to sit together and help each other. If he didn't know how to spell something he'd ask me, and if I didn't he'd help me out! I got through pretty good but he didn't, he didn't make it.'

Sam: 'Now she does all the writing, I do detest doing it now, I don't write any letters any more.'

'No, now Sam's retired and got all the time in the world, he doesn't do it!'

Looking back over the years Gladys is in no doubt as to which way of life she prefers: 'You never used to get a lot of money on the boats, but I reckon it was better. You could save, because you'd no rent to pay, and no electricity to pay and you could burn as much coal as you liked! What money you got was yours – you didn't have to pay it out to nobody else like you do now for gas, electric and rates; it was yours, no matter how little it was, you could do what you liked with it. That frightened me, when we come in this house and we had the first bill come. I thought, "Oh, my God, I'm not used to these things. I'll have to start saving for them" – and that's what I've been doing ever since!

'I liked the canal I did, I loved it. I don't regret being on it at all. If I could spend my time back, to like it was, I'd do it all again! But not like it is now, you couldn't get your living on it now, with all the pleasure boats.

'I used to love the boats. When we was teenagers we used to have so much fun on them. When you got to the ends of your trips nearly all your mates was there, and you could go to the pictures or off to a fairground. I used to love all that.'

A boatman's view of his wife, at the far end of seventy feet of boat towed behind him, attached to up to a further seventy feet of line. Gladys knew what had attracted Sam to take the picture, however: 'I'm sitting on the side because it's a straight pound washing all me legs. We must've been going out somewhere so I was getting ready'

Always on Hand

*Heather Wood: Shepherdess,
Hook Norton, Oxfordshire*

ALWAYS ON HAND

Although farming generally has changed dramatically since World War II, some things remain as important as ever. The new breed of highly educated agro-businessman may crop a better return on investments, yet never experience the real job satisfaction which his forebears enjoyed. Traditional farming should not be the plaything of profiteers, but rather an entire way of life based on subsistence and sustainable natural resources, and it is the man or woman who has true empathy with the seasons and animals who will reap the greatest rewards. Such a person is Heather Wood (née Thompson) who, among many other things, has cared for sheep for over half a century.

Opposite:
Bringing home the
sheep

While the tycoon may regard a flock of sheep as no more than X number of meat and wool units, to Heather every animal is an individual requiring year-round attention. Not surprisingly then, when it comes to lambing Heather regards 'always being there' as the most important thing.

A very modest and gentle lady, as befits the good shepherdess, Heather has always been close to the land and livestock, and immersed in Cotswold life. She was born at Elm Bank Farm, Cold Aston, Gloucestershire on 16 October 1935, and later moved to neighbouring Camp Farm, both places being run by her father. And when she married Nolan, in 1959, she moved only about 15 miles away, to Sugarswell Farm, a mile or two outside Hook Norton, where her husband is still the tenant. There, among the north Oxfordshire hills, sheep and warm stone cottages have characterised the countryside since the Middle Ages.

When I drove up to see Heather, late-July thunderstorms relieved the drought in many areas, although Hook Norton's hills remained stubbornly dry. As we chatted in her eighteenth-century farmhouse, Heather expressed her concern about weather trends:

'This is our third dry year in a row and our poor sheep have hardly anything to eat. Last year was even worse and they were ravenous, and we had to buy no end of hay when our own stock was exhausted. In the old days you would find lots of springs all over the place, but now they've mostly dried up. And with no piped supply your animals were always restricted to where the water was – that's why you had permanent pasture.

'In the early days here we had to carry our water from the spring – but then at least we didn't have to worry about frozen pipes because we didn't have any! Mind you, in the bitter winter of 1962–3, when we never saw a visitor and our Christmas cake was still in the tin at Easter, we had to thaw the dishcloth in the morning before we could do the washing-up!

'Our source of water is supposed to be the origin of the name "Sugarswell", because it is said to be a corruption of Sugre, the name of the man who looked after this watering place.'

Back in the war, *too much* water was once a problem, because when evacuees took over the farm bedrooms, Heather and her three sisters had to sleep in the basement, and this often flooded. Even so, they were very happy days, as Heather recalls:

'Dad gave us an old milk-float horse, called Betsy. She was *our* pony, though in fact Dad only let us have her because she was incurably lame and could never go fast. However, we often used

Heather and her sisters on the family donkey

to all get on her and ride her together, and one day she bucked, throwing all three of us into the nearby nettles!

'It was safe to wander everywhere then, and we went for miles collecting flowers, only going back home for meals. We often wore clogs and they were blinkin' rigid, but in those days children never dreamed of challenging anything they were told to do, unlike they do now.

'At Elm Bank Farm we had an old shepherd's hut as a playhouse and we even wall-papered it and hung curtains, but we were turned out when Dad let two German prisoners-of-war have it. They were lovely men who would repair

WANDERING SWALEDALES

'One time Dad bought 150 Swaledale ewes at market, probably because they were going cheap. Unfortunately they weren't used to southern fences and often wandered onto other people's land, and many a time I had to get up at dawn to retrieve them before they were spotted. Then one day a couple of these ewes really charged this wall, and in trying to jump it, flattened it. Yet when we saw the owner of the wall he never said anything – unlike a lady neighbour who was soon on the phone threatening to shoot our sheep if they went onto her land again.'

anything; they used our hut as their base by day, but they were taken back to camp each night.

'Dad had a lot of sheep – probably four or five hundred on his 450 acres at Camp Farm – and Mum always made lambs'-tail pie, which was a great delicacy. But it was cruel the way the tails were seared off with a hot iron. Nowadays, when the lamb is two days old a rubber ring is put on its tail, which falls away over several weeks; rams are castrated in the same way. They feel it at first, but it obviously goes numb quite quickly.

'Being girls didn't mean we didn't have to work hard. I had hoped to become a domestic science teacher, but I was needed on the farm and that's where I stayed. Yet we laughed each day through, and there were always lots of people about on the land; nowadays my husband sometimes comes home in his tractor and says he hasn't seen anyone all day!

'As there were four of us girls there was always a string of boyfriends calling – but Dad saw them as a source of cheap labour and they had to help us with jobs before we were allowed out. Once we even had to plant potatoes on Good Friday! It was very embarrassing.

'Another thing we had to do was work at the wheel of the mechanical sheep shearer for Dad, although you only had to turn it slowly, because it was geared to make the cutters go quickly. I also learnt to use the hand shears – I've still got the scars! The sheep had a fair few snicks too: it couldn't be helped if they suddenly jumped. In the old days on some farms it wasn't unusual to see shearing wounds just tied up with string to stop the bleeding.

'The most remarkable of the farm staff was an old recluse called Miss Williams, who looked after our poultry and had a cottage stacked full of Yeastvite tablets. She never had any company at all and lived by the daylight, just like the animals, always going to bed at dusk and getting up at dawn.'

When Heather was twelve years old, in 1947, she experienced one of the coldest winters ever recorded.

'I remember it very well because we were blocked in for weeks, and when one of my sisters was born, the doctor and nurse could only reach the house by walking along the top of the hedge, which was virtually buried by frozen snow. The frost got under some of the floor tiles in the house and when they lifted we couldn't close the door for weeks. We had to use a tractor to get the shopping, and I think we lost quite a few sheep. Under the snow they are protected from the icy wind and their breathing creates a little air hole above, but they soon die of starvation.

'Sheep suffer from the effects of hypothermia just the same as humans do, but they are naturally roaming creatures, and in the old days they weren't generally brought in for lambing like they are now; at Camp Farm all the ewes lived on the hill and we just went out at dusk and brought in any weak lambs which would have been at risk. In snowy weather we brought them in on a sledge, and I started doing this when I was a schoolgirl because Dad was laid up with lumbago.'

Among Heather's other tasks at Camp Farm was Cotswold stone walling, and if the fine example of ironstone walling in her present garden is anything to go by, she obviously became expert at this. She told me: 'Every winter the walls crumbled and fell, and every spring and summer we had to put them up again. The knack was to keep the middle filled with all the little stones to keep the rain and frost out.'

Laying hedges was another important job which Heather was obliged to learn, and she recalled this with mixed feelings:

'Dad would say something like: "See that tree over there? Well, don't stop till you reach it!" – so we always had plenty of practice! But it was a bloomin' cold winter job, so the first thing you did was to get the fire going; then you would break off to restore the circulation whenever you needed. But one time Dad had this splendid new white riding mac and he got so close to the fire he burnt it.'

With a tear in her eye, Heather told me what a 'kind and wonderful countryman' her father

Using hand shears to take off the fleeces

*Opposite:
Washing sheep
prior to clipping, a
common practice
in the 1930s*

was; so it was a great shock to the family when he died suddenly, at the age of 56: 'He alone was the farm tenant and we therefore had no right to stay on, so poor Mum lost both her husband and her home. It broke our hearts.'

It was in the same year that Heather married the son of her father's old friend, who had just 42 acres at Sugarswell Farm. As Heather explained: 'If you've got a thousand acres it costs no more to have a telephone than if you have only forty.' At Hook Norton, Heather continued to indulge her love of sheep:

'With a smaller acreage we only run a flock of about a hundred here, and we used to have all sorts. Then my daughter Sally became very interested and said we ought to have some decent sheep, so we decided to keep mostly North

NORTH COUNTRY MULES

The original mule sheep dates back to 1863 and was derived from a blue-faced Leicester ram mated with a Swaledale or Scottish blackface ewe.

Country mules, which are prolific breeders.

'Our system here is very traditional. We buy new stock in the autumn, from Banbury market or dealers who go north, and these are put out to rams at the end of October. Throughout the winter it's mostly constant checking and feeding, going on to trough food – cereals and so on – from late February. The lambs are mostly born in late March and April, and sold from July to October.' As lambing time approaches, Heather becomes very single-minded:

'You have to keep looking all the time for problems such as prolapsing, which is very common. I never go out at lambing and I don't like visitors. We have a multi-purpose shed here, and that's cleared to accommodate the ewes: even my husband's vintagetractors go out!

'All our ewes are brought inside every night, but with bigger flocks, where lambing is over a longer period, some farmers use different colour

raddle so that they know when each ewe is going to lamb and look after it accordingly. [Raddle, reddle or ruddle is a colouring material – often red ochre – applied to the chest of a ram so that those ewes which have been mated are marked.] One extraordinary thing that's always impressed me is how many of our ewes know their own spot in the barn.

'After lambing, each ewe and her offspring are put into individual hurdle pens for a couple of days, to make sure they are suckling and feeding well before they go out.'

Of course, during lambing Heather gets very little sleep, and after checking her charges last thing at night she may be lucky to get a couple of hours in bed before her 'body clock' wakes her again at 2–3am. But in recent years she has been greatly helped by a baby alarm:

'When a ewe is about to lamb it starts to talk, and when I hear this over the alarm it is important that I get out quickly to avoid mismothering. Where ewes are confined close together and, say, two of them have four or five lambs between them at about the same time, they can easily get mixed up. Also, ewes often do their damndest to pinch a lamb even when their own isn't due for twenty-four hours, so I want to be on hand to sort it all out. Incidentally, all this is caused by keeping sheep indoors. Outside, each ewe about to give birth would naturally find a quiet corner away from the others and there wouldn't be any problem. But overall, confining sheep is certainly worthwhile to reduce losses through difficult births, severe weather and predation. Luckily we have had no problems with foxes or dogs roaming free here.'

Heather's work has been made considerably easier by recent advances in sheep health care, as she explained:

'Nowadays we always have a bottle of penicillin at the ready, to inject at the first sign of sickness, and this has been a great saviour. Also, we have things such as Vetrazine to spray down the sheep's back and around the tail to prevent blowfly eggs from hatching. It's all very different from the old days, when all we had to control fly-strike, as well as many other things, was Jeyes Fluid – bottles and bottles of it everywhere, on walls and in cars. And whereas we now have scientifically developed sprays for treating sore spots, Dad relied on big brown jars of M & B Powder, which he mixed with lard to apply to wounds. And we both used Stockholm tar.

'Also in the early days, the local policeman had to come out and sign the book to say that he had seen every sheep dipped. When the Ministry men took over they were also meant to time how long each sheep was in the dip; but they didn't ever bother us.

'When I was a Girl Guide our captain said we should all go tracking and it was decided to do this on our Elm Bank Farm. When we arrived at the dip the sheep had gone and left the usual thick, grey scum on the surface. Unfortunately this looked just like concrete and one of the Guides stepped into it, right up to her waist, thinking it was solid! Luckily she wasn't harmed and we had a good laugh afterwards.'

Through orders and notices issued by the Ministry of Agriculture and vets, dipping has been an important and effective way to cure or stop the spread of diseases such as sheep scab, as well as to kill common parasites and prevent blowfly attack, but the chemicals used have caused much controversy. Dips containing Dieldrin were preferred to arsenic and sulphur as they persisted in the fleece, giving longer protection, but Dieldrin was banned in 1966 because it is highly poisonous and a possible meat contaminant. More recently, dips have contained mainly organo-phosphorus chemicals, but now

these have been widely linked with illness among people using them, so there is growing demand for their ban, too. Sadly, the warnings appear to have come too late for many handlers. As Heather explained, 'Protective gloves came with the packs, but these were unpleasant to wear and as there was no obvious health risk we used to use these for other things. There's no way I'd touch an OP dip now.'

Another thing for which Heather must be on the constant lookout is sheep on their backs: 'Sometimes they just roll over in a hollow, but it also happens quite a lot between lambing and shearing when they probably get itchy and turn over while trying to relieve themselves. For some reason it only happens to mature sheep, and without someone to help them back up onto their feet they can die very quickly in hot weather.'

Occasionally the sheep do not appreciate the care which Heather gives them, but she is never resentful: 'Some ewes bash you like mad, but never nastily, because they're only protecting their young. Sometimes I say I wouldn't like to be a fox when that one lambs! When I was young my nose was badly bruised when a ewe sprang up, and later a ram really clouted and hurt my hip.'

Given this background, I wondered if Heather still liked lamb and mint sauce: 'Oh yes,' she replied, 'but my husband doesn't like me cooking it. In fact he hates everything to do with sheep and much prefers the smell of oil and diesel. He always says that a ram sandwich is enough to put anyone off. Perhaps it goes back to his childhood, when farmers often did their own slaughtering and would even eat the sickly animals which they had killed!'

Heather on the combine

Not surprisingly, with a traditionally close working relationship, Heather has become very attached to some of her sheepdogs. She told me about two in particular:

'This is "Trim", who's twelve years old and came from a neighbour. At first she'd round up the ducks but not the sheep, so she had to go away with another shepherd for eight weeks. She's trained to the voice because I never could whistle, unlike my Dad. But her sight's not too good now. Sometimes, when I'm in the kitchen and look out I can see her following my scent where I've been to the washing line, and she never settles if I'm away. When she retires, I think I'll retire too.

'Before Trim I had Lassie – but perhaps Glen was the most remarkable dog our family ever had. He was blind when we had him, but he was a clever dog and worked the sheep well: he knew all the gaps in the hedges and had no problem bringing the sheep down the hill when required. He loved cars and our old Ford was the only place where you could shut him up. And you only ever tied him up once – there's the scars on my arm to prove it! He also took a huge hunk out of my sister Rita's leg because she got down-wind of the sheep. He'd round up everything, even the hens.

'One day Glen went missing and we drove all over the fields in the Ford Ten calling his name, into the woods and along the hedgerows. Then we came to this old, dry well, one of many dug in the Cotswolds in search of water, and we hardly dared peer in. But there he was, miraculously clinging to a piece of wood jutting out the side.

'We fetched a long ladder from the barn and gently lowered it into the well, but this was greeted by snarls and desperate growls because Glen couldn't see what was happening. So father gently coaxed and whistled and talked to him and we edged the ladder as close to him as possible. After a while, Glen put out a tentative paw, felt the hardness of the ladder, and then wrapped his front legs around a bottom rung, allowing us to pull him up, clinging on for dear life. It was a wonderful moment when he came to the surface.

'For a long time after that Glen wouldn't allow anyone near him except my father, and he continued to live in the old Ford until it was decided that he should be put down.'

Heather has also had some very unusual pets; here she recalls the most remarkable.

'On Dad's farm I had a lamb called Jill, which never left my side. Even when I went ploughing with the tractor she would always run along in front of the wheel. One day we had to go to my sister's school sports day and Jill was shut in. But as soon as we moved off she got out followed us, and this happened several times so we gave up and took her with us in the car. But at the sports field she had to stay inside the vehicle and wait for us. There were a few surprised faces around! One day she got into the garden and ate everything, so then Dad insisted that she had to go.

Since then I've had many other pets, including lambs called Lulu and Cilla.

'I also had a pig, a large white called Emily, although unfortunately I almost killed her! I fed her very well, but didn't give her sufficient water so she developed an oedema. When she was young she got to like sucking milk from a lamb's bottle, and she never forgot this. Even when she was full grown she'd sit on her haunches just like a dog and wait for me to give her a bottle! She was just like one of the family, and when we moved here she came with us. Later on my three children gave me a saddleback pig called Samantha and we bred a lot from her.'

Country life has certainly changed a great deal since Heather arrived at Sugarswell Farm. On the very day the Woods moved in, as they were taking the window out to get the bed in, the grocer turned up to take his first order! Contrast that with today, when most village shops have closed down and deliveries to remote places have become almost unknown. Yet while country folk generally must now travel long distances to towns in order to shop relatively cheaply, townsfolk are eager to get out into the countryside to pick fruit and vegetables such as Heather's strawberries. 'But I don't think it's a bargain they are after,' said Heather, 'it's more the space and fresh air they want.

'Some of these visitors expect me to know every birdsong they hear and every flower they see, and I'm always ashamed to say that I don't. What they don't seem to realise is that we have always been in the countryside to work and have just taken the things around us for granted.'

That said, there can be very few people who visit the countryside in search of 'nature' who can match Heather's love of animals, both wild and domesticated. 'Always being there' may have been for the mutual survival of both flock and shepherdess, but for Heather Wood it was never primarily for material gain.

A Royal Coachman

Arthur Showell:
Hampton Court Mews, Surrey

A ROYAL COACHMAN

A cobbled forecourt and rainwater pipes embossed with the date 1570 confirm the venerability of the place in which Arthur and Yvonne Showell live. The complex once formed the stables and coachhouses of one of the royal palaces; it still is, in fact, part of that palace, but nowadays the coachhouses are garages and the stables and grooms' quarters are comfortable flats.

Yvonne is a kind, hospitable person. She is quietly proud of Arthur's achievements in life and keeps a book of newspaper cuttings which mark occasions in his career. Arthur's life with horses deserves recording. It culminated in his becoming HM the Queen's head coachman at Buckingham Palace Mews. He held this post for twenty-three years before he and Yvonne retired to their flat by the Thames.

Arthur is compact in build. When he talks, his rounded features are bright with enthusiasm and he laughs cheerfully.

Arthur as a young boy in St Helier, Jersey; (previous page) Just one of the many horse-drawn carriages that made up the parade to celebrate the accession of Queen Elizabeth II to the throne in 1952

However, it is obvious that he can stand his ground when he feels it is needed.

For ease of telling, it is simplest to break Arthur's story into three parts.

Growing Up in Jersey

Both Arthur and Yvonne are Jersey born and bred, and they still visit and love the island. Jersey acknowledges Arthur too, for not so long ago when their Philatelic Bureau published a stamp to honour a royal occasion, they used a photograph of Arthur on its presentation pack: it shows him in full livery driving the Queen in the Ivory Phaeton to the Trooping the Colour. Arthur describes his early history thus:

'I was born in 1926. My parents never had any money and there was no such thing as the Pony Club, so because I loved horses, I used to go round all the local stables in St Helier just to get as much as I could of what in those days they called cartage. They'd let you drive the horses and I used to learn a lot from watching them. For example, the way they loaded their vehicles. They'd put two tons of coal or sand or gravel from the sea on a two-wheeled vehicle. It had to be balanced correctly so there wasn't too much weight on the horse's back. As the loaded cart approached a hill the carter would usually stand on the shafts; that stopped the shafts going up in the air when the horse climbed the hill and also kept the weight on its back. Some people would say, "Look at that lazy so-and-so making the horse pull him up the hill". They didn't realise that he'd walked a couple of miles, just to make sure that there wasn't too much weight on the horse's back during the journey.

'I'd help take the horses down to the beach on a Sunday morning, too. If the tide was right, the carters would get me to jump on their horses' backs and take them into the sea and swim them. The carters would each bring an old dandy brush with them and when their horse came out, brush all the feather on its legs and give each one a good clean up because they used to think that salt water was a good remedy. Nowadays people turn hosepipes on their horses' legs for tendons and suchlike, but in those days we took them into the sea.

'I spent a lot of time with a firm called Pitchers. They used to have horses what we called vanners which were a cross between a riding horse and a draught horse and which could be put into a four-wheeled van for haulage. They also had a livery yard with about twenty horses of all kinds, and they owned a bus company which did island trips. One of their vehicles was a six-teen-seater horse-drawn car called a "Tantivy".'

Arthur was thirteen when the war broke out. He describes the effect on Jersey when the

of vehicles like landaus, barouches, wagonettes, funeral carriages, horse hearses, more coaches and vans and a useful vehicle called a brougham, and went into the cabbing business. People could ring up for a carriage and pair or a single horse to go somewhere. Riding for pleasure completely stopped. The only time you got a ride in those days was when you jumped up and rode bare-back to the blacksmith's shop.

'One of the bad things was that there wasn't much food for the horses. You couldn't get a lot

Germans first moved in to occupy it: 'The island was in full swing with plenty of food in the shops, and when the German troops arrived and saw so much stuff they bought it all up quickly and sent it back to Germany. Well, it wasn't long before the shops were empty. Pitchers had a shop down in the Parade and they were sensible because before it was too late, they shut shop and took everything home. Put it under the floorboards.'

Pitchers and other horse haulage firms actu-ally benefited from the German occupation, because with petrol being short, horse-drawn vehicles were in demand. As Arthur recalls:

'Everybody started looking for landaus or any kind of horse-drawn carriage that was laid up in the manors around the island; there was quite a lot of carriages to be got hold of. Old Boss Pitcher was a bit shrewd and got himself a variety

of oats, and although it was grown locally, hay went up to £40 a ton. That doesn't sound much today, but in those days wages were 30s [£1.50p] and £2, so there's the difference. Horses were in such poor condition their collars had to be small so that they fitted around their shoulders. You had to force these collars over the horse's head – in fact you tried to open them up by putting them on your knee and pulling at them, and some people would put them on the floor and push down from the pointed end. It was always a struggle to get the collar on, but I thought that was natural, I just thought, well, the horse has got a big head and that's it. It was only after the war that I learnt different – in fact, when I went to work in Hampshire for Sir Dymoke White. His horses were in such good condition and their necks so big but the collars went easily over the

'FUZZ EATERS'

'We used to mix molasses with the horses' food, a sweet substance like black treacle, and were often so hungry we'd eat a bit ourselves! Mangolds was another horse food – a root similar to a swede – and the prickly shrub with a yellow bloom called gorse. We called that furze or fuzz. We'd bundle it up and put some risers on the van to cope with the high load. We put it through the chaff cutter, but because of the spikes on it we used to wear a pair of thick gloves and use a stick or something to get it through. Some of the heavy horses had a moustache on the upper lip and people used to say: "He's a good fuzz eater", because the moustache would protect him!' Arthur chuckles at this memory. Still considering gorse, he adds: 'Horses sometimes suffer from lampas, a swelling of the gums in the upper jaw. But it was said that horses fed on gorse never had it – and gorse was a good treatment for it, too. I also found out in later years that if you had a horse with severe colic and were lucky enough to have it recover, it would of course still be out of sorts and would take a long time to get eating again. However, if you got a nice bundle of gorse and strung it up in the corner of the stable, then a horse would somehow get some comfort from it and start picking away at it.'

heads and correctly fitted the shoulders. It was quite an eye-opener to me.

Going back to their wartime days in Jersey, Yvonne describes the household food they had: 'We were existing on swedes, a few potatoes, but mainly swedes. My grandmother could get Jersey milk, so she used to bring it to the boil and then skim off the cream and make butter; so she always had plenty of butter, but no bread so we fried the swede. We had boiled or fried swede for breakfast, and would then go out into the garden and be sick all the way.' Arthur takes up the tale: 'There was a curfew on the island. I think six o'clock in the morning you were allowed outside your house, but you then had to be in at ten o'clock each night or nine o'clock in the coastal area. It was a good job there was a curfew, otherwise the horses would have been worked both day *and* night!

'There were no lame horses on Jersey, they just all knew one another and were nodding, saying "Morning!" to each other as they went by. They really worked, those horses, I'll tell you that right now, even if they were bloody lame they still went. Actually the funny thing about a lame horse is, you can walk him along and all of a sudden he'll start bucking and kicking and when you move him on he'll still muck about. We had one horse that was definitely lame but it worked for several years like that. You see there was nothing to move anything and they needed transport. I mean, people were lame too, they were hungry and weak but everything had to be kept going.

'As I say, Pitchers really came into their own. They supplied the undertakers with the hearse and the funeral coaches, and they also did weddings, private cab work and supplied horses for the farms for doing a bit of ploughing.

'Although these horses were not in the best of condition by any means, they were fit and quite hardy, that is, they could trot for quite long periods and would very rarely sweat. But when you had a chance to stop and you threw a rug over their backs, we always used to have a knee rug for the cabbing work, that was their signal that they were going to get a rest and they'd stand really quiet.

'But occasionally a horse did take charge and gave you a bit of a frightening experience. I can remember a chap called Jack Coutanche and myself when we were both about sixteen or seventeen and we were both on a brougham with no passengers, returning to the stables. The horse was a rather well bred cob of about 15.2hh. Anyway, we hit this patch of cobbles, six to eight feet square, and as the wheels went over it vrrrhhmmm, suddenly this cob took off. I can remember the brougham started swaying from left to right and this horse was really galloping, you know his hind legs were touching the vehicle, with us both hanging on with a hand round the brougham lamps. I think we finished up with a rein each, pulling at it, but went another four or five hundred yards coming up to a rather nasty cross-roads until we managed to stop him – although he was on the pavement. I think I took the reins and Jack led us back home. We were both utterly exhausted – you'd be surprised how exhausted you are when you're frightened for your life!'

He did other jobs for Pitchers besides cabbing: 'You could be up at the gas works with a heavy horse carting coal. You'd load it with a sort of slack which was a dusty type of coal, then cart that and tip it around the purifyer. If you were on your own you would shovel and cart 12 tons, that's eight loads a day. I think I was about sixteen in those days. I used to come back of a night and put the horse in the stables with the other carters; and when I got home there wasn't always a lot to eat, and I'd be just about bushed so I used to have a wash and go to bed. Then my mates used to come round to meet me to go out, but I would be too tired to go – and I put up with all this just for the pleasure of actually working with horses, you know.'

There were also stints of coal hauling in the docks. It was dangerous work, as Arthur explains:

'You backed the horse and cart into the quay, and the only thing to prevent you going over into the boat below was six to eight inches of woodwork which went round the pier head.

Today it would frighten me to bloody death! And the noise was terrible, engines going and shovels. You'd stand in your cart and could just see the ears of the horse. For safety you put the reins through a piece of string which was attached to the high part of the riser, so if the horse made a dive forward you could make a grab for the reins. Men in the boat loaded the coal into baskets, and operators using a steam-driven winch and derricks would swing the basket at you, and you'd catch it and tip it in your cart; then you'd drop the basket down and it would go back to a chap to fill it again. A full basket weighed 3cwt. The great art of loading was to make a wall at the back of the cart: you'd put the lumps of coal there, or if you were loading slack, you would stamp on it to compact it there.

'It was a bit precarious when you got on to the top of the load and were getting the last two or three baskets. But if you had a good chap on the derrick, he could nearly hold the weight of the basket whilst you tipped it. Then the great thing was to try and prevent any of the coal rolling off onto the horse's back and frightening it.

'As soon as you were loaded you'd jump down and prepare to move off. You always started the horse off by going to his head. You never see

A Jersey farmer leads his horse onto the weighbridge

Arthur and his mates enjoying a pint after joining the army

If you had an obliging horse it would just lay on the collar – but a smart one who was sharp at getting away would make a plunge, and they'd all got to do it for the first time!

'You'd go onto a weighbridge, then on towards a store. Sometimes in summer it would be bright sun, but in the store there'd be no lights at all, just a few candles twinkling in the dust. The store was long and narrow, with often barely enough room to turn the horse round, and here there would be chaps called trimmers. They wore chokers, and they would throw the coal up high because the higher it went, the more they got in.

'You'd turn the horse and back the load up, and they used to hold their shovel on the near side of a sort of horseshoe hollow they'd dug out and say "On the shovel, son"! And you had to get your wheel in line with this chap's shovel as you backed it in. Then they would knock out the tailboard of the cart and the coal would come out – but you didn't want too much to come at once, and that's why the wall you'd made was useful, because that kept the cart reasonably balanced. If

people doing it now, but you held his head and felt his mouth so you'd got hold of him, then you put your right hand on the shaft and asked him to move by putting a fair bit of pressure on his mouth. If he decided to come towards you quickly with the weight, or stumbled and went down on his knees, you'd push yourself off him with your right hand – otherwise he'd fall on you, particularly as the cobbles were really slippery and also there was a crane track to get over.

SHOP DELIVERIES

'There was a chap on the island called Bert Mills, a bit of a flash character with a grey horse who used to do a shop round for a big multi-store called De Gruchy; they sold things like furniture and china, anything to do with the home. But after a period of time during the occupation the Germans decided to deport English-born people and Bert Mills was sent abroad; Pitchers took over the horse, and so then I drove it on the shop round.

'The horse was called Rosa; she was an exceptionally fast-walking animal, and this was good, because you didn't want a lot of trotting when horses weren't getting enough food. But I think she had kidney trouble, because about once a month or more she'd collapse, go straight down as you were walking along. I found the knack of unhooking her without undoing too many straps. I used to undo the back strap so it would free the breeching and free the hames from the hame strap under the collar, although the traces were still attached. Then I'd loosen the belly band if I could. I'd get two or three people to help me get on the wheel of the van and on the shafts and roll it back, and it used to just slide away. Rosa would lay quiet; and if, after looking her over, I couldn't see any injuries, I'd give her a shout and she'd get up, we'd put the bits and pieces on her and carry on as usual. In wartime people didn't waste their money on vets.'

the load shot out you had all the weight of the fore cart on the horse's back which would make it difficult to tip the cart. You also had to make sure that your horse stood still, because you didn't want it to pull forward and drag the coal out into the open area. If it did, the trimmer would probably have put his shovel on your head as he'd have the work of throwing it all back!

'Once the cart was tipped, you just moved the horse forward pace by pace very slowly until it was clear. When it was, a good thing to do was to put a lump of coal under one of the wheels and tell the horse to pull forward; as it went up and over the coal the jerk it made used to pull the cart back upright. If your face fitted and you did it right, possibly the trimmers would give you a hand to put the heavy tailboard back on. Then you'd come away, and then go back and do the same all over again.'

On one occasion in 1942 Arthur, Bert and Rosa were involved in an accident with a lorry on a blind corner; Rosa ended up with her two forefeet through the lorry cab window and herself on top of the bonnet. The accident was reported in the local paper and recently was re-reported in their '50 years ago' column. Family members on Jersey sent Arthur and Yvonne this latest paragraph and Yvonne has added it to her cuttings collection.

In quieter mode Arthur, Bert and Rosa used to deliver to a lady out on a farm. 'She'd give us a glass of milk and two little cakes each,' Arthur recalled. 'I can remember devouring my two cakes, but Bert used to always leave one of his for "manners". One day I didn't do the round with Bert because I got upgraded, and Jack Coutanche went in my place. I said to Jack "Did you have your cake?" He said "Old Bert said he'd better leave one for manners, but I told him 'Manners don't bloody need it, but I do', and I picked it up and ate it."' Arthur splutters with laughter at this memory and adds, 'I'd been dying to do that for years.'

In addition to working for Pitchers, Arthur spent some time with another Jersey horse firm called Martlands, which worked solely with heavy horses. However, it is Pitchers he remembers best, particularly the harness room and tack cleaning by a coke brazier. He also recalls how their horses were kept: 'Nowadays you don't see people grooming like we used to. Grooming was a ritual, and it was pleasant to watch a chap who could groom, you know, seeing him moving in a rhythm, and he'd "get a sweat on", as we say. The old grooms used to blow a bit, you know what I mean? Sort of "pwsssh" when they were grooming, and every time they touched the horse with the brush they went "prrrhh, prrrh"[Arthur vibrates his lips to make the noise], so the horse

Arthur in his army days: every inch the dashing soldier

half expected a hand on him, especially if they were doing the ticklish area around the stifle. I mean, those old grooms used to blow even when they carried a bucket. Sounds daft, but they did.'

In 1946, aged twenty, Arthur joined the army for a dare and came to England. He eventually ended up in a Royal Artillery Riding Troop at St John's Wood in London and in the King's Troop. In February 1952 he was selected to be sergeant in charge of the gun team which accompanied King George VI's coffin from King's Cross station to Westminster Abbey where it was to lie in state. He received the Royal Victoria Medal for performing this task.

After seven years in the army he left and did a couple of jobs involving horses. Then Yvonne's uncle died in Jersey and Arthur and Yvonne returned to the island. Their stay wasn't too happy, however; work was difficult, and eventually Arthur ended up working in the docks. But he still took the magazine *Horse and Hound*, and one day saw an advertisement which was to open a new chapter in his life.

Four in hand with Sir Dymoke White

The advertisement was for someone to look after hunters on the Norfolk estate of Sir Dymoke White. Arthur answered the advert. A letter came back asking if he knew anything about driving horses, to which he replied that he did. Sir Dymoke then wrote to say he thought him too experienced for the Norfolk job, but to come for an interview to fill the post of head man at his Hampshire estate.

Arthur recalls: 'I was working on a potato or tomato boat in the docks and that boat was going back to Southampton and I managed to book myself onto it.'

At the interview they spoke about driving horses, and Arthur told Sir Dymoke how to use couplings, the buckle on the top of the driving reins. He explained: 'If you get a horse that works harder than the other, you can pull him back two holes on his coupling to hold him back or

you let the other one out to let him work more, or if they're going along a bit one-sided, you can play with your coupling.'

This information was new to Sir Dymoke. Arthur then met Billy Belbin who had been stud groom on the estate for forty years and he showed Arthur the horses and carriages. Sir Dymoke was President of the Coaching Club.

Sir Dymoke's final comment was: 'You're a little chap you know, and these are big horses.' Arthur replied: 'Ah well, if you've any doubts best that we leave it.' Sir Dymoke didn't, and Arthur was engaged.

Looking back, Arthur says: 'I had nine and a half years there, and they were the happiest in my life.' Billy Belbin taught him to drive a four-in-hand and when another groom left, a friend of Arthur's from Jersey called George Abbot came and joined them. Arthur remembers some of Sir Dymoke's vehicles:

'He had a yellow and black coach, and a black Lawton coach which was the best one, the one used for showing; the yellow and black one went to Ascot or anything like that. Ascot week is in June, but on the Saturday prior to that there was Richmond Horse Show, and on the Thursday, the Coaching Club dinner at Hurlingham. We used to go up on the Thursday, the horses in a horsebox to be stabled at Roehampton, and the coach and harness on a long-wheel-based lorry. Sir Dymoke used to drive the coach to Hurlingham for the dinner, and then to Richmond Horse Show on Saturday; and on Sunday we'd load everything and drive to Victoria Street in Windsor where there was a pub called the Brunswick Arms. It had a stable yard attached to it. Then Charlie Fillbrick the lorry driver-cum-mechanic would take the best coach home and bring the yellow and black coach back for Ascot week.

'At ten o'clock in the morning we'd start from the Brunswick Arms on our way to Ascot. The Queen used to give us permission to go down the Long Walk. Some days we'd pick up the Queen's chaplain; in his garden he'd have a little table laid out with glasses of sherry, and we'd stop on the verge and the chaplain's wife would hand these round.

'The minute we stopped I'd jump down, because that's something that you do in private service. As the coachman, I'd hold the offside wheeler (one of the horses nearest the coach) so if Sir Dymoke wanted anything, I could talk to him. George would go and hold the two leaders. There was always somebody to hold the horses, and that's why we went nine and a half years with Sir Dymoke without any accident. If we came to any potential difficulty at all, at a cross-roads, for instance, one of us would get down and run ahead. Sir Dymoke was an old character and you got what you worked for, but he *appreciated* what you did, and that was the quality I liked in him.

'Occasionally whilst we were at the chaplain's, the Queen would arrive with a riding party. In those days it was quite a considerable party, the Duke of Beaufort and probably twelve or fourteen others. That's where I was first introduced to the Queen by Sir Dymoke; it would have been 1961, something like that.

'On Ascot race days we'd get to Ascot at twelve o'clock. Sir Dymoke loved going up the High Street with all the traffic and hustle and bustle, and he'd have George blowing the horn all the way! At the racecourse we didn't drive up the main drag, as the Queen does; we would take the horses and coach into the car park, and then had special permission to put the coach into the paddock. This is adjacent to the race course, so you could sit on the coach and watch the horses gallop by.'

PRIZEWINNERS!

Sir Dymoke, Arthur and George went to many shows – the Royal Show at Aldershot, Romsey, the White City – and won many prizes. They usually took part in the coaching marathon, which was judged on presentation. Marks were given for the condition and matching of the horses, the cleanliness of the harness, and the correct fitting of various appointments on the coach; for example, the whippletrees (or swingletrees), the pivoted crossbars to which the traces are fastened, had to be attached so that the screws faced the outside, and the umbrella basket had to be on the nearside of the coach.

Arthur carried on to explain that after he and George had put the coach in place and made sure that it looked tidy, they would take the horses to a barn in Ascot. It was Crown property, and was also where the Royal Mews horses were temporarily kept for the occasion.

After they had watered, fed and groomed their own horses, and rubbed up the harness, Arthur used to wander up and look at the royal ones. Colonel Miller (later Sir John Miller) was the Crown Equerry in charge of the Royal Mews,

and he'd say to Arthur 'Come and have a look' and Arthur would ask him all sorts of questions about the horses in his care.

The horses pulling an exercise brake was a familiar sight on the roads around Sir Dymoke's Hampshire estate. In Arthur's words:

'Stansted Hill was a lovely drag of about a mile. You could get horses pulling into their collars, the four of them, but they would be light in your hands, you didn't have to hold them back; we used to put about a half a ton of sand in bags in the brake, the equivalent weight of a full complement of passengers.

'The hardest thing when you're training horses is to get all their heads straight, and not "bossing" – that is, going to the left and to the right – and never mind how you play with the couplings, alter curb chains and lower or raise the bit, you can still have problems. A horse might be experiencing pain in the mouth, but it can't *tell* you what's wrong; this depends on your horsemanship, and learning how to cope with it.

'Some horses prefer one side rather than the other. If you've got a horse to go well on the left side, *leave* him, don't change him over. All horses to my mind like to go on the right-hand side, left is for traffic-shy ones.

'It's the two wheelers, the two at the back which do the pulling. They reckon that the one in the gutter moves you off, but how many times do you stop in the gutter?

'Another thing, if you had a big horse, say, half-an-inch taller than the other horse, you put him in the gutter so that the two looked matched to anybody walking round them. It was also the practice to have, say, 16.2hh wheelers and 16hh leaders, so that the leaders looked that little bit smaller and more cocky, you know.'

At this point I ask Arthur about the care of the coach.

'The Head Coachman looked after it, because you've got to wash it after every time it's been out – that night, if you can, even if it's only to wash the mud off the wheels. There's nothing worse than cow dung for sticking onto it! You must be

Driving in the Itchen Valley in 1958

careful cleaning that you don't bring the paint off. There's also little flints in the grass which chip away at the paint on the felloes – that's the wood-work which goes round the wheels – but there's not a lot you can do about that.

'We had a carriage jack, they're made of wood, for raising the wheels to clean them. We used a scrubbing brush on the ironwork. The iron on the outside of the old coach wheels is proud to the wheel, projecting about an $\frac{1}{8}$in to a $\frac{1}{4}$in so that if you came up against a curb the tyre would rub but the woodwork wouldn't. If people put iron on wheels today they have it flush, but it shouldn't be.

'Front wheels are always worst to clean; they're smaller than the back and they never have the brake block on them to help get rid of mud.'

I ask Arthur if he used detergent:

'You're not supposed to, they say plenty of cold water for varnish, but Charlie Fillbrick found me something called DEB. It used to really freshen the coaches each time, so I always used it – but Sir Dymoke never knew we used it, he'd have gone bloody barmy!

'What about looking after the interior – did you have to keep it aired?'

'Yes, coaches are few and far between, and there's not many that are really kept nice inside. You see, once you take away the inside they are not original any more, so you try to keep 'em to what they were, keep them hand-brushed and chuck in a dozen mothballs during the winter.

'On top of a coach the upholstered seats have straps to keep them in place. Sir Dymoke

Arthur on duty
at a show with
Sir Dymoke
White and his
sister Miss Pauline

was very keen that the straps were always buckled behind and not in front, because of the buckles tearing trousers or a lady's skirt. When I used to do a bit of judging, that was one point I used to go for.'

Arthur generally went with Sir Dymoke to Aldershot Horse Show; they usually showed the coach and horses there. It was normal practice that, prior to the show, the coach owners and their guests lunched in the officers' mess of the local barracks. Arthur describes the scene:

'At a given time, people like myself would get coach and horses together, drive it up outside the barracks and then the owners would come out, each to his own coach. Old Sir Dymoke would look along and say: "Arthur, you make me feel a proud man today." Things like that were marvellous, you know; and you hadn't even started, hadn't had a prize.'

On show day in 1968 Arthur was on the back of the coach as usual, with Sir Dymoke driving and his sister Pauline beside him. They approached the show ground, their progress being monitored, because a part of the judging was to appraise a coach's arrival to see if the horses were fit. Arthur goes on to relate what happened next:

'We were trotting, and I was sitting at the back, and the next thing I heard was Miss Pauline calling "Arthur, Arthur!" – and Sir Dymoke had

fallen backwards; and do you know, those horses stopped quick as anything, although we'd been trotting.'

A doctor was called and Sir Dymoke taken to hospital, where he died. Arthur finishes this sad incident:

'A chap came up and says to me "If I was you, the best thing to do is to load up and go home" – and that remark really brought me up short because *nobody* had told me what to do for nine and a half years. Sir Dymoke never told me what to do, he knew he never had to, we just talked roughly about what was going to happen. He used to say, perhaps to Miss Pauline: "I haven't seen Arthur for ten days but I bet when we get there he'll have it all put together."

Royal Coachman

Sir Dymoke White's collection of vehicles was dispersed to museums and Arthur was approached by several people offering him an appointment. Amongst them was Colonel John Miller of the Royal Mews in Buckingham Palace Road; he offered Arthur an assistant stud groom post, looking after polo ponies at Windsor. Arthur was taken on as royal staff, but for a while he had to stay on Sir Dymoke's estate; in the meantime he was sent various young horses to train.

Arthur's first meeting with the Queen was singularly lacking in pomp and circumstance. 'It was coming towards Ascot week, and it was decided that the horses should go up to Windsor so that the Queen could see them. I remember the Queen coming in when I was first there, and I was waiting for someone to introduce me and no one said anything. Then she came again, and still no one said anything. Anyway, the next time I just said to her "Good morning, Your Majesty"; and she replied "Oh, good morning, the horses are looking well". And we had a chat, and she asked me about different things, and that broke the ice. Princess Anne started coming down too, and she was quite friendly to talk to, so that helped as well.'

A little later Arthur was invited to come to London and take up the post as the Head Coachman. Arthur was delighted: 'I quite fancied myself driving the Queen up the Mall and carrying out all those sorts of duties as the Head

One of Arthur's proudest moments, driving the Queen at the Trooping of the Colour in 1987

ger brougham used to go out. It was drawn by a single horse and picked up the Queen's Messenger at the Court post office and took him around to various banks and offices. Usually it was a plain brougham, and the driver wore black livery in the

Coachman. To be honest I had criticised them in the past – I think all was not as efficient as it could be – so I said to myself, well go on up there, put it right, have a crack at it.' And so he did.

'For twenty-three years,' Yvonne explained. She had made some delicious sandwiches to sustain Arthur and myself through his reminiscences and, having cleared away the plates, had come back to join us.

I ask Arthur how he had settled into the new job:

'It was a case of going there and trying to weigh it all up. Horses are horses and harness is harness, although state harness has got ornamental pieces on it – ornate brass, and rosettes on special occasions – and of course the Mews were open to the public; this meant that I would have to allocate from my workforce men to stand around on duty. Part of the daily regime was that a messen-

summer and in the winter a drab coat. But on a member of the royal family's birthday, the messenger went out in a brougham painted in the royal colours, and the driver wore scarlet and had gold lace on his top hat.

'There was a lot to think about because there was the actual exercise of the horses each day, and vehicles for visiting dignitaries. For example, when an ambassador came to present credentials to Her Majesty, I'd arrange for a state landau pulled by two horses to take the ambassador to the Palace and return to his embassy. A High Commissioner had a semi-state landau, drawn by four horses. It was postillioned, that is, the horses were ridden. I'd also have to allocate horses for the daily jobs done by the brougham. Obviously the longer you were there, the easier it became to get into routine, but sometimes it was a job to remember that perhaps there was a covered brake wanted for the following day – that's a pair of horses – or horses required for an investiture. You really had to read your diary.

'For staff, I had three coachmen under me. A coachman is in charge of a stable with, say, eight horses and four men, that is a senior liveried servant and three men with him. New recruits were called junior liveried helpers. The next step up was to be a senior liveried helper, which was the equivalent to the rank of coachman. There was also a day man: his duty was to turn out the messenger brougham, then spend the day picking up droppings and keeping everything as tidy as possible. Talking of duties, after I'd been there a while I trusted certain men to do manes and

tails, and they did it well. In fact a lady wrote to ask me where I'd got the stocking netting which went over the horses' tails – but there wasn't any, it was the way they'd been pulled! We pulled the tails hard over the dock and kept them bandaged. On special occasions the manes were plaited and rosettes of ribbons were attached; usually these were crimson, but on the Queen's Silver Wedding we had silver rosettes.'

I ask Arthur how he coped with organising and preparing the horses for major ceremonial occasions.

'Well, there was a chap called Alfie Oates and he'd been there many years. I made him a coachman because he was quite knowledgeable about it all and helpful, and he showed me one thing and another. Also, I think when I went in there first, I earned the men's respect. I could ride and drive horses as good as anybody, if not better, and I knew how to feed and clip. They used to tip me off and say "Don't forget this or that tomorrow!"

'I did make some changes to bring things up to the standard that I liked and knew. Exercise on the road and in Hyde Park had been at half-past six in the morning but I found that, understandably, with such an early start, the men were keen to get back for their breakfast, and the exercise time for the horses wasn't as long as it should have been. So I made it a half-past eight start, after men and horses had been fed and watered, and then they stayed out until at least ten o'clock. There was a bit of opposition to this at first because the later they went out, the more traffic would be about; but when I was in the King's Troop we used to go out in the traffic, so I thought, we'll see.

'I made structural changes, too! For example, in each corner of the riding school there was a big lump of iron sticking out – I think lamps had hung on them years ago. I had these cut out because they were in line with the horses' heads. I gave some of the men riding lessons in their own time, and found that most were keen to learn.

'All the Mews bridles were blinkered – this was usual in a driving bridle, to keep the horse

INTERNATIONAL COMPETITION

'When the Fédération d'Equestre Internationale started, Prince Philip was the President and he asked Sir John if he would take part in FEI competitions: he said he would, and I started training the horses. It was a different thing altogether to the coaching I'd done with Sir Dymoke. For example, a lot more discipline was required in the horses. In a three-day driving event there would be dressage one day, cross-country the next and cone driving on the final day. For the dressage phase you used the best carriage and had nicely turned out livery; the test involved making circles and turns to the left and right. Day two was a marathon, a test of cross-country driving and you didn't turn out as smartly for this. It was usually over a distance of twenty-four kilometres, or fifteen miles, and was split into timed sections: one was straightforward driving, another at walk, a third at a fast trot. Cone driving on the final day was best 'bib and tucker' again in the ring, and it involved manoeuvring the horses and carriage round cones topped with tennis balls; if you dislodged a ball you were penalised. There was a time limit.

'We started out with Sir John doing the driving, and we did reasonably well, competing in Switzerland and Germany and winning gold medals. They have a presentation class at each show and we always had the best turn-out of anybody in Europe, and in the world, you know!'

looking forward and not shying at things going on around it – and in the riding school where it was the practice for a man to ride one horse and lead another, if you gave a bit of instruction, say "Turn left", the horses couldn't see each other and they would bang their heads together, which obviously they didn't like a bit; so I adapted the bridles to be open ones.

'I was also keen to use looseboxes as much as possible. Most of the horses lived tied up in narrow stalls, and big horses – and we had some which were 17 to 18hh – haven't got room to lie down in a stall. And just imagine it, if you were one of these horses, if you were lucky you had two hours' exercise a day and on Saturday just one hour, and if you were in a stall you spent all the other hours tied up looking at the wall! No, you'd be better off moving about, particularly if you were a bit arthritic, or perhaps you want to lay down and stretch out. So without breaking up the sets of eight horses too much, I tried to put all I could into looseboxes. The sets of eight were two teams of four which were kept together as much as possible because they generally worked together and would do so better if they knew each other really well.'

I ask Arthur if it was difficult to buy coach horses.

'Yes, very difficult. At first Sir John Miller bought the horses, but latterly I did and I travelled all over England, Holland and Germany to find them. It's nice if you can buy 'em all broken to harness but there's very few you get like that.

Arthur talks generally about horse-drawn vehicles today: 'Driving is really making a comeback. At Windsor Show there could be eighty turn-outs, and all beautifully presented and turned out. And it takes some doing to win in the private driving turnout because people who have just the one outfit really take a pride in it, and get the harness on the kitchen table and clean it all to the last buckle; and those who can afford staff have a groom to do that sort of thing. Yes, it's all coming back, which is rather nice.'

Kenzie:
Master Poacher

McKenzie Thorpe:
Sutton Bridge, Lincolnshire

KENZIE: MASTER POACHER

A time warp moves us from the wild men of the turn of the century, to one of the best known poachers who ever lived: the sturdy form of McKenzie ('Kenzie'): Thorpe of Sutton Bridge. He was of Romany stock, and his formidable grandmother – magnificently named Leviathan – could, they said, whip up a sitting pheasant, eggs and all, into her apron before the bird could squeak.

Kenzie started in a way his Victorian ancestors would have recognised as a bird-starver, equipped with a rusty old muzzle-loader.

His first, second and third 'proper' guns he stole. They were of a type known loosely as 'farm guns', kept in barns for shooting rats or pigeons and of no great value; but for Kenzie the price was right and he used them to start on what turned out to be an illustrious career. As a teenager he got to know the ways of the fen spinneys and the

pheasants that roosted there, learning quickly to discriminate between the silhouette of a pheasant, a magpie and a pigeon. Hares, rabbits and game of all sorts made its way to the Thorpe household, shortly followed by the local policeman who was to beat a well-worn path to their front door in the years that followed.

The series of stolen guns ended when Kenzie actually bought his first legitimate weapon; this was a .410, good enough for a start, but it lacked the power he needed so he soon changed it for a single-barrel 12-bore. He went where he wished and would come home loaded with wildfowl, pheasants and hares. He was a remarkable caller of hares, and this trick he demonstrated to millions on one of the several television programmes made about him, so that all could see how it worked. In fact there was no reason why the call should have been successful, for hares make no sound to resemble it. He had inherited the trick from his gypsy forebears. The noise is a peculiar moaning sucking of the lips which rises in intensity and volume, and when any hare hears it, it will pop up its ears in the corn and come lolloping to the place as though drawn by a magnet.

Escaping Flossie

Kenzie was calling hares, hiding in a dyke and drawing the hares to him. Two approached and he knocked them both down; he called again and two more appeared in the distance, heading

towards him. But at that moment he saw a black figure approaching down the bank, Flossie Longlands, the owner of the estate and a lady blessed with a fair turn of speed.

'I flew out, grabbed the hares, and ran back to the bank. I pretended to go east, but doubled back and went west, ran down the bank and nipped along the ditch at the bottom, and at last I threw her off. But when I got back to the boat it had tipped over with the falling tide and sunk. It took me three-quarters of an hour to bale her out – then I loaded the gun and the hares in her, and rowed across the river so that Flossie could not get to me and I walked two miles home.'

Such was a fairly typical day in his life, strenuous and with no respect for property; but it was an effective bag-filler, and he was no stranger to hard work.

Nabbed

Kenzie was caught many times in his career, once spending a spell in Norwich prison for a 'do' with a keeper; on this particular occasion he was out with a pal Arthur Porter in his timber lorry, enjoying a poaching safari through the Norfolk lanes, armed with a double-barrelled .410. In a field between Kings Lynn and Holt, Kenzie saw six pheasants all together; he 'gave them one', and stuffed three of them under the lorry seat. Two miles more and they saw another batch; two others joined the three beneath the seat. Almost into Heacham and he dropped another brace.

Then the law in the shape of the local bobby appeared, and stood his ground even when threatened to be run down by the lorry. There was a fight for possession of the .410 which Kenzie lost. The case came up at Kings Lynn, and Kenzie appeared in a dressing gown, old flannel trousers and carpet slippers; he was fined seven pounds and the loss of the gun. His travelling expenses in wartime with petrol rationing were sixteen shillings and Arthur got off with a pound. It was an expensive 'do' and all the gratitude Arthur showed was to buy Kenzie a single pint of mild beer at fourpence and he did not even say 'thank-you'.

Terrington Marsh

Inside the sea wall at Terrington was a newly reclaimed marsh which was a haven for roosting pheasants. Kenzie poached this regularly in spite of several run-ins with the venerable custodian of the place, who concluded that he had met his match. However, Kenzie decided that the place was being used by too many other locals so he organised a mass poach-in.

Running it as a parody of the squire's 'posh' shoot, he had his flanking guns and beaters and they started to drive the first hundred-acre bay. They were shooting many birds and hares when Kenzie realised that there was another rival gang at the other end of the bay doing exactly the same as he. His lot kept going until old Watson the keeper and some assistants added themselves to the opposition, and came in hot pursuit. Kenzie came to a wide creek against the bank of which was fastened an old punt fixed to a rope which Watson habitually used as a ferry to take himself to and fro.

Kenzie's party crossed on this punt in relays, the last batch arriving safely as old Watson came puffing up, threatening goodness knows what vengeance. Kenzie did no more than raise his gun and blow the bottom out of the boat, leaving his antagonists with a two-mile slog round the outside before they could catch up with him.

Not deterred, Kenzie and his 'shoot' continued with their sport on the other side of the water.

'And that's how it was in those days, poaching all over, going where I liked and doing what I liked. And the rougher the weather the better. That's how it was. We was chased and I was chased, hundreds of times, but we was never caught and nor was I, not until we got into the nineteen-forties. But that was the cream of it, round about 1928.'

Mixed Bags for Hard Times

In the war, rationing made meat a rare commodity and Kenzie shot anything on wings which bore a scrap or two of flesh and was, therefore, negotiable. He conveyed his week's bag on a rusty wheelbarrow to an eager market in the town, and the contents of that vehicle would have given birdwatchers as well as gastronomes quite a shock. It included Brent geese, shelduck, gulls of various sorts, ruffs and reeves, waterhens, black-tailed godwits as well as the more conventional rabbits, hares, pheasants, partridges and mallard.

His cartridges were supplied by the RAF (though without their knowing much about it) who kept a supply for training pilots in air gunning. He probably wasted fewer than they did.

The Record Year

A bumper year was 1942. Kenzie had been declared unfit for military service due to an old wound picked up in a family fracas.

His bag was as follows: September, 77 head, mostly partridges and hares. October, 108 head including 15 mallard, 9 wigeon, 24 partridges, and 18 pheasants. November, 185 head including 76 mallard, 72 wigeon, 7 geese. December, 183 head, a mixed bag of 81 pheasants, 40 geese,

52 wigeon and 20 shelduck. January produced 146 wigeon, 25 geese, 43 shelduck, 11 curlew, the total for the. month being 257 head. February concluded this marathon with 45 geese, 137 shelduck, 65 wigeon, 15 mallard, 2 curlew, 1 hare and 1 swan.

The total for this amazing year was 1,044 head to his own gun.

Swan Downing

The demand for fresh meat in those times of severe rationing caused Kenzie and his pal Horry Savage to stretch the rules. Swans there were in hundreds in the Lincolnshire fens, and the odd one had been well received by the game dealer. Kenzie and Horry therefore cycled the sixteen miles to Spalding, where they fell in with a good herd of mute swans. Armed with a .410 they knocked out seven of them, packed three into one bag and four in another, and set off home.

On the long road they came across another swan sitting by the verge; Kenzie took his torch, dazzled the bird and shot that one, too. Without doubt they were, as Kenzie would say, 'ver, ver warm' when they arrived back at Sutton Bridge.

An Embarrassing Moment

Kenzie was taking out shooters fairly regularly and had gained a considerable reputation as a guide of rare quality and character. The young Peter Scott learned his fowling with Kenzie, as did many other gentleman gunners of the period. On one of these outings Kenzie had with him two gentlemen used to the finer things in life, one being a recent Lord Lieutenant of his county, the other a considerable landowner. They recalled that Kenzie took them to a shed where he kept his gear, though they were not allowed so much as a peep inside. However, one of them craned his neck at an impossible angle and did manage to catch a glimpse inside as Kenzie slid through the quarter-opened door: the walls were lined with pheasants hanging up and ready for market. Not one of them, we may fairly guess, had been come by legitimately.

They were out shooting geese on a stubble in conditions of low ground-mist. They had had a number of shots when Kenzie spotted two legs approaching through the murk, and leaped out of his dyke yelling 'Run boys! here comes the keeper!' Those two highly respected men, JPs and pillars of respectability both, were obliged to flee across the muddy field, bags flapping and red in the face, to escape from the legitimate wrath of the gamekeeper. At home, each employed his own keeper; but as usual Kenzie was unrepentant, and offered no apology.

Folk learned to take Kenzie at his own valuation of himself.

Royal Poaching

Kenzie's most audacious feat was to poach the royal covers at Sandringham with his friend Horry Savage. Armed with a .22 rifle and the .410 and driving an Austin 7, the pair were afterwards stopped by Mr Amos, the king's keeper, and an underkeeper. There ensued a sort of wrestle for

The Slammer

Kenzie had appeared often enough at Holbeach Magistrates' Court for them to be heartily sick of him. When in 1945 he attacked a keeper and knocked him down he was convicted of grievous bodily harm and sent to Norwich prison for three months. This was a gruelling experience, but one which he survived unscathed; I have a clear picture of him gazing out over the walls and seeing a troop of green plover wailing by, high on their club wings. At that moment his situation struck him most forcibly, this free spirit used to roaming where and when it wished being condemned to a spell behind bars.

He was not reformed by the experience and continued to poach the large farms near his village, only abandoning the long trips to less familiar country.

the possession of the gun and a cock pheasant which lay under the seat. Kenzie was outnumbered two to one and eventually bested, for Horry was no fighting man; and to make matters worse, the trusty car – which till then had removed them in the nick of time from many a potentially difficult situation – failed to start, and both were fairly nabbed.

The subsequent summons included confiscation of rifle, £1 for possession of a firearm without a certificate, £5 for coming from land in pursuit of game, £4 for trespassing and £1 for opposing a constable, for Amos was a 'Special'.

Kenzie on Poaching

'You've got to be as cunning as a fox to outwit the keepers, farmers and labourers and anyone who lives inside your poaching area. You have to keep your ears and eyes open: notice any little

there with a .410 gun. That way they'll never catch up with you. Once you're on the job, keep to the fields and dykes and never cross a road. Never go near a cottage for, no matter if you're walking like a cat, some dog will give you away with his "yap, yap". And no matter how successful you've been, never visit the same place two nights running. If they know the place has been poached they'll be watching for poachers again — but they won't catch you if you're working five miles away on a different farm.'

Torching

'One of my favourite ways of operating at night has always been to take the roosting pheasants Out of trees with a .22 rifle. Try to spot the birds without using the light; there may be as many as ten birds in one tree. If there's a good wind blowing and the night is rough you can

sight and sound you have never heard or seen before. You've got to know your ground, your ditches, your roadways on which a car can approach at night without its headlights. You've got to know every bush, tree, every haystack. If there's a new object sticking up from a dyke or bank you must investigate it before you start work. If you don't you will be nervous, and this will put you off. At night don't think of starting until every light has gone out and everything is still.

'Outwitting a gamekeeper can be very simple if you stick to the rules. You've got to know his whereabouts, his movements, his habits and the company he keeps. Does he visit pubs? Does he have regular cronies? If he has, then with a bit of luck you've got him for you know where he'll be at certain times.

'Stay clear of estates with several keepers because they can run a duty rosta like the army, and keep guard four on and four off. Keep an eye on the keeper's cottage when you're out at night.

'And when you're out in the fields at night, have a shot here and a shot

sometimes get all of those pheasants without any trouble at all. The method is this: first show your torch on the ground. You look up and find your first bird with the naked eye – then straightaway cock your torch onto it and shoot, but leave it where it falls. You drop your torch again and switch off. Pick your next bird by the naked eye, too, then up with the rifle and repeat the performance. Don't move between shots; stand dead still and the birds won't take fright. I've had nine cocks out of nine in one tree, never picking the birds up until I'd knocked them all down.

'When I dussent use a torch for any reason I'd go round the trees with a .410 gun; this allows you to be just that bit more inaccurate. I use short cartridges loaded with number six shot. You aim by running your gun up the tree and firing directly the barrel blots out the bird.'

Torching on Grass

Kenzie would torch on short grass or stubble, and also on ploughed land, again using the .22. The best weather for this was severe snow, rainstorms and gales. The poacher had to walk into the wind with the torch strapped onto the bottom of the rifle, sweeping it from left to right to about ten degrees either side of the line of march. Walking very slowly he would never pass a bird and they would sit very tight; at times Kenzie had five or six pheasants 'jugging' within a few yards of him. Without moving he could get them all, unless one of them was wounded and started fluttering on the ground, in which case it would put the rest of them up.

However, the startled birds would rarely fly far, but would probably settle again in the same field so they could be attended to later. Walking at the correct pace, one man could cover a forty-acre field in about three hours. To take up to fifty pheasants in a night by this method was not uncommon; and that is a great weight of birds to carry, calling for more than one trip to take them off the field.

Torching Hares

Hares could be torched, but were harder work than pheasants or partridges which would sit and be slaughtered fairly tamely. For hares you worked at far greater range, about fifty or sixty yards compared with five or ten for birds. A powerful torch was needed, and when you spotted a hare in the form you swing the beam off her straightaway. Let it linger on her for even a few seconds and she would be up and away, scaring all the other pheasants and hares in her dash to get away. Swing slowly back to her, taking aim as you do so, and shoot the moment you can 'draw a bead' on her.

Calling Hares

Kenzie made the most of his remarkable ability to 'call' hares, using that strange, wailing cry which it seemed they could not resist. 'In the spring of the year I've stood in the middle of a grass field in pitch darkness and called hares all around me. I've knocked over seven or eight in five minutes. You call the hares across the field and then put the torch on them and, believe me, you can get them as easy as pie when you know how.'

Especially good times for him were the nights of full moon during February or March, hiding in a dyke armed with a 12-bore by a field of young wheat, for favourite. Sometimes they would come too fast to be killed, a swift right and left and barely time to reload before the next couple were on him – he once had eighteen hares from one dyke in little over an hour, without himself moving. Even he did not know why they came for his call, for it was unlike any cry made by hares – which are usually mute, except when wounded.

Trail-netting

We have investigated the Victorian method of trail-netting; it was an effective system then, and Kenzie was not the only East Anglian to use it later on. It suited the large, treeless fields where game birds roosted on the ground. Kenzie's net was fourteen yards by thirteen with the usual pole at each end, top and bottom lines and made of four-inch diamond mesh, or even better, four-inch square mesh (birds tended to become less tangled in square mesh than in diamond).

Carried at the customary ten degrees to the ground, the right-hand man had left hand forward, right hand down, the second chap the other way round, You laid the net on the stubble and the right-hand man took charge; poor communication meant tangles, and tangles meant a waste of time and much profanity, and in extreme cases the end of the night's work. The leader gave a twitch on his net as a sign to move, and off you went. When a bird sprang you felt a pluck, both dropped the net instantly, one man running to the front, the other to the back. The bird was removed, each returned to his pole, a twitch on the net and off you went again.

When you got to the end of the field you gave a pull on the net which made your mate stop immediately, two more pulls and he wheeled round you, one pluck and you were ready for the next swathe; in this way you combed the whole field.

'One night in a clover field with Horry a thick haze come over. It was very frosty and you could see your tracks so you could keep nice, straight paths up and down the field. We was

catching pheasants galore. The pheasants were that worried by the mist that they wouldn't get up. Some of them were letting the net go right over them. One particular time when we dropped the net we took the pheasants out and Horry took a step forward and put his foot on another cock just sitting on the stubble, and we caught that one, too. The pheasants were getting up and going down in the same field. They was properly scared that night, and we was properly scared, too, because we were catching so many. We took forty-three pheasants and four partridge that night, and we'd only done a quarter of the field.'

The modern antidote for the trail-netter was exactly the same as it was a century ago: the keeper who bushed the field or peppered it with stakes could keep the netters at bay. Kenzie abandoned trail-netting in the end, despite the great success he had with it over the years.

'We packed up trail-netting in the end. Hiding the poles was the trouble. Once we hid them in a tunnel, and the floods came up and floated them out and they were found. Another time we hid them in a wheat-straw stack, and we went by there one day and they'd started stripping the stack and we saw the poles laying out on the ground, so we lost that lot. And a third set we put in a straw stack that went on fire — so we packed up. It was a very exciting business, trail-netting, but we liked to feel free, and not have to worry about finding our gear.'

A Philosophical View

Kenzie Thorpe was an original, a rare bird treated with suspicion by keepers and landowners but one who occupies a niche in folklore as a man with rare skills; a man who cared little for authority, and who despite the strait-jacket of modern civilisation, lived the life of an untamed spirit. As time passed he 'became respectable' and established himself as a wildfowling guide. He became fêted as a conservationist, took films of seals on the Wash, and appeared on TV and

radio. However, I like to think that society never tamed him and that underneath the new veneer the old Kenzie still lurked, as wicked and unrepentant as ever.

A wonderful biography of Kenzie has been written by Colin Willock; it is entitled *Kenzie The Wild Goose Man* and may already be fairly termed a classic of field sports literature. I acknowledge this book with gratitude as the source of some of the Kenzie poaching adventures I have described. The last word on Kenzie and poaching I leave with the man himself.

'I have to admit that sometimes, afterwards, especially when I've been caught, I felt very, very ashamed of poaching. But I'd soon forget it when I got a gun in my hands again and a pocketful of cartridges and was out among the pheasants. It wasn't the money I made from it. All told I paid out £150 in poaching fines and I lost four good guns. Apart from that I used to give quite a few of the hares and stuff away. I'm not denying, mind, that I made quite a bit from my birds as well. But it wasn't the money at all, it was the sheer thrill of it. And I know if I had my time over again I wouldn't do it any different, except I'd be more cunning about it and I wouldn't go walking up a man's birds on a Sunday morning, which I used to do for the pure daring of it. I'd be a lot more cunning.'

A Farming Dynasty

*Dick Rowley Williams:
Denbigh, North Wales*

A FARMING DYNASTY

Blundell Edward Rowley Williams, who is ninety-one, might easily be described as a gentleman farmer. But if this is taken to mean a farmer who simply gets others to do the work for him, then it will not do at all. For Mr Rowley Williams is a man who likes to get his hands dirty, and as well as indulging his lifelong enthusiasm for the gentlemanly pursuit of foxes, he has kept his remote Welsh farm going for seventy years through his own resources and hard work.

Glyn Arthur is a lovely Regency house built by an ancestor, the family having owned the farm since the eighteenth century; it stands alone high on the Denbigh hills with glorious views of the town of Denbigh in the distance.

'Six generations of the family have now lived and worked here,' says Mr Rowley Williams, or Dick as he is known to friends and family. A quiet man who smiles readily and displays the formal good manners of a vanished era, he is proud of the family's long association with this part of Wales generally, and with Glyn Arthur in particular. 'My great-great-grandfather built the place using stone from a local quarry. We think work started on the house we see now in 1790, and it was certainly finished by 1800; but the old part of the house, to which my great-great-grandfather's house was "tacked on", as it were, has been here since about 1600. He could afford to build a new house simply because he had the good sense to marry an heiress. We haven't always been quite so sensible since!'

Although he is in his nineties, Dick still takes an active interest in the farm which is now run by his son Peter; farming seems to be bred in the family, although the different generations have approached it in markedly different ways. 'I suppose it was inevitable that I would be interested in farming, having been born here among farming people and where all the talk was of farming. But my own father was really what they call a gentleman farmer, in the sense that he had a private income and so didn't worry too much if the farm itself didn't make much money.

'I was born in 1903, and my earliest memories are of riding various ponies. I loved horses and ponies – still do – and looking back now I seem to have spent my whole childhood on horseback. I rode from the time I was a very small boy; in fact it was unthinkable then for a boy, or indeed a girl, not to learn to ride – it was how we got about, and of course you couldn't hunt if you didn't ride, and all our friends and neighbours hunted. Hunting lay at the heart of all our social activities. I was perhaps three or four years old when I learned to ride, and I was still riding in my seventies. I was joint-master of the Flint and Denbigh hounds for more than fifty years, and my son is now joint-master; so hunting, like farming, is very much in the family. I was very keen on hunting from an early age, it was just so exciting, but of course when I was sent away to school at Shrewsbury I couldn't do much.'

After Shrewsbury, farming wasn't an automatic choice for a young man with good connections and a good education, and like many well-off country families, the Rowley

An early Fordson tractor in action at Glyn Arthur

Williamses decided that their son would benefit from spending some time abroad. 'When I left school I was sent to Rhodesia, largely I think because no one had the faintest idea what to do with me! I worked on a remote farm owned by a friend of the family, and all I remember is that after clearing the scrub using oxen, we grew tobacco and maize. I was also sent to France for a while to learn to speak the language. If you were brought up as a gentleman these were things you needed, and I suppose I could have gone into business and made a lot of money; but even then I dreaded the idea of working for someone else on a sort of five-days-a-week, nine-to-five basis.'

For Dick, the attractions of making money were as nothing compared to the attractions of hunting and shooting. 'Yes, I might have made more money if I'd done that sort of thing, but I realised pretty early on that I would be far happier farming, even if it meant making no money at all. The fact that I loved country life and everything it entailed also came into the decision, of course. If I were asked to sum up my life, I'd say that I didn't make much money but I enjoyed myself.

'I was also very keen on training and working sheepdogs, not to win competitions, but simply because I enjoyed it – sheepdogs, and breeding and schooling horses. However, from an early age I worked on the farm, although we did employ farm-workers. I had to help with the horses, and with the sheep; in fact with just about everything, at one time or another.

'When I was a young man, shearing sheep was a far more exhausting and difficult business than it is now because it was all done with hand shears or clippers, like a big pair of iron scissors; a good man might shear forty sheep in a day, whereas nowadays a good man with electric shears will do three hundred sheep in the same time. With hand shears before you could do anything you had to lift each sheep onto a special bench and then tie its legs. It was a laborious business.'

The Rowley Williamses are not by any means self-sufficient but they are, and always have been, quite happy to go for weeks without visiting the town; and several generations have always lived happily in the house together, making their own amusements. At the moment there is Dick and his wife, and also their son and daughter-in-law living in the house together with *their* four children. 'Long after the electricity came we still had to resort to lamps and candles in winter when something went wrong, and

TRAVELLING IN STYLE

Glyn Arthur has always been a remote farm, and the passage of time since Dick was born there has done little to change that; the only difference between isolation at the turn of the century and isolation now is that the spell is more easily and perhaps more comfortably broken. The narrow mountainous roads are no longer made from pounded stones, and in a car, the town is only ten minutes away. However, the Rowley Williamses were always able to travel in some style – in those days the family had their own phaetons and broughams, gentlemen's carriages whose names are now quite unfamiliar to the vast majority of the population.

'Yes, when I was a boy we had a number of different kinds of carriage. The phaeton, I recall, was a rather grand thing. It had four wheels – unlike the dog-cart or the gamboge which had two – and was pulled by two fine horses. It was a very comfortable, sprung affair which would easily carry four people in great style and comfort. The dog-cart could also carry four. It had two seats in front, and the underlings – the groom or the children – sat on a sort of box at the back; below this was a board on which you rested your feet. None of the roads was metalled then, as you can imagine, and we were often cut off – we are still often cut off in winter by drifting snow; and when the valley flooded even the carriages were hopeless, so when I was a young man we used to go by sailing boat to Denbigh to the hunt balls.'

although we are isolated here there was always plenty to do; we had lots of friends to go and see, we visited each other's houses, as we still do, and there was hill hunting, tennis and rough shooting. And of course as a child one could be mischievous and invent one's own pastimes. I used to get up to lots of pranks. I remember once as the maid was serving us at dinner – the whole family had sat down – I produced a live slow-worm out of my pocket, and a great pile of plates crashed to the ground from the maid's hands. I was reprimanded rather severely for that!

'In my youth it was still the custom in many country houses to say morning prayers in the house. The head of the household, – one's father, would lead the prayers. One morning during prayers I found it difficult to take it seriously because I had noticed that our terrier was taking a great interest in a big old cupboard in the corner of the room, what we called a Jonah cupboard. As soon as I could I opened the cupboard door and spotted a big rat. I prodded him, he leapt out and our terrier caught him in mid-air. That, I'm afraid, was of far more interest to me than the prayers on which I should have been concentrating! Like all children I used to do some pretty mad things; I was terribly fond of chickens, I remember, but I couldn't afford any of the fancy poultry which I loved, so I used to buy ordinary chickens and paint their legs bright colours! However, even while I was very young I was helping out around the farm and learning the ropes.'

As farm incomes dropped and the family money began to diminish, the days of farming in what might best be termed a rather amateur if gentlemanly fashion had to come to an end, and Dick soon found that farm work had become a serious, full-time business. 'I used to get up at five and ride down to help with the milking, which of course was all by hand; then I'd help feed the pigs. Our pigs weren't like modern pigs, they were damn great things that used to attack me when I went in to them! During haymaking time we worked from dawn to dusk for seven shillings and sixpence a week, and at lambing time we'd be up half the night wandering the fields.'

Although they have lived in Wales for generations, the Rowley Williamses sound thoroughly English, and their outlook is far more cosmopolitan than that of other local people who have never left the area even for a few weeks. In fact isolation and insularity inevitably produced a certain amount of eccentricity among the local population, as Dick remembers: 'Our blacksmith, for example, was a rather odd chap. I remember chatting to him one day and telling him that he ought to get married. He said in his lovely Welsh accent "Ah, but you don't know what you're getting, do you, when you get

Mrs Dick Rowley Williams at work on one of the steepest parts of the farm

married." All right, I said, get a housekeeper then. "Oh, but I'll have to pay her, won't I?" he said. I thought that was terribly funny.'

On a hill farm where every bit of grass was needed, the rabbit was considered a serious pest, particularly as the species seemed to be most prolific in Britain just at the time when farm incomes were at their lowest, in the thirties and forties. So when myxomatosis came in the 1950s the family welcomed the rapid and almost complete disappearance of the rabbit population, and Dick is still grateful that myxy did what no amount of shooting and gassing could ever have managed. 'We reckoned that four rabbits would eat as much as a sheep, so we were very glad when myxomatosis came in and virtually wiped them out. It was particularly important for us because on a hill farm it's a constant struggle to make ends meet. When I first really got to grips with the land here it was during World War II. I had been a captain in the Royal Welch Fusiliers but I was released because they thought I would do more for the war effort on a farm than in uniform.

'Farming was at its worst in the 1930s and

THE MAN WHO 'CULTIVATED A MOUNTAIN'

'We knew that in spite of the hilly country we had quite good soil, so we tried to eradicate the bracken; and although people said it could never be done, and that even if we could do it, we'd never be able to plough and harrow the steep hillsides, we thought we'd have a go. And we did it. I'd done similar work in Rhodesia so I hired a tractor with caterpillar tracks and used a horse-drawn plough on the really steep bits'.

Thus Dick's greatest moment on the farm undoubtedly came when he created useful land out of what had been bracken-covered hillside, and the story of how he did it made him something of a celebrity, whose activities were described in glowing detail in local newspapers in the 1940s. But of course the incentive was there, because for the first time since the Great War the nation needed as much food as it could produce itself; and suddenly, after the long years of agricultural depression, the farmer was a very important man indeed. After one particular feature in a local paper Dick became known as the 'man who cultivated a mountain'.

A splendid litter: 'Our pigs were damn great things that used to love to attack me!'

be able to help others in similar circumstances. But farmers lived isolated lives then as now, and they didn't always take kindly to my advice. Bad reactions to a visit never went beyond rudeness and bad temper with me, but we knew of other advisers who were threatened with guns. Mostly we just asked them to upgrade their cattle and improve their land; and remember, this was a time when we were all being asked to dig for victory, so it was important work.

'As this is predominantly a sheep area, one of my jobs was to assess a farmer's rams. If the ram was good enough I'd put a mark on it; if it wasn't, I'd suggest to the farmer that he get another. One chap I talked to about this had already threatened an official with his gun, but I found I got on all right with him. I told him he needed a new ram, and he just said "You give me one, then". So I told him he could have any ram of mine he liked, and that seemed to do the trick.

1940s. You had to accept that one year you made a bit of money, and the next you made none. We schooled and sold horses when things were very bad, but farm wages were minute then – thirty bob [shillings] and a cottage. And you could buy a sheep then for thirty bob, though a cow might cost £20.

'I was a farming adviser during the second war, partly because we'd done well here in difficult circumstances and so they thought I might

'Like all farmers before the last war, we walked all our animals to market along the roads. To get to Denbigh with twenty or thirty sheep would take about two and a half hours, but many times we'd drive the sheep there, fail to sell them and have to drive them all the way back again! And with geese on the old drovers' roads, we'd dab their feet in pitch before we set off so they wouldn't wear raw and bleed on the stony track.

'If the ram was good enough I'd put a mark on it...'

'Farm incomes improved immensely after the second war, and in 1959 I bought another farm some miles

away for £10,000. That was a lot of money in those days, but I sold it thirty years later for £300,000, so I didn't do too badly!

'On a farm you never know what you may have to do – I remember my wife coming back from a hunt ball in a rather lovely dress and then, still in the same dress, having to help with a sow that had got into the wrong pen. We had about thirty sows then, but we never really made any money with them.

field, and must have covered as many as forty miles in it in a day.

'My mother always hunted, and rode side saddle which has virtually died out now; she was a marvellous horsewoman. She would always go to and from the meet in the carriage with the horse tied behind; but I often hacked ten miles to a meet and then ten miles back at the end of a long day's hunting. People thought nothing of such distances in those days. Our

Clearing bracken: 'They said it couldn't be done.'

'We had a car quite early on, an old Austin that lasted for twenty-three years. Then we had a Morris 8, but we had to get rid of that because the nanny got too fat to fit in it! In the days before the motor car we thought nothing of travelling long distances by carriage. The dog cart could seat four comfortably, and we might go twenty miles in it; and when my father stopped riding to hounds he used a carriage instead, and raced about the fields in that. He always managed to keep up with the

hunting country has been badly cut up by roads; people think the antis will stop hunting, but I think it will be the roads.

'In the 1920s you might have paid £30–£50 for a good horse – a working horse, that is – and it would probably keep going until it was twenty. We'd usually give it lighter duties then. I remember we had two Suffolk Punches, one of which ran away with me one day; it just made a dash for the road with me hanging on to the harness. I stopped it after a few hundred yards, but by then we were virtually wedged in the hedge!

'We had six men with six horses as well as a land girl and my wife, and we all worked full time, but it was still slow going. What we called the teamsman looked after the horses, but at harvest-time all our friends would come to help and we could all turn our hands to just about

'I often hacked ten miles to a meet...'

anything round the farm. We used to cut the hay, give it two days to dry, and then turn it with a horse-drawn turner, a clever mechanical thing which would just flip the hay over as it lay scattered about the field. When both sides were dry we cocked it, which basically meant we piled it up in little heaps. We used what were called tripods for some years, which helped the hay to dry more quickly; as the name suggests, the tripod was a three-legged device designed to keep the air circulating under each pile of hay, and they worked very well indeed. We always called our haystack the Queen Mary, simply because it was so enormous. Even in the early days we were

rather modern here, and one of the things we had was a hoist for the hay which was operated by a horse. Before we built our Queen Mary we'd cover the floor with brushwood first to keep the hay above the damp.

'Hay-carrying waggons were built specifically for that one task, having flat bottoms and very high sides. Even so, the hay would be loaded until it was so high that it could become unstable if you didn't know what you were doing. I remember once I was right at the top of a full haycart when the lead horse turned too quickly and I came off – I was lucky not to be injured. Farms are dangerous places, or they can be. On another occasion I got pushed right into a thick thorn hedge by a bull. I was in my suit as I'd just got back from town, when I found that our bull had got out of the field he shared with some heifers. I prodded him with a pickel, a small pitchfork, to encourage him to go back in through the gate, but he turned and chased me. I almost made it to the gate by the road, but not quite, and he hit me in the chest and ripped a great hole in my smart jacket. I was all right, but I was furious about my suit so I turned and shouted at him and waved my arms. I was so cross it worked and he turned and fled! But I must have looked very funny running across that field in my suit with my two dogs and a bull right behind me!

'In total I followed hounds from the age of six until the age of seventy-six, which may be some kind of record. I hunted with several packs and was chairman of the Flint and Denbigh hounds for many years. I had many falls, but few nasty ones. Once I went down with a horse that rolled on me, and had such a terrible bruise on my face that I couldn't shave for a week; it made my neck very bad too, so I went to an osteopath, but I think his treatment was worse than the injury – I thought he was going to wring my neck! Another time I was brought down by a pheasant, of all things, which flew through the horse's legs and made it stumble and down we went.

'Today we have just under one thousand sheep, and they graze our 380 acres as well as a sheep walk that we rent. We still have one farm-worker, but we couldn't afford more and there'd be little for them to do because mechanisation, electricity and machines have made everything so much easier. We used to have a cook, two maids and a nanny, but those days are long gone. The nanny, who lived in, was paid £16 a year.

'The only labour-saving device we had in my youth was a waterwheel. It was set up on the stream to drive our wood saw and to grind our corn. You just pulled up a sluice, the water came through, hit the wheel and you were in business.'

Like many country houses, Glyn Arthur had an inside loo by the turn of the century but it was reserved strictly for use by the women of the house; the men still had to go outside, and they continued to do so well into this century. The staff had another, entirely separate loo, which was also outside. Dick laughs indulgently now at how different things were in his youth; but he is proud that, however much things have changed, the presence of another generation of his family in the house is assured. He has four children: Peter, who now runs the farm; Richard, a civil engineer; Elizabeth, a solicitor; and Edmund who lives and works in London.

One characteristic of the Rowley Williamses which non-hunting people find curious is that, like most country people who love hunting they are very fond of the fox, and over the years have

Broadcasting seed on a typically steep Welsh hillside

kept several as pets. 'We had one for a number of years when I was young, and if I shouted "Come on, Charlie!" he would rush over and jump into my arms. However, every fox will wander away eventually; I think the mating and travelling urge is just too strong and eventually they just have to go.

'Other foxes we kept used to wander around the house and sleep with the dogs. One used to play with the hounds – the fox would hide in the shrubbery in the garden while the hound puppies tried to find it. They'd draw for him in the undergrowth while he sat, with a rather superior look on his face, bang in the middle of the lawn!'

Towards the end of my day with Dick he confessed that, great though his love of farming is, he does occasionally regret that he did not devote more time to his other great love: art. From the back of a dusty cupboard he revealed an ancient sketchbook filled with exquisite pictures of horses and ponies, sheep and other animals, as well as drawings of landscapes and the hills of his beloved Wales. 'Yes, I studied art at an art school in the Home Counties for a while in the 1930s, because I had found I was quite good at it; but the farm was so busy that I did little over the years before Peter began to take over. But I have this book of drawings, and several of my pictures are framed on the walls here in the house, so there will at least be something of my artistic side when I'm gone.'

Opposite: A land-girl at Glyn Arthur during World War II

A Life
on the Roof

Ernest Sharp: Master Thatcher,
Wokingham, Berkshire

A LIFE ON THE ROOF

A twentieth-century bungalow in suburban Berkshire is not the sort of place where you would expect to find in retirement a man who has spent most of his life perpetuating the chocolate-box image of Old England. But, master thatcher Ernest Edward Sharp has never been one to romanticise about the English countryside. Even at school, he regarded following in grandfather's and father's footsteps as 'just hard work, not something you wanted to do'.

Today this very well-preserved septuagenarian, who retired from the rooftop at the age of 65, presides over a family thatching business which is now in its fifth generation. With his son and grandson now firmly on the rung of thatching success, he is very much the middle man, linking the craftsmen of two centuries through family tradition.

Ernest has always lived in and around the Wokingham area, but it was a much more rural Berkshire when he was born on 22 February 1920. He was one of eight children six boys and two girls — and remembers getting hay-waggon rides to school, although most of the time they had to walk everywhere. 'You could have walked up the middle of the main road without any fear in those days.'

When he was about 7, Ernest started to help his father with the thatching of hay and corn ricks. 'My brother and I used to harness an old carthorse up and on the cart was a big old water-tank, which we used to take down to the ford at the river and fill the tank up, using a bucket on a rope. Then it was back to the farmyard, where the longstraw was in bundles. It was our job to shake it up with a pitchfork into a bed and every so often throw water over it. Wetting the heap helped to bed it down and soften it. Then we'd start drawing it out by hand into a nice line, the idea being that the wet and weight helped to straighten it out. We drew out bundles 2½ft wide — yelms — then it was onto the rick. Father did the actual thatching and it was the same procedure for rooves.

'Even as kids, we used to spend a lot of time working. During the summer holidays I used to go away with father rick thatching, to Sir Robert Percer's at Colnbrook. We cycled over at first, stayed in a tent and came home at weekends. The work lasted about a month.

'Eventually father got a motorbike and side-car — a 1,000 twin James — and we was in luxury. But this was nothing compared with his first car. He was doing ricks for the doctor who owned Warfield Park. There was this old Wolsey in the barn and dad asked the doctor what he was doing with it. He said you can have it for £3 10s, and so he did. It was a French-built car and the doctor had collected it from the dock. Funny thing is, father drove it home on Saturday and

With fox terrier
and cider jar:
Ernest Sharp's
father (aged 17)
and grandfather
in 1913

we all went to the seaside in it on the Sunday, even though he'd never driven a car before. I was about ten then.'

Before the days of easy travelling, most countrymen had to be very adaptable to keep themselves in work, and the thatcher was no exception. 'Right up to the war the average thatcher was no businessman, just a tradesman. Most of them regularly had to do other work, especially hedging and ditching in winter and helping with the harvest. There just wasn't the money being spent on house thatching then, but in the Thirties a rick thatcher – provided 'e could do the job right – could earn more than most people.

'And just after the war, too, it was a good living. I used to get £5 for a big rick and £3 10s for a small one, and as I could do one a day, £25 a week was a mighty good living. But there was no rush to do it because most people were being lured away into industry in those days. Anyway, it was a good thing that many thatchers packed it in after the war because there were too many of us.

In April 1940, Ernest volunteered for the Grenadier Guards and, after postings at Chelsea and Windsor, saw service in North Africa and Italy, during which time he was caught up in the horrors of Anzio. Fortunately, he escaped injury, although he did cut his head when he drove his lorry over a cliff. He was in a convoy travelling

SELF-SUFFICIENCY

Like most country folk, the Sharps were fairly self-sufficient, with about five hundred chickens and some two dozen milking nanny goats. 'And we used to eat the young billies at six months – lovely meat, absolutely beautiful. I remember during the war being sent with a pony and trap to pick one up for my brother's wedding reception.

'We used to kill the goats by tying a rope round their legs, stringing 'em up and slitting their throats. Grandfather was a pig killer too, and went all over the place. Sometimes I used to help him. The last one I remember was while I was still at school. It was in the dark and I held the torch while two or three men held the pig down and grandad stuck the knife in.'

along a mountain road in Algeria when the lorry in front broke down. 'I stopped, then pulled out to go round him, but we slid over the edge. My mate was asleep but that soon woke him up.'

But Ernest hated the Army and left as soon as he could, in 1946, having married a local girl, Iris, in 1945. So it was back into thatching with father and brother.

One of the more unusual jobs which Ernest used to help his father with was well-digging. 'He did the digging and I used to help lug the clay out with a bucket and rope. The depth varied a lot, according to the water-table. The one in the garden here is just 21ft, but one at Barkham was 100ft. I suppose most are no more than about 20ft deep. They are lined with a single layer of bricks.

'I suppose well-digging can be a bit dangerous, but the worst that ever happened to me was knocking a thumb-nail off when I was breaking up the top of an old well. Mind you, my uncle dropped half a brick on dad's head when he was labouring for him once.'

From those early days, the number of insects about stands out in Ernest's memory, 'especially the dragonflies down by the river'. But insects have caused a few problems in his thatching career, during which he has been stung by wasps on many occasions. 'Once I went to do a little repair job for an ol' feller, and I went to bat up under the eaves. The old devil, he knew that nest was there but never told me. All he did was laugh when I got stung, but a kind woman next door came out and rubbed half an onion all over

Master thatcher Ernest Sharp working on a kiosk along the towpath at Richmond in the mid-1960s

the swellings. I was ill for a week. In most cases a wasp nest is in the roof space, but this one was in the thatch.'

Unfortunately, Ernest has never found any treasure in a thatch, although his son Geoff recently found a bundle of love letters in one made of Norfolk reed. This is by far the best thatching material and when well laid should last for over eighty years. 'But it's also the most expensive and with all the drainage water reed is increasingly hard to find. Sometimes we have to go over to France to get supplies.

'Longstraw is the cheapest of the three main types. Made from threshed wheat straw of fairly good length, this is the traditional thatch of the South, South East and Midlands. It is recognised by the split hazel rails at the eaves, inset with cross spitting, and when thatched by us can last up to thirty years.

'Devon reed – combed wheat straw – originated in the West country, but has spread over the Home Counties, is recognised by its smooth mushroom-shaped thatch, and has a lifespan of up to forty years. The Norfolk reed is found mainly in East Anglia and the Home Counties and gives a smooth thatch with angular lines.

'Costwise you are talking thousands for a complete new thatch, but it might be ten or it might be twenty; the price varies enormously according to the size and the number of complications as well as the type of material used.'

Now Ernest proudly relates that his son has re-thatched some longstraw work he did over 35 years ago, 20-30 years being the average for this cheapest of thatches. His son has even thatched in France, but generally they stay within Hampshire, Gloucestershire, Surrey, Oxfordshire, Berkshire and Buckinghamshire. He has never been tempted to move to an area with more thatch 'because there are certain to be more thatchers there. It's got so much more competitive over the last ten years. Everyone thinks it's a goldmine, but nobody wants to work the five- or six-year apprenticeship there used to be.'

Apart from the family trio, the Sharp business employs four other men, 'and there was a

FALLING OFF!

Despite all his rushing, Ernest has survived to tell the tale, although he has fallen off the roof quite a few times. Once when he was working at Ascot he was up and down a ladder all day before it broke and he fell some 15ft, but he got away with only a broken ankle. And on 1 August, 1985 (he remembers the exact date because they were due to go on holiday that night) he broke an ankle when he jumped down off the straw on a pick-up truck. His foot twisted when he landed on a ball of straw. So instead of going on holiday he began a seven-month lay off.

A more serious accident happened in his early thirties when he was cutting holly. 'The holly was in great demand for wreaths and crosses and we used to make hundreds of 'em. But it was mother's trade really and we used to take them to Brentford Market. Anyway, this particular year I stepped on a dead branch when moving between trees and fell 20ft straight down. Somehow I managed to drive the motorbike and sidecar home and when the doctor came the next morning he told me I'd broken two vertebrae. I ended up in plaster for four months'.

time when my wife Iris used to labour for me too. But she could only do ground work because she didn't like coming down the ladder. And it's best if everyone in the team works at about the same pace. Mind you, I'm a bit of a rusher, always wanting to get the job done. But I suppose it's been a business for me. Those old boys certainly worked longer hours than the men today, but then they were only plodders.'

Despite smoking from the age of 22 until he was 68 ('I used to roll my own'), Ernest never set a thatch afire. 'Of course, I never smoked on a job. But I do remember when a steam-engine went through and set a thatch ablaze.'

During his long career, Ernest has worked for many distinguished people, Berkshire being a renowned haunt of the rich and the famous, close enough to London but with a generous sprinkling of old cottages. Among his clientele have been Tiny Rowlands, King Hussein (at Windsor), the Sultan of Oman, actress Beryl Reid ('do call me Beryl') at Wraysbury, Hollywood actress Jacqueline Bissett, and even the Queen, for whom he re-thatched the princesses' play-house at Windsor.

Apart from houses, Ernest has thatched all sorts of buildings, from the barn at Eton College to a school at Hartley Wintney in Hampshire. 'Sadly, it was knocked down years ago.' He even thatches new buildings – 'We've done four in the last year'. And sometimes he is asked to make animals and birds from thatch. 'One American got me to make two thatched pheasants for him to take back and put on his shingled roof!'

Fortunately, the thatch does not have many natural enemies, 'though rats and squirrels will

All this activity has certainly left Ernest with a sparkle in his eye, which is just as well as he believes that 'any thatcher must have a good eye for lining things up. And the other essential quality is a head for heights; you never hold a ladder, always working with both hands.' But as well as his trade skills, Ernest always had a good business sense, unlike 'some of the best thatchers I knew, who didn't earn any money. Trouble was they didn't know when they'd done it good enough.' And it is this ability to combine quality craftsmanship with business acumen which has enabled the Sharps to survive in the profession for over a century.

Three generations of thatchers: Ernest Sharp (right), with his son and grandson, and their binder for cutting straw, summer 1991

chew holes in it. It's not our fault, though, but where the owners are not aware they have pests in the building. You can thatch a roof well and go by soon after and see where rats have punched holes in the wire-netting, from the inside. It seems incredible that the owners don't know they are there. Oh, and then there's bloody magpies, which I've known to pull out long reeds for no apparent reason. They simply kept returning to the same spot in the thatch, pulled out the water reed and dropped it on the ground.'

But these have been minor problems in what has been a generally successful thatching career. 'You didn't get a lot out of life much of the time, but we had a lot less hassle than many people.' And years of running up and down ladders obviously still left Ernest with enough energy for recreation, as his main hobby has been cycling. Before the war this involved time trials, but with the arrival of Continental refugees road racing started. 'In the old days, under National Cycling Union rules, no bare legs were allowed, so we wore black tights and an alpaca jacket. It was nothing to go 50 miles, but it was immensely enjoyable then as there was so little motor traffic.'

Their Majesties' Keeper

Jack Clark: Gamekeeper, Sandringham, Norfolk

THEIR MAJESTIES' KEEPER

When Jack Clark marched behind the coffin of George VI along with the other Sandringham keepers there were tears in his eyes, for he had seen the passing not only of a great shot but also of a man devoted to shooting and all its followers. Jack's father was also in that procession from Sandringham Church to Wolferton Station in 1952, marking a long family commitment to the royal family.

Previous page: King George VI and his daughters, Elizabeth and Margaret, cycle behind Queen Elizabeth as she crosses Sandringham estate to inspect the harvest in 1943

'George VI really liked duck shooting and rabbit shooting best', Jack told me at his very attractive Victorian retirement cottage at West Newton on the Sandringham estate. 'We often had to walk the woods for him in between main shooting days, so we was never done. But he had to slacken up in the last few years when he became ill.

'I spoke to him on the hare shoot the day before he died: he said goodnight to us and we said goodnight to him. Everything seemed much the same as usual.

'Next day we was pushin' a load of rabbits home on a bike when we met the farm foreman He said "I suppose you know the news" "No" we all chirruped together. And with a lump in his throat he said "The King's dead. The valet found him when he took up his cup of tea".

Christened John Edward, Jack Clark was born on 29 April 1923 at Great Wilbraham, Cambridgeshire, where his father and his grandfather before him had been keeper for Squire Hicks.

In 1934 the family moved to Sandringham, when Jack's father, Nobby, became beat keeper at Flitcham. And after schooling at Flitcham and West Newton, fourteen-year-old Jack not surprisingly started work in 1937 on the Wolferton beat, where he was to remain for the whole of his working life, apart from war service. 'In those days there were very few job opportunities so you took what you could. I might have gone in the Army, but you had to take a test and I weren't too good at arithmetic'.

For a month or two before starting on pheasant work Jack worked as houseboy for the retired schoolmaster who looked after the King's racing pigeons. 'When the old boy died the lofts were closed.'

Working under his father, Jack did a lot of vermin trapping and, as 'the junior', he was heavily involved in the routine feeding programme which included the usual mix of eggs, rice, scalded biscuit meal and 'hundreds and

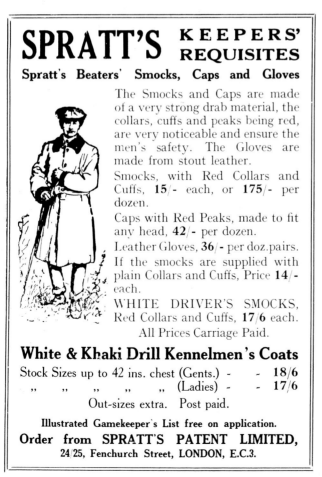

SPRATT'S KEEPERS' REQUISITES

Spratt's Beaters' Smocks, Caps and Gloves

The Smocks and Caps are made of a very strong drab material, the collars, cuffs and peaks being red, are very noticeable and ensure the men's safety. The Gloves are made from stout leather.
Smocks, with Red Collars and Cuffs, **15/-** each, or **175/-** per dozen.
Caps with Red Peaks, made to fit any head, **42/-** per dozen.
Leather Gloves, **36/-** per doz.pairs.
If the smocks are supplied with plain Collars and Cuffs, Price **14/-** each.
WHITE DRIVER'S SMOCKS, Red Collars and Cuffs, **17/6** each.
All Prices Carriage Paid.

White & Khaki Drill Kennelmen's Coats

Stock Sizes up to 42 ins. chest (Gents.) - - **18/6**
" " " " " (Ladies) - - **17/6**
Out-sizes extra. Post paid.

Illustrated Gamekeeper's List free on application.
Order from SPRATT'S PATENT LIMITED,
24/25, Fenchurch Street, LONDON, E.C.3.

hundreds of minced, boiled rabbits. We fed three or four times a day and the food stove never went out, even if it was pissin' with rain.

'All the coops were kept in a great big shed and for days on end we had to scrub them out with Jeyes Fluid, and then they were lime-washed. And all the runs had to be creosoted.

'Each clutch was made up to about twenty eggs and it was very important that the broods were kept separated. So we put each chick in a little marked bag to make sure they all ended up with the right hens after being crated to the rearing field about a mile away — the hens would brain the wrong chicks.

'Each coop contained a faggot of rhododendron for the chicks to hide in till the grass got high, and we moved the coops every day. The chicks demanded a great deal of attention so we used to pray for a cold night so that we could shut them up early and not have to watch them.

'Days were specially long if there was big vermin trouble and we sometimes had to stay in the cabins all night. And you know what it's like working for father. Not only did he make me gather all the firewood in a pony and cart, but I had to take him his dinner on me bike, too!

'We were on the rearing field for six to eight weeks as there were two hatches. When the first lot went to wood it was often two weeks before the others would be off. One of our biggest problems was that if they was sick there were no

The Sandringham gamekeepers marching behind George VI's coffin from Sandringham Church to Wolferton Station in 1952. Jack Clark is pictured second from the left in the second row, his father front right

drugs to dose the birds up: all we could do was shift 'em to fresh ground and hope they would get better.'

Rearing stopped at Sandringham with the outbreak of war and there has been none since, though a few pheasants were reared in 1940 on another beat.

When the war started in September 1939 Jack's father immediately joined the Army. In fact Nobby had a distinguished military career. After 12 months he was selected to train Special Operations Executive agents – such as Odette Churchill – in survival techniques, and was eventually commissioned. He had also been mentioned in despatches in 1919 during the Afghan War: Jack still has the framed citation signed by Winston Churchill, who was then Secretary of State for War (And Air).

Jack joined up at the end of 1941, serving with the Norfolks (his father's regiment) in North Africa, Italy and Europe, the Sherwood Foresters (with whom he was wounded in Italy), and the King's Shropshire Light Infantry. He returned home in 1946.

Shooting had continued at Sandringham during the war, when there were some good partridge years – about 6,000 were shot one season. 'With the let-down of the war, wild pheasants and partridges found ideal conditions here and really came into their own. There was no going back to the old days of heavy rearing, when they thought nothing of shooting 2,000 pheasants or 300-400 brace of partridges on a single outing. The total number shot must have been enormous and we always wondered how accurate the gamebooks were. Large quantities were sent off to market and we always reckoned that somebody must have made a fortune somewhere along the line.

'In those days neighbouring estates too were taken for the shooting, but that all finished with Edward VIII. On some beats, if they didn't kill more than 2,000 the first time over then someone was for the high jump. Anmer was probably the best beat. But I was only a lad then.

'Father had a lighter suit for partridge shooting, which often took place in fine weather early in the season, but for pheasant days he wore a big, dark-green beatkeeper's coat, cord breeches gaiters and a hard bowler hat with gold braid sash and two acorns around. It was ever such a heavy coat – what it would cost today goodness only knows.'

Before the war the beaters wore blue, numbered smocks, 'and there were two gangs of them on partridge days as there was no transport to whizz people around in. In fact there were still two gangs for a while after the war.'

In those days the keeper's lunch consisted of 'a great chunk of bread – about half a cottage loaf, cheese, meat, beer and mince pies – all wrapped up in a little parcel. The Guns had a special marquee for lunch, and headkeeper Bland had his own little tent adjoining it. Mother did out our big front room for the loaders of the guests, but we used to be all right for grub for about a fortnight afterwards, what with sauces, cold meats, pickles, chutneys and suchlike.

'Headkeeper Bland was not a popular man. He looked just like George V and rode about on a pony checking up on everybody. All the keepers had to call him "Sir" – you wouldn't have dared address him by his Christian name in those days.'

Like other headkeepers of the period, Bland made spot checks on the partridge nests marked on each beatkeeper's map, looking at perhaps three or four hundred nests on one beat as often as he could. 'There were so many birds here then. Why, on my mile and a half walk to school I could spot about thirty partridge nests in the hedgerow, but today you would be lucky to see half-a-dozen. Of course, you spotted the most in a good nestin' year and when the growth didn't come too soon.'

As a junior, Jack's other jobs included 'putting out hundreds of yards of sewelling to stop birds breaking back, and taking out lunches to as many as twenty "stops". The stops were mostly older men who found it hard to keep up with the line, but some poor devils had to stay put all

*Even in retirement, Jack Clark of Sandringham
remained closely attached to his dogs*

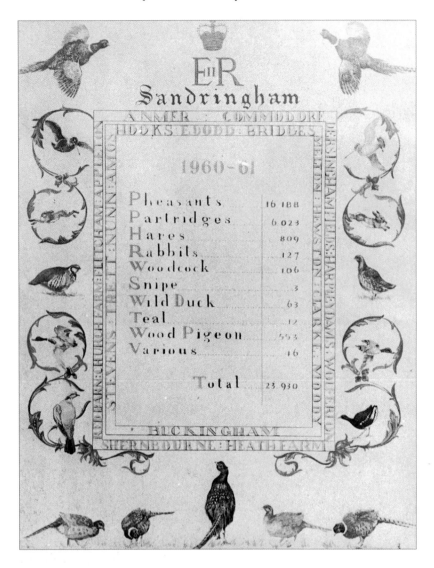

EIIR

Sandringham

ANMER : COMMODORE

HOOKS : EDDD : BRIDES

1960-61

Pheasants	16 188
Partridges	6 023
Hares	809
Rabbits	127
Woodcock	106
Snipe	3
Wild Duck	63
Teal	12
Wood Pigeon	553
Various	16
Total	23 930

BUCKINGHAM

SHERNBOURNE : HEATH FARM

At Sandringham, some of the best seasons' bags were commemorated in special colour paintings by Lady Fellowes, wife of an old Sandringham agent, Sir William Fellowes

day, gently tapping to stop the birds running out the sides.'

At first Jack earned 'Ten or twelve bob a week', but after paying his keep ended up with 'only about two bob pocket money', so he was much better off in the Army, when he had the whole of his ten bob pay to spend.

A bachelor most of his life, Jack married in 1980 – quite a change for the man who, prior to retirement in April 1988, lived for fifty years in the same cottage in Wolferton woods, where he still does a little vermin control. He gets 'a decent pension' from the estate, 'and there was a lump sum on retirement', but now he has to pay some rent, whereas it used to be free.

The cottage is crammed with photos and other reminders of the shooting life. Included

among the treasures are Jack's royal Victorian medal, which he received from Her Majesty the Queen in 1986, and the CLA keeper's long-service award, which he received at Chatsworth in 1987. 'It was for forty years, but actually I had done forty-nine then.'

But the objects of yesteryear mean no more than the memories – clearly stretching back to the day when George V handed Jack an orange on a visit to the local school. 'I never saw him shoot, but from what I've been led to understand he was a pretty good Shot.

'The Duke of Edinburgh and Prince Charles are excellent Shots, though Charles doesn't do much shooting now and Philip gets bad arthritis in his hands: you always know when it's playing him up on a cold day because he misses more than usual and then swears a lot. Lord Brabourne is perhaps the best Shot I've seen, though he can be a bit greedy. Today I would say that the three best regular Shots at Sandringham are Hugh van Cutsem, Anthony Duckworth-Chad of Pinkney Hall, Norfolk and Lord Tollemache of Helmingham Hall, Suffolk. Prince Edward is not a particularly good Shot.

'Most shooting at Sandringham takes place in January now. The Queen never shoots, but what a keen gundog lady she is. All the dogs love her and make a great fuss of her. She had handled my old bitch Pendle and now whenever the dog sees Her Majesty she will make straight for her – even if she is a hundred yards away. All she wants is a bit of fuss made of her and then she comes straight back to me.

'Overall, it's been a good life, but I've certainly had some hassle. I'm the sort of bloke who worries and would have been no good as a headkeeper. I don't know if I'd do it all over again. I missed the Army you know, especially when I was demobbed. When you came back to a little ol' bloody village like Wolferton after years abroad nobody knew you, and you couldn't join up with the regulars if you were all crocked up like I was with my injuries.'

Jack died in July 1997.

BEWARE! POACHERS!

No doubt his Army experience helped prepare him for the inevitable occasional brush with poachers. Jack's worst experience was in 1955, when he came across a gang of three at night. 'I fetched one bloke down but the other buggers came back at me. I was on the ground when I saw the raised gun and instinctively put my hand up to defend myself. I'm sure that saved me from having a clobbered skull, but the rifle butt did smash several ribs.

'But I had my own back once or twice. Father did too. Take the time when he struggled with a man holding a 410 and the gun went off right next to his head when he was holding it by the muzzle. The man got away, but next day they found the gun's fore-end along with a box of matches at the scene of the incident.

'The following Sunday a gang of five from Wisbech were seen poaching on another part of the estate and were picked up by the police. Next morning the police inspector found that one of the gang's guns matched the fore-end found the week before. The police knew one of the gang well – a seventeen-year-old – so put the heat on him and he coughed the lot. Just before the war that was'.

As Jack told me this story in his pretty little cottage, swifts continually swooped past the windows. 'How lucky you are', I remarked, but Mrs Clark interjected 'I don't like 'em bombing my washing line though'. 'You should like birds, dear', said Jack quietly, but firmly.

The Dukes of Gloucester and Edinburgh walk solemnly behind the funeral cortege as a respectful local turnout line a country road to watch King George VI's final journey from Sandringham Church to Wolferton Station, in 1952

Son of the Soil

Tom Long: Nurseryman, Hillier
Nurseries of Winchester, Hampshire

SON OF THE SOIL

Tom Long was born in Winchester in 1936 and grew up during the war. His family were ardent supporters of the 'Dig for Victory Campaign' and they all looked forward with enthusiasm to the regular weekend expeditions made to their allotments. Tom's mother and grandmother would pack up picnics and the whole family would go off to enjoy a day's gardening and doing their bit for their country. Tom and his brothers all developed a profound interest in plants and gardens; Tom, however, was the only one to take up gardening as a profession: 'I didn't look at the money side, I didn't really take any interest in how much it was paying at the time, although now I sometimes wish I had done.'

*Previous page:
Chelsea Flower
Show 1951*

When leaving school, Tom applied to Hillier Nurseries for his first job and has been with them ever since, except for the compulsory period of National Service. He started at Hillier's Saint Cross Nursery, Ghost Corner, on the 1 January 1952. There was no bank holiday in those days, and some say the first day of the year became a bank holiday because so many people were late for work, or did not appear at all, staying at home to recover from the revelry of heralding in the New Year.

However, Tom arrived on the dot of twenty-past seven, after a long bicycle ride in the cold from his home in Winchester. He reported to the foreman, Mr Woodland, and was put to work tending herbaceous, alpine and water plants. 'I got to like the herbaceous and alpines because that was the section I was put on. It does grow on you,' laughed Tom in his usual jovial manner.

Looking back, Tom considers himself fortunate in that he was allowed to spend several years at one crop, and was therefore able to get to know herbaceous plants well. 'Now, if I pick up an herbaceous plant, I'll smell the root and people will say, "What are you doing that for?" It's amazing how many different herbaceous plants, even Michaelmas daisies, have a different smell to

the root. Perhaps when it was dormant and you were lifting, you'd reassure yourself you were lifting the right side of the label. I remember the "Ballards"; they stuck out quite well as having a different smell to the root. Not many people do this, but I still do. It's the same with the iris, the orris root, it's quite distinct, and the Gladwyn iris, which you find in the hedgerows in Dorset.'

Through the winter, time was spent lifting orders, and then the herbaceous plants had to be split and laid in for spring planting. In those days everything was dug by hand, and hand-planted. If it was a really big field, Hillier's might use their plough and harrow and it would be dug by hand afterwards. After 1953 a rotavator was used, but plants continued to be dug in by hand.

'There were usually about a dozen garden staff – Mr Woodland and his assistant, Martin Drew, about six blokes dealing with the herbaceous field planting, three in the greenhouses, and there would be a specialist propagator. That was all very cloak and dagger in those days and you would have to do so many years before you could get in on propagation.' The girls did the lighter work and were kept occupied in the alpine section where they would handle only 3in pots, that is 7cm today.

Tom at work at a
Hillier nursery

Hillier's shop at 95
High Street,
Winchester, where
Tom Long
weighed up seeds
and learned to do
'floral work'

Tom Long enjoyed his work with plants and being in the open air. 'They weren't a bad crowd of people. In those days they were more happy with their lot and most of them were doing the thing they wanted to do.' He does feel that Hillier's staff were perhaps a very insular crowd of people. 'They knew themselves to be the best nursery in the country, and then the staff of each department took such pride in its work that a great feeling of competition between themselves was generated.' Tom's was 'No.3 Nursery' and they considered themselves the best. The competitive spirit meant that each department did its best to keep its nursery at the top, the firm seeming to foster this *esprit de corps*.

H.G. Hillier (later Sir Harold, and affectionately known by the staff as H.G.) was the boss in those days, and although his presence was rare, he engendered an aura of authority befitting a person of seniority. In turn, the employee knew he must obey a certain code of behaviour.

'You did not leave a mess behind you, and you knew you had to keep yourself tidy. It was expected of you and it was all part of that generation. You had come through a war so you did not waste things; things were still hard to come by. If you had a tear in your trousers you had it sewn up – your mother saw to that – so that they lasted a bit longer and you were tidy for work.'

When Tom came upon one of H.G.'s catalogues he felt he was part of something big, but was not really clear what this was. 'When my old neighbour asked me, after I'd been there for a few months, "Are you going to Chelsea?" I did not even know that Chelsea was the Royal Horticultural Society Flower Show. So I went and asked and was told: "One day when you know a bit you will be able to go." So, to get to go, you had to show willing and keenness that you were interested in the job. You just did not get picked if you were passing the day along and worked with your clothes torn and that sort of thing.'

Tom went to Winchester home-base nursery in the winter when it snowed; that was the garden centre now opposite the county hospital. 'They did house-plants, bedding plants, chrysanthemums and so on, and we helped them prepare for the following spring. Sometimes we did planting and because it was cold we would cover the ground with straw overnight and rake it off in the morning ready for carrying on the next day's work.' Now with hindsight, Tom thinks this was a very slow operation compared with modern times.

'Sometimes we were sent up to the shop in Winchester High Street where they weighed their own flower and vegetable seeds. There would be two or three of us weighing up eighths of an ounce of seeds from a hundredweight sack of carrot seeds. It's grammes today, but then it was ounces. You would have a spell at that and while you were there, they would show you how to do a bit of wreath work, making holly wreaths at Christmas, for example, or if it was Mothering Sunday time, making sprays. Occasionally they would send you out with the bike making deliveries to local customers; that was to save the van going.'

In those days they used to start lifting the water lilies in late spring when the water was warming up and the leaves were forming. There were paths nine inches wide between the tanks, and it was Tom's job to make up the baskets with wire-netting and line them with turf to stop the roots going into the water:

'One day, it was just before twelve o'clock, and Martin Drew, the under-foreman, and myself were doing the orders for water lilies and getting the baskets ready. I turned to him and said "Which one?" and he said "That one in the next pond". I put my foot out on what I thought was the path, and of course, it wasn't – it was just a leaf, and I went in up to here!' Tom drew his hand across his neck.

'The old fellow in the packing-shed looked over and he told the foreman I did it on purpose so that I could have an extra hour for dinner, because I would have to go home and get a change of clothes. But I can assure you I didn't!'

When Tom started work, the hours had just come down from a 47- to a 46-hour week. They started at 7.10am in the summer time and finished at 5pm, and on Saturdays at midday. In winter time, when there was no light, they started at 7.20am but they had to make up the time, and could opt either to have less time for dinner or to work longer on Saturdays. Tom opted for the shorter dinner hour as he played football for the Winchester league on Saturdays. His wage at fifteen, when he was still living at home, was £2 16s a week, and he qualified for the

H. G.

H.G. Hillier, now remembered for the greatly renowned Hillier Arboretum, Ampfield, near Romsey in Hampshire that he started in January 1955, was extremely industrious. He did not work by a clock: He used to say that he worked twenty-four hours a day' but Tom remembers 'When we got a bit older we used to say, "Well, you're getting the money, aren't you? We're not!" H.G. did not have too much contact with the staff because his catalogues, notebooks and collecting plants took a hell of a lot of time. He relied on his foremen to run the departments, and usually all they got was a message on the back of an envelope, to save a new piece of paper. That was his filing system. When you think of the range of plants we had – and although we still have a big range, it's not so big as it was – and that man was doing it without a computer. Just think, he was doing it manually on rough paper and odd notebooks! If he lost one of those, it was something to lose – where a cutting had come from, who sent it, what date it was. He seemed to will a cutting to take, because it was the only one to have been given to him.'

agricultural wage increases each year. In later years he enjoyed the extra money that was 'the right of a man travelling the shows', but the men would be questioned as to why they thought they were worth more.

When Tom came out of the army he had no intention of going back to the same job, but then he took a bike ride out into the country and came across Hillier's new herbaceous and alpines nursery, and was invited to take his job back. He says if he had ridden off in the other direction he would not be where he is now. 'They had grown and had got up to twelve acres of herbaceous plants, and supplied the shop with flowers for weddings and so on. Now they have an even larger organised programme of selling flowers. Yes, everything had got bigger. There was a packing shed, they had gone over to rotavators, and they were doing their own shows. They also had a bulb catalogue and potted up a lot of spring bulbs; there was a bulb store in the old stable at one stage. They did about five thousand

bulbs, and after the flowers had been cut off, they were sold off very cheaply as mixed bulbs. It did not seem much, but it saved them going on the bonfire heap.

'The department had gone up to about fifteen, with the girls still working in alpines. The girls had to use the toilets of the local householders, but they didn't mind – it was a chance to have a cup of tea with their friends.'

In the sixties Tom took a job as foreman in the landscaping department. He enjoyed the work because it got him out and about meeting people. He did all sorts of landscape work, 'from gardens for old ladies to that one in the park where the parks' superintendents stood on their

A group of staff in 1932. Sir Harold Hillier remembered the 'good old days' thus: 'I remember the days when my father, my uncle and the staff worked from 6am to 6pm, finishing at 4pm on Saturdays, using hurricane lamps in the winter, early mornings and evenings, in the days of Shroner, this meant a walk of six miles before 6am. Only if one was lucky was there a lift in a wagon. After a high tea, my father would work in the office at the back of 95 High Street, returning home in time for bed at 1130pm'.

brooms watching you, you know.' One job was at Winchester College, where the art master had initiated a fund from amongst the old Wyke- hamists as he thought there was not enough planting being done for future generations: he raised £800 to be spent on its development. At that time Tom was earning about £8 a week, so £800 seemed a lot of money to him then. They planted a lot of unusual trees around the old col- lege buildings and cloisters and the sports fields. On the edge of the cricket field at Gamier Road they planted five *Cercis siliquastrum*, (the 'Judas tree', so-called because it is the species from which Judas is said to have hanged himself), and they are there to this day.

Tom and his team did a variety of landscap- ing jobs around the country. He would take a few men in his car, because not many people had a car in those days, and they would leave in a gang at five o'clock in the morning and would not get back until nine o'clock at night. One client, Mr Leighton, the optician at Hove, was particularly pleased with them and wanted them to enjoy themselves. He encouraged them to have plenty of time to eat and drink, and when they were finished he invited them to stay longer. 'You don't have to rush. Get a bit of over- time – I'm paying the bill!' he said.

Tom's last landscaping job was a big one at Christchurch for the town council. They had demolished a lot of old houses and made a traffic island, and instead of just grassing it over or planting it with heathers, asked Hillier's to landscape it.

'The winter of 1961, it was, and it was hard work! They had made the island of reclaimed sewage sludge that had been sterilised, and it was on a steep slope. They put the soil on the island without any supervision and they had dumped it all on the bottom of the slope, it was a wet month, and when we went to start, a load of it had to be brought up the slippery slope on planks to get the site firm and ready for planting. One day H.G. came down and helped build the rockeries himself.'

THE CHELSEA FLOWER SHOW

Tom has worked at three Chelsea Flower Shows. In those days they had separate stands for shrubs, roses, herbaceous and alpines inside the tent, and one year Harold Hillier also organised a stand of hollies in the avenue outside. 'They used about 150 different varieties of hollies. That was when Roy Lancaster joined Hillier's and he helped run this. It would be a different genus of plants each year.' Tom enjoyed show-work, and found it not so much hard as tiring.

The men would design the stands between them. At the provincial shows they would do a stand of cut flowers some thirty feet long; preparation for the Chelsea Flower Show, however, would be more rigorous. Potted plants were put on show there, specially raised and started early in the previous autumn.

'Some would have to go in the freezer, some didn't. Some in the full shade, some put out in the full sun. I never pulled my hair out, there was no point because you couldn't always make them bloom, and if they didn't come out you couldn't use them. There's a lot of camouflage goes on at a stand. Something may not have leaves on, but it can have a good flower stalk, so you camouflage the fact.

'It was work, eat and sleep. There wasn't much time for a joke. Clearing away was far worse than putting up. They sold most things off on Friday night and the public would buy at an inflated price just because it was from Chelsea, but anything still looking good went off to the Bath and West show that followed on.'

They did summer shows every fortnight around the country. 'A showman's lot is a hard lot, and hard on his wife because he is never home.'

When Tom finished with show-work he took over the herbaceous section, and because the firm had grown so big, they took on a man from Wisley to manage the alpine section. Tom has an apprentice nowadays, and when he last took the boy's papers home to mark he found his spelling was atrocious: 'He writes as he speaks, and even created different hybrids just by bad spelling!'

Tom made a request to remain permanently on landscape work, and even thought about moving to a landscaping firm. However, in 1961 he married and the move was forgotten, and he went back to 'herbaceous' and became involved with 'Shows'.

Together with his team of twelve people, Tom is always busy getting orders 'off the beds and off to the packing sheds'. This is his main job, and he is quite happy to do this until his not-too-distant retirement. 'Every man is

Queen Mary at Chelsea Flower Show

dependent upon the man before him doing his job satisfactorily. The packer is dependent upon the propagator and he in turn is dependent upon the cuttings man. If the material is not up to standard, it will be sent back.

'In the old days H.G. would come along with a packet of seeds that perhaps he had collected in Korea. "Raise all you can." "What's all you can?" "Every single one of them, they are gold dust." You didn't know if you were going to sell them. He kept a mystique really, and he sold on mystique. If you had five plants and he brought a party of people round and there was Lord Avon and Lord so-and-so, or perhaps it was a princess, he would play one off against the other. "I'm sorry, I've only got five and Lord Lonsdale said he

would like one." In his way he was a good salesman, wasn't he?'

Tom looked thoughtful: 'It's the older generation that generates the money in gardening. Some military people want to put something back into the world that perhaps they feel they have been mangling up. When they were away on their campaigns they must have seen the most wonderful plants. Perhaps at one time they might have pitched their tents amongst magnolia trees. Yes, perhaps they now want to make up for any destruction they may have contributed to.'

Tom also believes there has been a lot of unnecessary desecration of the countryside, particularly with ploughing up of hedges and felling of trees, often without planning permission. "Capability" Brown, the landscape designer, was responsible for a great deal of destruction in the eighteenth century, but he left gardens for those who came after him and yes, he was moving large trees, even in those days.' Today, Hillier Nurseries are renowned for their work with trees, both raising new stock and transplanting very large specimens, some 200 to 250 years old. 'What started H.G. off, was that he was called in to camouflage aerodromes during the war. They were moving things during the night and they even had their own small-gauge railway for doing it on. The trees were situated around the hangers to disguise them and make them less obvious from the air.

'Winchester chalk was ideal because the soil is only about eighteen inches deep. You only had to go down to this depth and you would hit the pan where the root fibred out, and you could get the winch and pull the tree over and it would break away as clean as a whistle. It's very difficult to move the trees from some types of soil and it cannot be done if the weather is too bad, because

as fast as a hole is dug it fills up with water and a pump has to be used to drain it.

'Now Hillier's have an area like a big stony beach, divided into avenues by huge poles concreted into the ground and linked by ships' hawser wires strained to take the weight of the trees; these are usually finished off in one thousand litre pots, which are more convenient. The pots are wire baskets lined with polythene, and to make the job easier, they are filled with potting compost from bags. It's big business! The trees are allowed a minimum of three years to become established and sometimes they are left for several years, and then, when the weather is fine, they are lifted.'

In the late sixties Harold Hillier went to the Isle of Wight to give a talk when the hospital for tuberculosis sufferers at Ventnor was about to be demolished. It had been suggested that the grounds *should* become a botanic garden, but Harold was not too enthusiastic about the idea and thought it would be better as a sports field. However, the town council contacted him a few months later to say that it had been decided that it should become a botanic garden, and would he go over and help. Hillier Nurseries therefore started to shift all their greenhouse stock of Australasian and New Zealand plants – some they donated and others were supplied at a premium rate.

'We were allowed to go there to collect cuttings, and whenever we went to get them we always took a carload of new plants. We'd collect osteospermums, eucalyptus, we'd collect the seed of them *grevilleas*, and South African stuff, *euryops* and so on. It wasn't long before the old stone walls were covered with climbers donated by Hillier Nurseries and other interested people.'

Hillier Nurseries have ceased to visit since the death of Sir Harold Hillier. 'We don't grow so much Australasian stuff now. He was a different chap when he was there. He always used to go over on a Thursday and stay with a relative and I would meet him with the head propagator on a Monday morning at the boat and he would drive us down to Ventnor. We would go and get the cuttings and that. When he was about the garden in the day he became a down-to-earth type of man on those occasions, He enjoyed it. The first time we were there, it got to ten o'clock and the head gardener said, "Come on Hillier, it's cup o' tea time." "Ooh, no time for that," he replied. Then it was three o'clock. Well, after the first time, he looked forward to going to tea. We took three men over once and they were frightened when he said to them "Come on, what kind of cake do you want? Do you want a doughnut, do you want a cream bun, or do you want an ice-cream?" When he'd gone they said, "Oh, we didn't like to say yes!" He said to me once *"You had a cake with me, Long, what's the matter with those others, aren't I good enough?"*

Sir Harold Hillier died at about the same time as the head gardener retired and another man was brought in from Kew to run the botanic garden, and things changed. They built a grotto and a greenhouse and they made a charge to go into the greenhouse. Unfortunately, the national press has reported that a great deal of pilfering of plants goes on at the botanic gardens,

RARITIES

In the late seventies Harold Hillier started a rare plant unit. There were thousands of varieties of plants and seeds collected abroad and delivered to the nursery, and the job of dealing with them and labelling them was allocated to Tom. In one season he sowed 1,200 different varieties of plants. With all these seeds from all over the world it would have meant so much writing that a number was put on instead. Every plant was coded and listed in a book shared by Tom and Harold Hillier. Plants were listed alphabetically and each nursery had a number. Every place, source, plant and seed had a number. The stock on the ground was sectioned and numbered, too. Tom attended to this task in the evening, when he also made a point of looking up the places the plants had come from. The altitude was also coded and Tom could tell if the specimen could be grown in this country. He was later to find that many plants could be grown on the Isle of Wight that would not grow on the mainland.

even from the greenhouse, but Tom is sad to say that this has always been something of a problem with gardens opened to the public. 'It's pilfering to order — what is being pinched is for somebody's collection. I found this in the nursery at one time. Somebody said to me "Would you leave the gate open at night?" And I am talking about a really rich person. "Would half-a-crown be enough?" That was when it was half-a-crown, now twelve and a half pence. I told him to get lost. He was a *sempervivum* expert and we had a good collection on the alpine section and there was half-a-dozen varieties he wanted. In them days they were 2s 6d each and he was prepared to come back and filch them! But it wasn't worth worrying the old boy about it, else he would have had us all standing guard at nights. This is why gardens are numbering plants and not naming them nowadays. It's sad, isn't it?'

Tom says he does not worry over things, he switches off when he goes home. He might read his books on plants, but he says this is being switched off. At work he is content to go on meeting orders, so long as he can depend on the men behind doing their bit and the men in front having enough pallets ready for him to fill. Nevertheless, he looks forward to the day when he retires because there are so many things he wants to do. Who knows, perhaps he will get around to putting that stuffed koala bear in the eucalyptus tree in his garden, and when the men come out of the nearby inn, The Potter's Heron, they will see what could be described as the alternative to pink elephants!

Much More Than Rubber Stamps

Elizabeth Williams &
Joy Johnson: Postmistresses,
Shropshire & Oxfordshire

MUCH MORE THAN RUBBER STAMPS

The village postmistress has often been caricatured as a shrivelled, embittered, grey-haired gossip, one who is quick with a rubber stamp but slow with help and advice. Yet generally, nothing could be further from the truth, as most postmistresses have been caring members of close-knit communities, serving very wide cross-sections of society.

Two excellent ambassadors of the profession were Elizabeth Williams and Joy Johnson, both of whom set up sub-post offices in their homes during the 1940s and 1950s; they became closely involved in village life and were constantly helping others. For example, Elizabeth was a great friend to the illiterate gypsies who called in from time to time: not only did she read their letters to them, she also wrote their replies. 'Generally these notes were just enquiries after family health and news of new arrivals. The Romanies were always polite and very grateful for my help.'

If anything it was the postmistresses who were likely to be treated with disdain, rather than the customers, as Joy recalls:

'It was soon made clear to me that the regulars expected me to be a mind-reader, to know exactly what they wanted without being told. A stranger would stare in astonishment when a regular came in and without saying a word, put money down on the counter. Then I'd have to think… "Now that's Mr So-and-So and he wants a two-shilling postal order for his football pools and a stamp." And I'd hand them over with no word spoken except the customary "Good morn-

Homebrook House, Hinstock, where Elizabeth established a post office in 1948

Hinstock.

ing!" and his "Thank you, my duck," or whatever. There were many permutations of that, ranging from one lady just wanting a stamp for a monthly letter to Aunt Flo in Canada, to another pushing her family allowance book across the counter for me to date-stamp, tear out the counterfoil and hand over the 8s – all in silence!'

Neither Joy nor Elizabeth had particular ambitions to be postmistresses, but rather just drifted into it; in fact Elizabeth had wanted to be a teacher. One of three children, she was born on 27 March 1923, at Hinstock, near Market Drayton. Her father had been a coach-builder at Crewe Railway Works, but did not go back to this after the General Strike of 1926; instead he bought a 60-acre farm.

After school at Hinstock and Sambrook, Elizabeth won a scholarship to Newport (Shropshire) Girls' High School. On leaving, she kept house for a relative for some months, helped to nurse an invalid, and worked on the land before taking on the post office at the age of 25. Here she explains how this came about:

'The first post office that I can remember in Hinstock was started by a lady who had it until 1940. Then somebody else ran it with a shop but this got into difficulties, so I was able to start up in 1948. I was still living with my widowed mother at home, the eighteenth-century Homebrook House in the centre of the village, and it was there that we set up the post office, clearing the scullery and taking out the old sink, copper and bake-oven to make room for a counter and shelves.

'Hinstock had a population of about 600 and was a pleasant village with a war memorial on the green, a parish church, a Methodist chapel, a school, two general stores, a sweet shop kept by an old lady mainly for the company of her customers, a vet (at first my grandfather, later my cousin), an undertaker and carpenter, two blacksmiths, a butcher who killed his own meat, and three pubs. My customers were nearly all connected with agriculture: farmers, farm workers, millers, milkmen and cattle hauliers.'

Unlike the postmaster before her, Elizabeth did not run a shop in conjunction with the post office; she did, however, sell some postcards and stationery, although there was not a great demand. Elizabeth's post office pay was only £22 a month, and out of that she had to pay for an assistant and provide a property. Her enterprise concentrated on basic post office business, as she explains:

The village postman was often a close friend

'The post office was very important to the village for the sale of postage stamps (a letter then cost just 2½d, except for papers and unsealed envelopes which cost 1½d), for the parcel post, for postal orders, payment of pensions, savings stamps, saving certificates, and savings bank deposits and withdrawals. I sold a great many dog licences at 7s 6d and gun licences at £1, though very few game licences at £5. Road tax licences were not issued by post offices then. With the family allowance there was nothing for the first child, but 5s each for the others.

'I had to be up at 6.45am to receive the incoming mail, but once the letters had been sorted and the letter carriers had left, the office was closed until 9am; then it remained open until 6pm, except on Thursdays when it closed at 1pm. On Sundays I opened from 9am until 10.30am for the sending and receiving of telegrams.

'My mother helped in the post office, and my sister was a letter carrier, who once earned just 6s 6d a week, working two hours a day on six

---

A CAST OF CHARACTERS

With customers ranging from eccentric to uneducated, Elizabeth often had reason to chuckle as she went about her business. Here she recalls a few of the more memorable villagers:

'The local squire was quite a character who had trained to become a priest but did not finish the course. Sometimes when the rector was on holiday he would take the church services, with much throwing around of arms and almost shouts. During the summer he used to walk around the village swinging a white horsehair fly-switch. He was held in little esteem and lived at the hall with his mother, while his wife lived at the neighbouring village hall.

'Then there was the old boy who used to be a road length'sman. He looked after a stretch between two convenient points, trimming the hedge banks, picking litter and so on, and was paid very little. But he was a very conscientious worker whose length was always clean and trim although he was almost bent double. He was a regular ringer of one of the church bells, and his philosophy was that there were just two things from which there was no escape: one was rent day, the other death.

'There was also a man who was mentally retarded, who always took his place to blow the church organ; even after we had electric put in for the bellows he would rush into church and sit in the back pew ready to man the pumps if necessary.

'But the funniest thing I remember was when an unmarried mother asked for a form to claim family allowance, then brought it back and asked me to check that it was properly filled in. Against 'Name of father' she had written 'No father'!'

---

days. By 1946 her wage had risen to 22s a week. All four of my letter carriers were local people who did this part-time in conjunction with other work. In my time they all used bikes, but shortly before one went on foot. When one of the letter carriers retired I had difficulty in filling his place, so head office sent a man to do the round. When I discovered he did not know the area I sorted the mail for him and tied it into bundles, sending him off thinking that he could not get into too much difficulty. However, late in the afternoon someone came in for stamps and said that at lunchtime they had seen the man in a corner of a field with letters spread all around him. But next morning, when I asked him if he could cope, he assured me that he could.'

Elizabeth was always closely involved in village activities. For example, she was on the committee to raise money to build a new village hall, she was also a member of the local church council, and she sang in the choir for twenty years. Today the church holds both happy and sad memories for her:

'One evening at a church meeting, the question was raised about what day in the year Jesus was born, and one lady was most upset when the rector said that the actual date was in fact not known, but that 25 December had been appointed because it fitted with the church calendar. Then on another evening, after the clocks had gone forwards, a lady came into church and walked up to the front pew as we were singing the final hymn, much to the amusement of the choirboys.

'On the Friday evening before Rogation Sunday, the church choir and congregation would make the traditional walk from the church. The route went past this piggery, and it was ironic that as we filed past it we were usually singing "Brothers, we are treading where the saints have trod"; there was usually quite a smell in the air, too! We then had a short sermon by the pool, finishing with a hymn at the war memorial.

'On 3 September 1939, when everyone was expecting war to be declared with Germany, our morning service began at 10.30am, so the rector's

sister remained at home to hear the announcement at 11am. She then came to the church door and nodded to the rector with a pre-arranged signal, to say that war had indeed been declared. The rector then passed on the news to the congregation, and everyone knelt in prayer.'

During her time in the post office, Elizabeth was lucky in that she did not have any really awkward customers, although there were some who genuinely needed help; for example there was the lady whose hands were so crippled by arthritis that Elizabeth had to feel in her pockets for the money. However, Elizabeth herself was gossiped about from time to time – 'as were most people in the village; but it was mostly ignored, and soon passed.'

Elizabeth gave up the post office in 1956, when she married and moved away. The business carried on in the same place for one year before the new postmistress moved it to a local shop. Today Hinstock has only one shop and one pub: the butcher, the baker, the undertaker and

THE VILLAGE BOBBY

Crime was never a problem at Hinstock either, and the postmistress was never robbed or attacked. But in those days most villages had the benefit of a resident policeman. Elizabeth recalls the man at Hinstock:

He was a good friend to many people and after a whist drive or dance would often walk my sister and I back home, especially if there were strangers about. One night after he had met his sergeant on point [a pre-determined meeting place], he was cycling home when he met a crowd of airmen on cycles, and none of them with lights. He turned off the road to let them go by, but they called him over to ask if they were going the right way for their base. Unfortunately he had to tell them that they had already cycled six miles in the wrong direction! They had been to a dance at Newport, and when they came out they had seen some planes going over, and had followed their flightpath – the wrong way! So the bobby put them right, but asked them not to tell any other policeman that they'd seen him because he should have reported them for not having lights.'

Over the years, many village post offices have been combined with shops. This picture was taken at Shipbourne in 1935

carpenter, the blacksmiths and veterinary surgeon have all gone. Elizabeth reflects sadly on the decline of village life.

'Most villages are now experiencing a great influx of people from towns, people who neither know nor wish to know about village life, nor to take part in local events. Their incursion is also making it very difficult for the young local people to find affordable homes, or even accommodation, so many end up moving away; this means there are few left who care about the closure of shops, churches and schools.

'In the old days everybody got involved with everything, and consideration for others and helping anyone in trouble made for a happy village. There was great community spirit when I was at Hinstock, which I suppose carried on from working together during the war; besides which the church and chapel congregations always co-operated for the good of the village.'

Today Elizabeth lives at West Felton, near Oswestry, and her husband has a 60-acre farm.

Although Joy Johnson was born in Birmingham on 6 February 1922, she spent all her school holidays on a Worcestershire farm: from her very first visit there she knew that her heart was in the countryside. Thus in 1947, as a young wife and mother, she seized the opportunity to move to a Cotswold village where she learned to enjoy a relatively primitive lifestyle. Her husband had contracted a serious form of recurring malaria while serving with the 1st Army in North Africa, and had been advised to live in the country after he was demobilised. So under the government's war agricultural training scheme the couple moved to Spelsbury in Oxfordshire, to a tied cottage 'like something out of Hansel and Gretel'. It was a big change for the daughter of the managing director of an engineering firm, one who had studied at King Edward VI Grammar School and was used to comfort! The new home had no electricity and no water on tap, and sanitation was a bucket privy down the garden. Water came from the village fountain, and all cooking and water-heating had to be done on the old black-leaded fireplace.

A year later Joy's husband took a farm job with a tied cottage in another part of Oxfordshire, and they moved away from Spelsbury. But in 1952 they heard that a church bungalow was for sale, and so took the opportunity to return to the place they loved. They had an acre of wilderness and worked a sixteen-hour day rearing hens, ducks and pigs as well as growing all their own produce. At the time, all the other houses in the village belonged to the owner of Spelsbury House.

But the 'good life' venture was not enough for the workaholic Joy, so when yet another unexpected opportunity arose, she welcomed it. She explains how fate took a hand:

'When we moved to Spelsbury the post office was run from the hallway of a cottage and dealt basically with stamps, pensions and family allowances. But it served a most useful purpose as the nearest shops of any kind were in the market town of Charlbury, well over a mile away.

'In 1953 officials from Oxford head post office visited every cottage in Spelsbury trying to find a replacement for the retiring postmistress, then in her eighties. I was the only person prepared to consider it, so we had a lean-to built on to our kitchen.

'It was very much a sub-post office, dealing only in letters, parcels, stamps, pensions, postal orders, family allowances and national savings certificates. No licences of any kind nor post office savings books were handled. I had to requisition everything I required from head office at Oxford, when I submitted my weekly return of transactions.

'I had no other staff, but on the whole the work was very light and I had plenty of time to pursue my other activities with livestock and produce and so on. My hours of opening were 9am to 5pm on weekdays, and 9am to 1pm on Saturdays – until they persuaded me to sell newspapers on Sundays!'

Joy's parish included the hamlets of Ditchley, Taston, Dean and Fulwell, but Spelsbury was the recognised centre of activity as it boasted the church, the village hall, the school (later closed due to a lack of pupils) and the post office. The nearest pub was over half a mile away, the nearest policeman and doctors in Charlbury, and there were no shops of any kind in Spelsbury. The post office at Charlbury also acted as the area's telephone exchange, and the postmaster there connected all calls manually.

The entire parish contained only a few hundred people, many of whom were related through inter-marriage, but until Joy became

Traditionally, the post office has been at the heart of village life, as seen here at Hildenborough in 1936

postmistress she did not realise just how broad a cross-section of humanity rubbed shoulders in this kind of cloistered community:

'We had the lady of the manor, the vicar and his wife, the schoolmistress, two farmers, the inevitable spinster sisters, a retired tea-planter and big-game hunter, employees of the manor farm, the elderly folk in the almshouses, and the occasional tramp begging for a cup of tea. There were also gypsies, some of whom tried to convince

The postmistress has always played an important part in the life of a village; her position enabling her to get to know everybody in the village community

me that they were of true Romany blood and could tell my future; but most just tried to sell me odds and ends they had made.

'What fascinated me most was the village social structure, which seemed to have been set up by self-appointed "elders". Everyone was categorised according to a sort of "points" system depending on social background, education or wealth.'

Every few weeks an inspector would descend on Joy to check that all was running correctly; usually she was given warning of these visits, but on one occasion she was not, and the inspector in question was given a cool reception, as Joy relates:

'He said that he was from Oxford post office, and that he had arrived without warning to

ensure that I had no time to prepare or to hide anything. Admittedly he produced an identity card, but I was not convinced. With outward calm I asked him to stand outside for a few minutes, which he did, and then I locked the door, rushed to the telephone and checked his description with Oxford. When I was satisfied he was genuine I let him in, allowed him free access to my papers, apologised for my suspicion and gave him a cup of tea. To my relief he smiled kindly, saying that he'd made many surprise visits to post offices, but that this was the first time anyone had checked on him!

'One of these inspectors had been responsible for my several days' initial training in post office routine and duties, the most vital of which seemed to be remembering to change the date stamp before opening each morning. Until then I hadn't appreciated the power one can feel wielding a date stamp! I soon came to realise why people the world over fear or respect rubber stamps: just one thump of authority and your entire way of life can be changed! At the same time it was important that the rubber stamp's date was correct, to prove when something was posted.

'Having to sign the Official Secrets Act also gave me an inflated sense of importance for a while, but it was in fact an asset when I refused to involve myself in local gossip; for instance on family allowance or pension days the locals from the other four hamlets converged on my post office, and if it was raining or bitterly cold they would congregate inside to exchange news and gossip. Clearly they expected me to know all the local goings-on, and were very disappointed when they learned I was treating all information and activities as confidential.'

Another occasion on which Joy had a slight 'brush' with authority involved the police, as she explains:

'After helping to organise a large village fête at Spelsbury manor house I was asked to keep the takings – many hundreds of pounds and a positive fortune in those days – until the bank opened on Monday. But with so many people knowing about this, and because my premises were situated right on the edge of the village, I was rather apprehensive and decided we'd better take the cash to the nearest police station, at Chipping Norton, and ask them to keep it safely until Monday. They readily agreed, but it was such a large amount that, stupidly, I asked the desk sergeant if it would be safe there. With great patience he smiled, and said: "Madam, one hears of people trying to break *out* of a police station, but I've never heard of anyone trying to break *in*!"

'That was the only time I ever needed the police, as I was never threatened or frightened by anything. In those days you could safely leave the place unlocked when you were perhaps engrossed in work, right at the far end of the garden, and I could even leave the post office unlocked while I went to other rooms in the bungalow. Having to be anxious about security, as such, simply never occurred to anyone there, and most people didn't even bother to lock their doors at night.'

When food rationing ended in 1954, Joy was often asked by the locals if she would supply various items. As a result she had the post office enlarged to enable her to stock a small selection of food, toiletries, stationery, sweets and

Inspecting the books: every few weeks an inspector from head office would descend on the village postmistress to check that everything was in order – not always with due warning, when he might be given a frosty reception!

ice-cream. During the summer she started to provide ice-cream sodas, but came to regret this as there were so many glasses to wash. She also rued the day she agreed to make someone a few cakes, because her reputation for this soon spread, and she felt obliged to provide home-made cakes on a regular basis. Regulations concerning food hygiene were far less stringent then, and she was able to put out her produce in a glass display case specially made for the purpose. Christmas was a major challenge, as she was inundated with orders for cakes and mince pies; and in the summer there were large orders from Scout parties who camped in a nearby field. Everyone welcomed this new source of supplies as few people had cars and there was only one bus a day to the nearest market town.

Access to basic supplies was always a special problem during severe weather. Joy particularly remembers one bitter winter in the mid-1950s:

'For a few days we were totally cut off. Then a tractor somehow managed to break through to Charlbury and bring some basic necessities to us

all. But with the telephone lines still down we continued to feel very isolated; when the postman finally managed to get through after six days he found the village postbox full of snow, ice and rotting mail! However, one of Charlbury's doctors captured everyone's imagination by using skis and snow-shoes to reach some of his patients. Most villagers were still dependent on the central fountain for their water, so they organised shifts to try to keep it from freezing completely. Even so, by the time some of them had staggered home with their buckets they found their water covered with thick ice which then had to be melted by the fire. When a lorry laden with supplies eventually got through there were loud cheers all round!'

When Joy first moved to Spelsbury she soon realised that the war had not touched the people there in the same way that she and other town dwellers had been affected. As she explains:

'This was largely because they hadn't known what it was to live through the blitzes or to queue endlessly for essential food. Although rationed to some extent, they had been able to have milk and eggs, and occasionally meat when a stock animal was slaughtered, as well as keep bees for honey; they also had the space to grow plenty of fruit and vegetables. Indeed, the only thing they really shared with townsfolk during the war was the separation from their loved ones, and the trauma sometimes of the tragic death of family members or friends.'

Among Joy's most unforgettable customers was the village 'Mrs Malaprop', who was a constant source of amusement and delight:

'She used to ask for items such as dislocated coconut and perforated milk, and once she announced that "The condescension on our windows is something awful". She also excitedly brought me the news of the local council's promise that the village was to be connected to mains water at last: "It was agreed anonymously," she said in triumph, "so they must all realise it was high time we had it." And then there was the time she commented on the Vatican's strange custom of sending up smoke signals whenever they "erected a new Pope".'

After six years Joy's circumstances changed dramatically and she had to give up the business. Fortunately, by then another villager was prepared to run the post office – though not the shop – from another cottage. A year later Joy moved to Oxford, as breadwinner to her two daughters. She now lives in Tring, and looks back with great affection on those Spelsbury days, 'when there was great community spirit and everybody shared and cared as though they were members of one big family'.

In rural areas the method of postal delivery could be quite imaginative. A stout pony was a more reliable form of transport than a van, and less hard work up the hills than a bicycle

Keeping the Peace

Marjorie Hardacre:
Landlady, Somerset and Wiltshire

KEEPING THE PEACE

It was in the light of considerable first-hand experience that 77-year-old Marjorie Hardacre (née Southway) told me: 'When the drink's in, the wit's out', for in some sixty years service behind the bar she has witnessed many volatile situations. Indeed, one was literally explosive and happened right where I was sitting when Marj told me about it at the Crown Inn, Pilton, near Shepton Mallet:

'One of the farmers put some gunpowder in the ash tray on his table and sat round with his friends till *wooomph*! – someone put a lighted cigarette in it. The result was obviously much more violent than the farmer had expected. The fluorescent light on the ceiling shattered, one man had a hole blown through the rim of his trilby and another was so startled he sat with his mouth wide open for over half an hour. Mum and Dad had been sleeping upstairs and came running down to me in a panic, and not only was I completely stunned but couldn't hear for two days.'

But that prankster hadn't meant any real harm, any more than the drunk who once poured Guinness all over Marj for no reason at

Christmas Eve festivities, with Marj (left), Jack Cox and the 'gleanie', and 'Little Billy'. (previous page) In some old inns horses have a traditional right of way through the bar to the stable at the rear of the premises, a right asserted by this carthorse and his owner at the New Inn, Monkton in Kent, in 1951

The Crown Inn when Ken and Marj Hardacre (centre) first knew it in 1950

all. However, there were many times when Marj really did need to run for help.

'When I was ten, in 1931, Father became tenant of the Railway Inn at Wincanton, and that could be a very rough place. Lots of tramps came in as they had a lodging house along the road, but they always had to go in the special room Dad provided for them. When they were drunk, and he told them they weren't having any more, they'd throw their glasses in the fire or even through the window. I should like as many pints as times I had to run for the police there.'

Marj started serving at the Railway Inn (now demolished) when she was only twelve, when her mother went into hospital. This was a daunting job for a girl, as no women customers at all went in that pub until the outbreak of war in 1939, and it was also in a very basic environment:

'There was sawdust on the floor and spit-toons which Father emptied and blackleaded every day. But it was always filthy, of course, as lots of men used to chew tobacco.

'Livestock were auctioned close by, so on market days, when we were extra busy, Dad kept the swing door in the passage open to make access easier. One day a cow got away from a drover, came in that door and got stuck. There was no way it could turn round so the drover got a mallet and pushed the animal forwards – all through our back room and beer cellar, until it was free.

'With the cattle market opposite we did a lot of food there and we were open from 10am to 10pm, but there was only one little bar. The rest of the pub was just rooms where the farmers would sit around with their drinks, and I had to take them their bread and cheese, for which Dad used to give me a penny for sweets.'

Marj's parents, Jessie and Lilly Southway, behind the bar at The King's Arms, Market Lavington

Right: The Crown in 1963, when Marj's father had to drive along the tops of frozen hedges to collect the beer

When war broke out, eighteen-year-old Marj remained at Wincanton to work as a book-keeper for seven years, while her parents moved to Market Lavington, Wiltshire, where her father became tenant of the King's Arms. After the war, Marj went to help her parents at the King's Arms, but times were still very difficult.

'We could open whenever we wanted to within the legal hours, but with the rationing still on there was only enough drink for us to open three days a week – usually Wednesday to Friday. We'd put up notices saying open at eight in the evening, and you should have seen the tremendous queues that formed!

'But one person who didn't go without his booze was the butcher. He always came down at eight in the morning and had his two double Scotches – and then we'd be sure to get the meat we wanted!'

When Marj married Ken in 1946, she went back to live at Evercreech (some three miles from Pilton), the village in which she had been born on 12 August 1921. There she and her hus-band lived with her mother-in-law for 3½ years, before fate took her back into pubs.

'My husband came home and told me the Crown was going, but I didn't really want a pub as you couldn't get any time off – my parents hadn't ever had a holiday! But in the end I agreed, and in 1950 we moved into the Crown as tenants of the Charlton Brewery, later George's, then Courages and now Ushers.

'It was very different with the old breweries,

when it was less big business. Then it was always Mr and Mrs Hardacre, but now you're just a number. Also, they actually used to come and collect the rent and always left half a crown for us to have a drink on them.

'We used to get through a lot of rough cider at the Crown – sixty gallons a week from a local farm. And back at the Railway, Dad used to keep ginger to sprinkle on it. We still have some of the old cider cups here, one printed with "Crown Hotel, Pilton", and one or two are still used. And that conical copper container hanging up from the beams is what they used to warm the cider in.

'And there's been quite a few years when our customers really did need warming up, such as in 1963. That year, to get the beer, my husband had to borrow a Land Rover from a farmer and drive into Shepton on top of the hedges – the snow was so deep and frozen hard. And we were extra busy because so many local people couldn't get to work and just sat around drinking.'

Marj has also had a great deal of fun at the Crown. For example, one Christmas Eve Jack Cox decided to pluck a gleanie (guinea fowl) in the bar, just for a laugh, and when Marj came down on Christmas Day 'there were feathers everywhere'. Then there was the customer who, without asking, brought his horse into the bar to make a point to a friend, as if it were something you did every day.

The inn and the easy going way of life had changed relatively little since Fred and Alice Harvey ran it from 1908 to 1919, and made their own cider there. During their tenure Pilton boasted its own brewery as well as seven pubs, but when the Hardacres moved in, the Crown was the only pub left in the village. The Harveys continued in the cottage opposite, where Fred had been born in 1873, but by then Fred had become very wary of the greatly increased traffic, so Marj used to 'see him over the road to the pub at twelve o'clock and back again at one'. Today he would be even more concerned. 'So many more lorries now thunder through the village,

especially since the tolls over the Severn Bridge have become so expensive and drivers look for alternative routes.'

Ken Hardacre died in 1988 and in 1989 Marj's son-in-law, Tony Sherwood, became the new licensee, ably partnered by Marj's only daughter, Pauline. Today, with a skittle alley where the old coach house and stables used to be, the sixteenth-century inn continues to thrive and the youthful Marj remains as busy as ever, pulling pints.

Marj and Ken with Mr and Mrs Harvey, who kept the Crown from 1908 to 1919

Harewood House

Country Estate: Yorkshire

HAREWOOD HOUSE

I remember being taken to see Harewood House as a child, by my parents, when I was around seven or eight years old. My father was a north Yorkshireman but had worked as a solicitor in Leeds and obviously felt a great deal of pride in this nearby mansion. Returning to the place nearly forty years on, I found that I remembered much of the atmosphere. Of course, at that time I couldn't have told you anything about the architect, the landscape gardeners or the history of the family, but it is the spirit of these houses that is probably the most important issue.

On a summer's afternoon in 1998, Harewood struck exactly the same response in me as it had done years before: somehow, its grandeur manages to remain friendly, accessible. Harewood is a place that could be daunting and remote, but somehow it manages to avoid this. Perhaps you sense that it is a family home – perhaps you appreciate the care that goes into the upkeep of the buildings and the gardens. It is as though you somehow pick up on the fact that this is a place loved and cherished by owners and servants alike.

Harewood itself is little more than a couple of centuries old, though the Lascelles family, who built it, had lived in the district for two hundred

This illustration, published in 1779, shows Harewood House, seat of Edwin Lascelles

years before that. The magnificent interior was largely created by Robert Adam; it has superb ceilings and plasterwork, and it houses one of the finest collections of English and Italian painting in the country. There are also exquisite examples of Chippendale furniture, and extensive porcelain collections. The grounds were landscaped by Capability Brown, and are particularly famous for their lakeside and woodland walks.

The Earl of Harewood is the son of the late Princess Mary, daughter of King George V, and is therefore a cousin of Queen Elizabeth II. Princess Mary lived at Harewood for many years, and some of her pictures and possessions are still on display in her rooms. For most of this century this connection with royalty has been an important aspect of life at Harewood; certainly for those who have worked there it has given life an extra dimension, an added dignity, and none has felt this more acutely than the now-retired head gardener, Geoffrey Hall.

Geoffrey Hall, Head Gardener

Geoff Hall is one of the most charismatic men I have ever met. Is it his smile, or his deep, rich voice? His fund of stories or the twinkle still very definitely alive in the eyes of this eighty-some-thing-year-old? Geoff's father was head gardener at Harewood before him, and Geoff himself has had a legendary influence on the gardens at Harewood, and their commercial development; however, here I wish to concentrate on Geoff's childhood at Harewood during World War I and through the twenties.

A recurring theme in my research was that childhood on an estate is quite different from the norm. Discipline and standards were definitely a part of it, but a vital ingredient appears to have been a sense of identity, a spirit of belonging that is so often absent in the larger, outside world. Everyone who has spent their childhood on a country estate speaks warmly of it. Perhaps this is nostalgia – but do we all remember our earliest

years so fondly? This is especially so as we reach the end of the twentieth century and children are increasingly restricted and controlled in their way of life. Geoff Hall's childhood was not without duties, obligations and restrictions, but he still seems to have enjoyed a freedom that many of our children today would not know how to cope with. And perhaps it is this freedom from an early age that leads to self-reliance and the ability to see through problems for oneself...

'I was born in 1914 in the head gardener's house – my father had taken the position in 1912. I was about eight when my sister Margaret was elected from amongst Harewood school children to present a bouquet of flowers to Princess Mary as she and her husband, Viscount Lascelles, arrived at Harewood village soon after their marriage in London. I was one of the boys who had the honour of being chosen to pull the Rolls-Royce car by ropes down the mile-long carriage-way to Harewood House, where the couple were met by the fifth Earl of Harewood and his wife Florence. I well remember the occasion, because Lady Harewood had a dachshund dog that decided to take a nip at my ankle and for a little while all the main celebrations were forgotten and I was the centre of much ado and attention.

'It was about this period of my life that I had my first taste of horticulture. I was on holiday

Geoffrey Hall outside his house on the edge of Harewood House

As a young boy, Geoff Hall spent much of his time with the estate horseman

a plantation of hazel bushes behind our house, and we had to select our own cane, a most ignominious task!

'Another of my stamping grounds as a child was the laundry – as you know, every major estate had one of its own, a gaunt, spacious-looking place. A dear old battle-axe whom we knew as Old Ann was in charge of ours, with Lydia the second-in-command; both were of Scots descent and with strong Quaker beliefs. The laundry lasses who worked with these old dears must have experienced a tedious, uninteresting and sheltered life because they were never allowed to mix with the local people in any form of social activity whatsoever. In part, the local lads were considered socially unworthy, a rough, rude, unruly lot! Then again, you've got to realise that in those days there was no reliable form of birth control, and the last thing any housekeeper wanted was one of her lasses in the family way – life was difficult enough without any unnecessary

from school and wearing a pair of new trousers, and as I climbed my favourite conker tree I tore the backside out of them! I pleaded with my granny to do the necessary repairs before my father came home, but alas, it was too late for that. Not for me the usual one or two clips behind the ear or three or four on the bottom, but three days weeding the asparagus beds! Rough and ready justice was how it was in those days, and I was always up to some mischief or other around the estate. Very often my father would hand me his pocket knife and say, "Here, go and cut one to suit yourself, lad!". There was

THE HORSEMAN

'As a young lad of about ten I would spend most of my time with the estate horseman, Dick Kettlewell. I can hear him now as he groomed Major, the heavy shire, and Jack, the lighter horse we used for trap work. Not many of Dick Kettlewell's calibre are to be found today. You've got to realise that these men were extremely dedicated, practically born amongst boots and harnesses – though not saddles, because there wasn't much time for riding. No true horseman would retire for the night unless he knew his charges were properly fed, watered and bedded down – except in the summer months, when after the day's work the teams were turned out into the fields to graze until the following morning. The spring and late summer periods were arduous times for the farm horses, and both men and beasts would be on the move early: preparation for the day's work would have to be in hand soon after five-thirty in the morning in order to be ready for the manual workforce that started at seven o'clock.

'Many times I would rush from school and make straight for the potato field or wherever the horse was working, just so that I could ride or drive it back to the stable when work finished at five-thirty in the afternoon. I remember with much respect many of the twenty-odd gardeners that worked in the department, but Dick Kettlewell was the outstanding favourite. It was always a safe and sure thing that if ever I went missing my mother had only to ask father where Dick Kettlewell was working to know where I would be.'

complications! Woe betide any girl who did fall for a baby, especially if the father didn't come forward. The chances were that she would lose her position entirely and be sent back home, if the family would still take her in. All the laundresses wore clogs, I remember, which made a great clatter if work was in full progress. Every week on Saturday afternoon or Sunday morning, my sister and I would have to take some seasonal vegetables to the laundry, and we'd always bring back some treacle toffee and one or two magazines or journals that had been sent down from the House itself. Sometimes it might be a *Tatler* or a *Country Life*, and it would cause a family row as to who should have the first look!

'I was always hungry in those days, but there always seemed to be somebody who would provide me with an extra bit of food somewhere!

Harewood House

The gardening staff were housed in the bothy. Geoff Hall recalls that this life created a real sense of comradeship amongst the men

For example, I'd make a habit of drifting down to the stable just before twelve o'clock and would wait until Dick Kettlewell came in with the horse because he'd always give me a piece of cold pasty from his lunchbox. Then I'd be off to the laundry where a dish of soup or sago pudding would generally come my way – and if I was still hungry, I would see if there was any milk to fetch from the dairy, for the dairymaids would always supply a cup of milk to drink on the spot! Only then would I move off for my lunch!

'Equally there always seemed to be somebody ready to give me a clip round the ear. I used to sing in the church choir, like most of the estate workers' children; I remember I was paid 2s 6d [12½p] annually, a princely wage, but I was always being pulled up by Canon Lascelles, a really strict disciplinarian. Then there was Mr Wadsworth the headmaster who used a cane even more than my father.

'When I was on holiday from school my father would see to it that I was kept out of mischief by giving me jobs of work; these were generally to do with gardening, pigs or poultry. It was customary in those days to have a household pig, and nearly every house had its own pigsty. A week or two before Christmas would be the time to kill it, and for some weeks after, meals would consist of pork, pig's trotters, pig's offal, or anything else connected with the sad animal, until everything except the bacon and the hams had been eaten. These were laid on stone shelves to await the local butcher who would do the necessary curing by applying salt and saltpeter to the meat; it was then left to pickle. Father's flock of one hundred hens, would keep me busy too; in fact I really enjoyed this work, and at one time thought very seriously of becoming a poultry farmer, so great was my interest in rearing chickens.

'Although I was always out and about on the estate, I never got away with that much. I remember once coming back proudly with a swan's egg that I'd nicked from the nest when the adult birds were away. My father made me put it back, and this time the birds were in residence! That wasn't nearly as easy a job, let me tell you.

'In 1928, at the age of fourteen, I left school and started work under my father for a weekly wage of 10s 6d [52½p] – all of which I had to give to my mother. My starting status was that of "crock lad": most large estates of that time would use thousands of clay pots each year, and each had to be crocked – this meant putting a few broken pieces of pot over the plant-pot hole at the base for drainage purposes. Hence the name "crock lad"!

'The centre of everything in those days was the bothy, where the gardeners of varying experience were housed. Generally the squad would consist of one or two foremen, the first and second journeymen, and then all those still in their apprenticeships, called in those days "improvers". It really was a hub of activity. Each would take his turn to be the "duty man", and this was a truly terrifying experience because for one full week practically the whole gardening department was your responsibility. You would get up at six o'clock in the morning, light the bothy fire and put the kettle on to boil, then be off at the double to do the rounds, especially if it was a cold frosty morning. First you had to stoke up the boilers and check on all the greenhouses, hoping that the thermometer in the tropical house was showing a reasonable reading; if it had dipped overnight there would be a real dressing-down by the foreman and then by the head gardener, particularly if the temperature had fallen to below the required minimum. Then you had to get back to the bothy to wake all the rest, make the tea and cook a breakfast that would have made Fanny Craddock weep, I tell you! I've seen some of the weirdest concoctions on breakfast plates ever to grace any table: bacon and eggs cooked by fantastic methods and served in most colours – mainly black.

'During the weekend further chores were thrust upon the poor duty man's shoulders: he'd have to fetch the milk from the home farm and sometimes deliver produce to the big house. He'd post letters for the head gardener who always seemed to do his correspondence on a Sunday; then perhaps he'd have to water plants if it was a hot summer's day…whatever was needed, the duty man would do it. Still, bothy life was a good

thing for young men, creating a real comradeship and even brotherhood. As you can guess, there would be plenty of mischief, but there was no badness. Work and discipline there was in plenty, but very little pay: 34s [£1.70] a week was considered tops, and if you wanted a holiday the same time had to be worked back as overtime.

'Of course, it helped if you were good at cricket! Then you'd be well in demand right the way through the summer. Estates in those days always had their cricket teams – especially up in Yorkshire which has always been cricket-mad – and generally the aristocracy would take some sort of part in the game; often the captain would be a lord, or a high-up official of the estate, and you had to be pretty good to keep your place in the team. However, a certain amount of animosity could creep in at times, particularly if the gentry had a friend to stay, or perhaps a lord's son would be home on holiday – then no doubt a regular would be dropped, or if playing, would be demoted in the batting order or not favoured

---

AIR RAID!

'I was only four when World War I ended, but I can still remember the bombs dropped from German Zeppelins; to this day there remains a depression in the church path where one of them fell. Two further bombs were dropped on the estate, one falling near Harewood House and the other on the clerk-of-works house – this went through the roof of the toilet and actually landed in the water tank! I still remember sitting by the fire in the kitchen and listening to the drone of the engines above. Mr Deakin, the Harewood blacksmith, would always warn people of any imminent raid: he would cycle round the district telling everyone that Zeppelins were about, so then we had to get blacked out and show no lights. Old Ann and her staff would come up from the laundry to keep us company, and we'd sit by the fire with one candle flickering on the sideboard. Father would be relating some of his personal anecdotes to the laundry girls, but Old Ann was more concerned about keeping a firm grip on her bible!'

to do any bowling. This happened to me once when I was on an estate and the three sons came home for the holidays; they did all the batting and all the bowling, and the opposition had a field day.

'They'd over two hundred runs for hardly any wickets, and the captain eventually threw the ball to me – after all, I had taken six wickets in the previous match! But I kicked the ball back to him and said, "Not bloody likely, you do the bowling yourself!" Not only was this rude of me,

Cutting the grass using horse power

but in those days it could have easily got me the sack – I was lucky to get away with it.

'Sport played a big part in our lives – that is, for those few hours a week we had a bit of time off. When I was a lad there was a very severe winter, and skating was in full swing on the 40-acre lake. I would take every opportunity to have a go, and I soon became pretty good, or at least I was one of those who managed to keep his feet. I would have half an hour's skating during my dinner break, and it was during one of these sessions that I was approached by the princess herself: she asked whether I would mind helping George who was skating for the first time – this was the present seventh earl, George Lascelles, and he would have been about eight years old. Of course, this suited me fine because it gave me a good excuse to be away from work for a spell!

'They were good times, those: I remember Lord Harewood arranging an ice-hockey match for one Saturday afternoon, and teams were selected from all those present. We had about sixteen players on each side. The princess was in goal on my side, and the sixth earl was in opposition. His lordship was an exceptionally good skater and never once did I see him fall on the ice, despite the attentions of one or two lads like myself who desperately tried to bring him down during the match.

'Before any skating could take place on the lake it would be my father's job to test the ice and make sure it was safe. Don't ask me why, but this seemed to be very typical on most estates, and you'd often find head gardeners talking about the job and comparing methods. Anyway, anyone caught on the ice before my father's declaration of safety would get a severe ticking-off. The testing of the ice was quite a performance. Father would muster about six gardeners of different weights and acquire a ladder with a hundred-foot rope attached. The lightest gardener, usually the garden lad – often me – would step on the ice and take the ladder, aeroplane-fashion, and push it forwards. All the other gardeners would then follow at twenty-foot intervals until the last man, the heaviest, would be well on the ice. Then at my father's command – who, incidentally, would be quite safe back on terra firma – everyone would have to jump up and down. Thank goodness the ladder and rope were never needed, even though I'm fairly sure Father had the situation well in hand because he knew the lake as well as he knew his right hand.

'A lot of responsibility came my father's way. Most large estates like Harewood would have their own fire brigade, and my father was the captain of ours for most of my young life. He would get the first call by telephone, and then it was his job to round up the rest of the firemen in his area; this meant a two-mile bicycle trip. On one particular occasion the fire was on one of the estate farms, and father received the alarm call at four-thirty in the morning. Off he went to his first call, Tom Baldwin the blacksmith: on arriving at the house he saw a light in the cowshed, and there was Tom, milking away. "Come on, Tom, there's a fire!" he shouts. Tom just nodded and said he'd come once he'd finished milking. On went father to the plumber, George Baldwin, and after knocking on the door several times, up came the bedroom window and a voice shouted down, "What the hell's up?" Father gave the instructions, whereupon George replied that he'd be soon on his way. Finally after getting the brigade mustered at the station, the team set off. The engine was drawn by the best of the farm horses, and after just a few hundred yards of galloping full tilt, the farm bailiff came tearing alongside shouting angrily at my father; in short, he didn't want the horses galloping and getting into a sweat. When the outfit finally arrived at its destination the farm was just smouldering charcoal!

'Estate life: yes, it wasn't all work, and there were many good times. For example, how I would look forward to the big shooting parties that took place during my career as a garden lad. I relished the chance to go bush beating, and would be dismayed the times when my name was not on the list to go. Generally, three-quarters of the whole estate staff would be assembled for the occasion. Each bush beater would be given his own package of sandwiches, and his drink which would be a bottle of cold tea. It was horrible stuff but it helped to wash down the dripping "butties"! So long as you had a Woodbine cigarette to finish off the day, everything had gone satisfactorily!

I took the photograph of Geoff Hall outside his house on the perimeter of the estate on a warm, sunny evening when the garden was streamed with light. Flowers, vegetables, rolling hills...it seemed so fitting that Geoff Hall should be back at Harewood where he so definitely belongs.

PRINCESS MARY

'Once World War II had ended I was just delighted to come back to Harewood, the scene of so many happy memories for me. Of course, again it was work that dominated my life, but there was still such a great deal that was of interest and pleasure there for me. Princess Mary was still in residence, and I think it would be reasonable for me to say that outside the household staff I probably had more conversation with her than most. The princess would rarely miss her daily walk, a distance of nearly two miles, half circling the lake and returning to Harewood House. Her walk would follow a distinct pattern: in the afternoon she would be accompanied by her lady-in-waiting, but in the evening she would often be alone with her dogs. I could never really understand this, and it was my impression that our princess was sometimes quite lonely; I felt this on many occasions when I was at work in the summer evenings, and she would come along and just sit down and have a chat. Perhaps she would discuss the work in hand, or talk about some new plantings by the lakeside, and then both of us would go along to assess the situation. Very often the royal lady would trail me back to Harewood House, which meant climbing a rather steep hill. I was fifteen years younger than the princess, but I can honestly say that it was Geoff Hall who did the puffing and blowing, and not the elderly lady when she said, "Goodnight, Hall!"

The princess was a tremendously generous, warm-spirited lady, and I think all of us on the estate cherish her memory very fondly to this day. When she died, I was detailed to take charge of all the floral arrangements at her funeral; this included receiving all the floral tributes, and displaying each in proper order as it arrived. Some of the great names from the Continent were on those tributes: the King of Norway, the King of Denmark, the King of Sweden, the Queen of Holland and the King of Belgium. Such tributes, right down to the tiny bunch of primroses from the not-so-well-off, made it clear just how widely she was loved and respected. Oh yes, the 27 March 1965 will always be a black day for the estate people here'.

Frank Widdop, Butler

My second meeting at Harewood was with Frank Widdop (pictured left), the butler at the house since 1978. Frank is in middle age, bright, bubbly, and very much the new breed of butler. Much like John Savill at Syon House, Frank does not come from a background of service but came to Harewood after a period in the Royal Navy. In his own words:

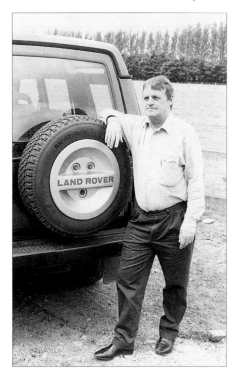

Frank Widdop

'I think you'll find a lot of ex-servicemen going into jobs like this, and I often compare my job here at Harewood as butler with running an admiral's mess. Certainly I had a great deal of experience of this sort of thing during my Navy days. For example, way back, lying off Gibraltar, I was looking after Harold Wilson and Marcia Williams during their negotiations with Ian Smith, leader of what was then called Rhodesia. I remember that we put Wilson into a really plush cabin, but Smith had to put up with something way down the scale! I think that a life in the Navy teaches you to get on with things, and to accept anything that a job can throw at you, and this is invaluable when it comes to butlering. For example, when the family are in residence – a time I always like – you can easily work sixty or seventy hours a week: that's nothing. But if they are away, then your hours can plummet dramatically, and twenty to thirty hours a week is probably the norm. But you just don't watch hours – it's simply not an issue. This again is like being in the Navy, in that the job is there to be done, and you just get on with it; it's all a matter of "if and when" and "give and take".

'Occasionally I'll travel with the family to London, but most of my work is done up here in Yorkshire. I'll probably start at about six forty-five in the morning, just getting things ready and thinking about breakfast. Then I'll work through to round about eleven-thirty, have a bit of lunch till about twelve or twelve-thirty. Then I'll be on again, with a short break through the afternoon, until dinner's over, which is generally about ten-nish but this depends greatly on the number of guests that are here to stay. I've got all sorts of jobs – I'll clean some silver perhaps, certainly wait at table and generally lead the team of housekeeper, cook and housemen.

'You could say that it helps that I'm married to the housekeeper! We live in the west wing; we've been there for twelve years and we love it – even though the steps are something of a nightmare. But then, our flat has four bedrooms with an absolutely spectacular view. I think it's good that we're attached to the house so intimately. The wife's jobs tend to include table service, ironing and looking after Lady Harewood's personal belongings. But we very much work as a team, and I'll help her just as she'll help me. We'll probably move when the time's right, but I'm quite sure that it will be to a cottage on the estate. It's become our life, you understand. For this reason I'll always work at the house, even when I retire, or so I hope.

'The houseman basically serves at table and does quite a lot of the cleaning. I suppose he does far more cleaning than I . . . but then again, I'm the boss and I've got to have some perks! We don't really socialise as a staff team – though I do genuinely think of us as a team. There will be an annual staff barbecue, but it's very difficult to fraternise with people under you, and then tell them off if there's a problem. I've always felt that you've got to keep things professional, and that very probably comes from my background in the Royal Navy.

'You get quite a turnaround of staff. A good number come into it not knowing what to expect and then leave shortly afterwards, not really happy with things. Then a lot of assistants we train up to know the job soon move on. What we like to do is take people with some sort of

A young gentleman arranges his social affairs, while his man fastens his spats

catering background, someone we can really teach. During my time here I've had ten house-men under me; the last one went to an MP's house in Oxfordshire, and a lot do go on to other jobs in service. Just a few opt out altogether because they decide it's not really the sort of thing they want.

'We've seen times change just in the period that we've been here at Harewood. Back in the late seventies, the heads of all the departments were called by their surnames, but now the fashion seems to be to use Christian names...though I'm still known by my surname, and like it. I get on very well, I like to think, with Lord Harewood, but I'm still employed by him: there will always be a gulf, and it really doesn't bother me to be known as "Widdop".

'I would say that we've always got on well with Lord and Lady Harewood. They are exceptionally special people, and will always find the time to discuss anything with you. I've been

very satisfied personally throughout all my time here, and I would never, ever consider moving. I just couldn't say anything wrong about them, even if I wanted to.

'Of course, one bond that we have is the football. One of my duties – if you can really call it that! – is to take them both to Elland Road to watch Leeds United play. Of course, Lord Harewood has been the president of the club for many years. I'll also take him to test matches whenever they're up here at Headingley. This Leeds United connection has led to Howard Wilkinson coming here for dinner, and I do recall that he's particularly fond of pheasants. When Lord Harewood was head of the Football Association we used to go to the England matches as well. I suppose that's another part of butlering today – you find that you do a lot of general driving, whoever your boss might be.

'I feel I have grown close to Lord and Lady Harewood, partly perhaps because they've never

entertained on what you might call a grand scale, and things are kept fairly intimate. They have a lot of family and many very close friends, so most dinner parties rarely number more than fourteen or fifteen or so. Both of them are very much into music and there's always a very civilised atmosphere here. Neither of them look their age, and they're both well and happy. I'd certainly be happy to serve Lord Harewood until my time is up, and I'll do anything I can for them – they've just been so good to both me and my wife.

'I have no doubt that butlers will go on well into the next century, even though the role changes constantly in slight ways. Probably a butler's life today is less formal – it's more about sorting out affairs for the people he works for. I feel that my job is not so much running a huge team as making life easier, ordering train tickets for example, just ironing things out through life.

'As far as I'm concerned, it's a lifestyle that is enjoyable and secure, and you can't say that about all jobs in this day and age. You've got to be sensible, of course, and you've got to be really trustworthy: that's vital. I've got the keys to every part of the house, and to the safe, too. You know, once upon a time butlers actually used to sleep outside the safes! Either that, or they'd put up a bed by the vaults. It's important, too, to maintain standards. Again, I really like my beer and my wine, but I'd never think of drinking on duty: that sort of thing is just not acceptable at all!

'Sometimes my wife and I go out, and in the early days especially, our friends used to ask me why I stayed. They'd point out that I'd earn a lot more in London working perhaps for industrialists or something like that. But I ask you, what good would that do us? What more could I get out of life than I do already? My life's interesting and I work in a very good atmosphere with people I'm tremendously fond of and towards whom I feel enormously loyal. I've never regretted spending a single day at Harewood, and that to me is the real test as to whether a man has enjoyed his life or not.'

John Lister, Clerk of Work

I met John Lister, the recently retired clerk of work, in one of the old stables on the Harewood estate, recently renovated into a block ideal for corporate meetings, parties or even shooting lunches. He was admiring the way in which some of the old woodwork had been rescued and integrated with the overall, modern look. It's very easy to think of life on the great estates as simply revolving around the titled families, a strictly people-orientated type of life, when in fact it is often the actual fabric and structure of these estates that is of more interest to those that understand them. From an early age Lister demonstrated this sort of bent, and a singular determination to achieve his objective:

'I was only a lad when I experienced a real setback. Mr Baldwin, the sexton of the church, had got me taking the ashes from the church boilers down to the old quarry, and the cart that I was transporting them in somehow got out of control. Anyway, in the resulting crash I lost my thumb. Everybody said that this would be a major problem to my becoming a joiner, and they tried to make me into a painter. But I was determined, and I stuck out to be what I wanted. It was a bad start all right, but I made it, and then lived my life doing exactly what I wanted.

'Mind you, I had the very best of help, and if we look back to the war years there were some great craftsmen, and they taught me everything I knew. For example, there was Mr Wilde the foreman: he was over sixty-five when I knew him, and he worked on into his seventies; he was responsible for the staircase that's now in existence, and the sash windows. He lived on until he was ninety-six, and you'd see him on his bicycle anywhere around the estate. He was also into boxing and teaching the sport, and on his ninetieth birthday the *Yorkshire Post* featured him thwacking into a punch ball! He loved to set out the elliptical arches that you see all around the village here. It's funny, but when I look at the structure of the houses or anything around the estate, that's when I tend to remember people from the past. When I began – and we're looking

Opposite: Mrs Arnold Ross wearing a headdress representing the 'World of Opera' at the Countess of Harewood's Annual Opera Ball, held at the Dorchester Hotel in 1962

John Lister examines some recently restored woodwork

Opposite: Harewood House was given over for use as a convalescent home during World War II

back over fifty years now – there were seven or eight joiners on the estate: Mr Pinch, and Archie Ambler who was the house carpenter, and Jack Baldwin the wheelwright, and altogether twenty-four on estate maintenance in those early days. When I became clerk of works there were still fifteen.

'All these men in one way or another managed to leave their mark. For example, Mr Brayshaw was the stone mason early on this century, and the stone heads that you see all over the estate were his work; there's one in front of the laundry. It's a similar case with the porches that were built, and the lovely estate walls; these were perfectly done with no joints whatsoever, rather like drystone walling. Over the last thirty

WORKING WITH QUALITY

'For a craftsman like me, the best thing about working here is that you can appreciate the real quality of everything that you work with. Stone and wood I love – even though I'm a joiner, I love stone. It's a material that you have to carve and work with to understand. Harewood stone is a little soft, but when you understand it, it's got real character. Jimmy Woodburke was a great stone mason here, and people used to ask him whether his work would last a lifetime; and he'd look at them and laugh, and say, "Aye, perhaps, – it'll certainly last mine!"

'We have a lot of Chippendale stuff here, and I was very lucky to be able to work with it as an apprentice around the time of the war. There was a back room to the joiners' shop, and that was full of beautiful things; I found them all fascinating. There were boxes of the stuff – gorgeous mirrors all allowed to go to rack and ruin, all sorts, but I helped with the restoration. So I was very fortunate in that I was as good as brought up with beautiful things. Mind you, so was Chippendale himself, and he was fortunate in the time that he inhabited because granted, he had the design, but there were also first-class tradesmen in London in those days – he had the material as well as the people who knew how to work it. Today you maybe have the designs but not the craftsmen to put them into effect.'

or forty years cars and crashes have gone a long way to destroying this work, but it's still lovely to look at.

'Mind you, my life hasn't always been dealing with the finer sort of things. I've made hayracks, trusses, even entire barns during my time here. I've always liked roofing – in fact anything to do with joinery. In 1947 we had a really terrible winter here, and the buildings were literally falling down. Set rooves were sagging everywhere, and I spent all summer putting up new trusses and rescuing one building after another.

'I think I really began to understand wood during that period. But I just love trees – I like to understand them, and I like to talk to old Geoff Hall who was the gardener here and knows absolutely everything there is to know about a tree itself. You know, that's the great thing about these estates, something that people tend to forget: I see them as oases of hardwood – ash, oak, beech and so on. The Forestry Commission simply plants more and more softwood, and there's no real worth in it. That's where the estates come into their own and are so important. If you work on an estate with the sort of wood you can find here, you're into real joinery. I love walnut, mahogany, limewood, oak and rosewood. Hornbeam is attractive, and laburnum, too: that's a lovely wood, even though it's a bit hard. Still, all woods are worthwhile to my mind, if you treat them properly.

'Over the decades I've become very interested in how wood grows. And I know a lot now about the diseases in wood; death-watch beetle, for example – and I'm used to woodworm, all right! From loving wood like this it's easy to become fascinated with the craftsmen of the past, and for this reason the wood and the stone of Harewood have always fascinated me in their every respect. There's so much beauty here, so much understanding, and I'm just grateful to those great craftsmen of the past that taught me so much and helped to give me the most satisfying of lives.'

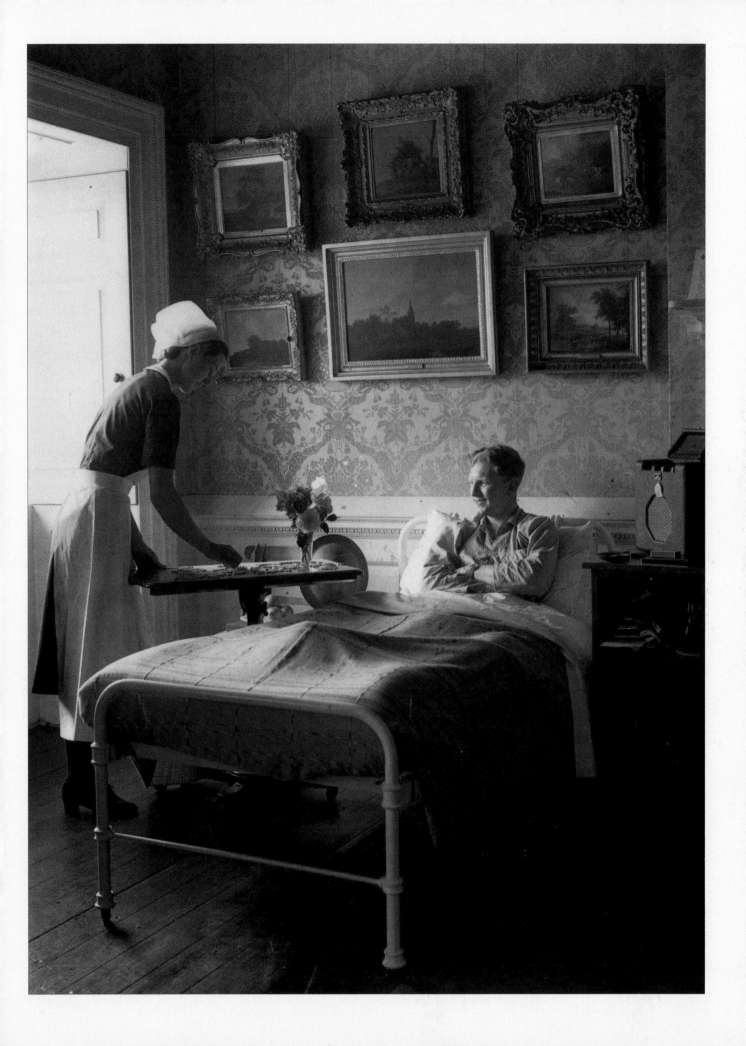

Tied to the Soil

Violet Clarke: Farm Labourer,
Wooler, Northumberland

TIED TO THE SOIL

Violet Clarke (née Watson) grew up in an isolated community where it was always 'make do and mend', where she cleaned her teeth with soot until she was thirty, and neighbours really believed that 'sheep jumping high meant bad weather'. When she attended Sunday school in a little corrugated iron hut of a church, she dreamt of escaping to become a hairdresser or a nurse, but there was almost no choice for a poor country girl in the wilds of Northumberland early this century. 'It was either service in a big house or farm work'.

Opposite:
Blackberrying:
still popular with
children

Violet chose farm work, and has lived and laboured on farms all her life, both before and after marriage, just as her husband, her two brothers and her parents did. She has toiled long and hard, from the last days of the bondagers – in near-slavery conditions – until the times when machines dominated. Her home has never been her own, and she has always lived in tied cottages within a dozen miles of her birthplace. Hers is a story of considerable hardship; yet on reflection she admits: 'I cannot say I was unhappy'.

One of four children, Violet was born on 26 May 1928 at Thornton Farm, Norham-on-Tweed, close to the border with Scotland. At four years old she started school at Thornton, near Berwick, but owing to the insecurity of her father's farm work she went on to change school three times. Here she explains why:

'March hirings were held in all the villages, and men and women walked miles to be looked over by farmers who wanted a likely-looking person to be his employee for the least possible wage. It almost amounted to slavery for the long, hard hours and no holidays. But you had to take what you could get. And when Dad changed jobs at flitting time – 12 May – all our family had to move to the new tied cottage. This meant I had to go to Norham-on-Tweed school first, and then when we flitted twice more I went to

Doddington School, and later to Hazelrigg, where the schoolhouse and school were surrounded by farms.'

Violet always walked to school, generally about three miles away, but along the way she took the opportunity to pick primroses from a dene near the banks of the Tweed, and to hunt for birds' nests. She also enjoyed 'seeing larks rise up to sing before dropping down into the heather on the moors, the crying of peewit flocks, the croaking of corncrakes, yellowhammers in the hedges, and the occasional hawk hovering. Sadly most are now gone, but the swallows keep appearing.

'The wild flowers were plentiful too, with cranesbill, agrimony, ox-eye daisies, foxgloves, tansy, ragwort, campions, willow herb and many more. They all suffered with the new farm methods, but now I'm pleased to see them making a comeback. We even have wild flower seeds being sold in the garden centres.'

In many ways, this natural wealth and joy in simple things helped to compensate for the lack of material possessions. Violet recalls: 'When I was seven Father earned just £1 12s a week, so there was no money for luxuries. Mother made most of our clothes, or altered from ones too big for us: I always had my sister's outgrown hand-me-downs. But later on I did get sixpence (2½p) a week for delivery papers.'

THE 'NETTY'

'Our netty [toilet] was a sort of sentry-box built onto the side of the pigsty, and to visit it at night in winter was a major exercise. After putting on my outdoor clothes, I used a spluttering candle or hurricane lamp to light my way through mud, slush and water which constantly ran off the bank next to the house. And when I arrived I still had to wrestle with a door that opened inwards and barely allowed enough space to squeeze between it and the plank. Then you sat on this box-thing with a hole on top, a bucket under and newspaper cut into squares for toilet paper. And rats squeaked and rustled under the plank, so I didn't waste time there. I had the unsavoury task of emptying the bucket, too, as well as mucking out the pigs and hens regularly. At some of our cottages the toilet had two seats, and then you had to share.

'Sometimes when I went to the netty at night I heard the German bombers going over, on their way to Glasgow, so then it was even more scary as we had to be very strict with the blackout. Nearby was Milfield aerodrome, where they trained Polish, American and French pilots. We often saw them practising, dropping sand bombs on two old tanks on the moor. One day, when we were out working, we saw a Spitfire and Hurricane collide and my friend and I were the first on the scene, but there was nothing we could do. One pilot was still in his cockpit and the other had his parachute on, but he was too low to bale out safely so both men were dead.'

'Berwick-on-Tweed was the fair, with all sorts of entertaining events such as strong men with a board on their chests with others standing on it, or breaking huge stones, as well as swings and roundabouts and all the usual things which were magic to a seven-year-old. Unfortunately, the fair was held just once a year and it was the only big one in the area.

'In those days our farm still had two or three bondagers [female outworkers in the Borders and northern England; every male farm worker had to provide one bondager for the farm work]. They still wore the old uniform, with a heavy brown skirt and apron; a home-made, navy blue raffia hat lined with pink, and a pink-and-white scarf fastened over the head and around the chin and sides of the face. When they took this off you always knew what they were because their faces were very brown at the front where they were exposed to every weather, and this contrasted strongly with the pale skin always hidden by material.'

When fourteen-year-old Violet left school in the summer of 1942, she was lucky in being given the choice to work 'in a big house or on the farm'. She chose the former, and went to nearby Hetton House Farm, where she worked both indoors and out. However, this lasted for just one week, for which she earned only 6s 6d (32½p) before she had to start work on the farm where her father and two brothers were already employed. She became part of a way of life which had scarcely changed for many generations:

'With the war we all had rationing and coupons of course, but our family were not too badly off compared to the townies as we had fresh eggs from our few hens, milk and butter from the farm cows, and bacon from the two pigs which we were allowed to kill each year by permission of the Ministry of Food. We also had lots of myxomatosis-free rabbits, mushrooms, crab-apples and brambles, all growing wild.

'Our cottage had no electricity, no piped water, no bath, no kitchen and no indoor toilet, only two small bedrooms and a small living room where my parents slept, so it was fairly cramped. The living-room fireplace had an oven at one side and a set-pot at the other, which was meant to heat water, but it was cracked, so Mother had to cook and heat water in a yettling [three-legged pan] – no mean feat when catering for six people. The kettle was suspended on a swey [the horizontal, iron chimney-bar which could be swung over the open fire], from which pots also hung for most of the day, with contents for the pigs and hens as well as us. Mother was a good, economical cook and she often made a big pan of soup which would last for three days or more. Food was always basic; lots of porridge or crowdie, broth, potato mash, stovies and rhubarb dumpling, always something filling and nourishing. Sometimes we had beef or bacon, but most common was herrings cooked on top of tatties.

'Our work started at 6am, and at 8am we stopped for breakfast. Our bait [sandwiches] were thick slices of home-made bread spread with cold dripping from the eggs and bacon we had at night. With this we each had a tin bottle of tea, wrapped in an old sock to keep it warm – some hope! When the bottle got old the tea was black, but you didn't notice this when drinking straight from the bottle. And there was no nice warm place to enjoy this meagre fare – I was usually huddled behind a wall or hedge, or sometimes against the cart if I had the horse yoked. Out in all weathers, I was either frozen or fried. I wore ex-army trousers and battle-top jerkin. I was too young to get the Land Army's special uniform.

'The odd horse used was one that could not work as a pair and was generally old and good-natured. My old nag was kept in the far end trivage [stall] of the stable, and as the whole place was lit by a single hurricane lamp it was very dark in places so I often had to go by touch. I would wake the horse with a "Keep up! Keep oot!", and a slap on the rump to let him know I was there. Then I would proceed to harness him, although this was very difficult because I had to squeeze between the trivage and this massive Shire, which was the size of an elephant to me, as I was not too big then. But gradually I would manage to get the saddle on his back, fasten the britchin [breeching: the straps to hold the harness together over the rear end, with chains to fit to the cart], tighten the girth, get the collar upside-down over the head and then swing it up so that the narrow, pointed piece was at the top. Then I fitted and tightened the hame sticks [the two curved bars of the collar], also with chains, for the shoulders to pull; then the bridle, and the bit with rings either side to hold the reins for "steering". All was then set to lead the horse out through the narrow door to be yoked to whatever implement or vehicle was needed for the day. It was always short carts for winter, long carts for harvest, and bogies [low, heavy trucks] for hay.'

In those days Violet and her contemporaries were very much at the mercy of the weather, but overall they followed the age-old pattern of farm work dictated by the seasons. Here she describes in detail the relentless slog of life on a Northumbrian farm over half a century ago:

'In spring, men with furrow ploughs pulled by pairs of horses prepared the land for planting potatoes, corn and bagies [swedes], after the harrowing and rolling were done. With no protection, the poor ploughmen were constantly "whitewashed" by the droppings of hordes of seagulls which followed in search of ploughed-up worms.

'The corn seed was sown by a ribber [drill], also pulled by horses. I used to wait at one end of the field for my father or some other worker to dish the seed out from a sixteen-stone bag into the ribber. A round wooden bushel was used for this, and it was quite heavy even when empty. It was often cold for this job, so if my father was working with me I sometimes drove the pair to and fro while he sat on the plank at the back for a smoke.

'When the bagies had grown big enough, the drills were cut down by the horse-pulled scarifier,

which made it much easier to thin the plants out with a hoe – a job known as singling. There were acres and acres of bagies to deal with, though we did get help when the farmer employed gangs of piece-workers, often Irishmen. They were paid 1½d (½p) a hundred yards.

'I planted potatoes from a pail or bag slung over my shoulder, hanging down my front like a

kangaroo pouch, which I filled from a cart going in front of us down the drills. If I tipped too many into my pouch I staggered along bent double, dropping a tattie every twelve inches or so. As soon as my bag was empty I started all over again, toiling all day long in that back-breaking position. Behind us planters came the "double" or "drill plough", splitting the drills to cover the tatties.

'In early summer the hay was cut by a reaper into swathes and we had to go round and round the fields turning them with pitchforks. When they were dry enough they were horse-raked up into rows to dry some more, before being drawn into small heaps called kyles. Then a man with a horse-drawn contraption called a tumbling tam – a pronged wooden affair – gathered up the kyles, from which we made big, cone-shaped heaps called pikes [haycocks]. These pikes were also in rows and built to stand the weather, so they were trampled firmly and shaped to a peak to run the rain off.

'To lead the pikes home to the shed or stack-yard was an operation in itself. I would take a horse and bogie to the field where a man and horse were waiting with a big chain to pull the pike onto the upended bogie backed into the pike. But first the bottom edge of the pike had to be kicked up to loosen it from the grass all around it. If the pike did not sit properly on the bogie – that is, if it was too far to one side – I'd have to watch the gateposts on my way home. If it was too far to the front I'd have nowhere to stand because I'd be too near the rear end of the horse, and then I could be knocked off the limmer [shaft] where I had to stand to drive. Fortunately I never had a coup [spill] in all the years I worked with horses and wagons, and later with tractors.

'At harvest-time, men with scythes cut a width all round the headriggs [headlands], next to the hedges where machines couldn't manoeuvre easily. The bondagers followed behind and tied the cut corn into sheaves with wisps [bands] of straw; this ensured that no corn was wasted through trampling when the horses and binder went in. Workers were in pairs so that the sheaves could be picked up two at a time and stood up together in eights, to form stooks; these faced east to west in straight rows to get the most of the sun and wind into them. And great pride was taken in making the best row.

'After drying, the corn was taken on long carts to the stackyard, where it stayed until threshing time. The forker was always a strong person, and quite skilled in throwing up the sheaves. And I had to be a good stacker on the

Violet's father in the 1940s

cart to stop the sheaves falling off. If the cart was overloaded at the back there was a danger of strangling the horse through lifting it off its front legs by the harness attached to its shoulders – I actually saw this happen once.

'Back in the yard, the men built the stacks going round and round on their knees all day, packing the sheaves tightly in a spiral, one layer going clockwise, the next anti-clockwise. When the required height was reached a roof shape was formed to keep out the rain. My father was an expert at this and all his stacks were clipped and tidy. Anyone who didn't do this properly would be very unpopular because if the stacks became wet in the middle the grain would be ruined, and then he'd have difficulty getting another farm job because his reputation would go before him.

'Some stacks were round, and there were other larger, oblong ones called sows. All had to be thatched after the leading was finished, and three people worked on each: one on the top, one on the slope and the other forking up big bunches of straw. The top man received each bunch, cut the twine around it and handed down fistfuls to the "roof man" below, who fanned it out and pushed it into the stack, overlapping all the time. When it was completely covered, it was roped in a criss-cross way to hold it in place. Most ropes were made of hemp, but some were still made of straw, usually on wet days in a barn or shed, using a tool called a thraw crook. Then the stacks would be left till threshing time.

'Winter work was mostly feeding sheep and cattle, leading bagies and hay to outside animals, and mucking out the inside hemmels [cattle courts]. I would back my horse and cart into the hemmel where the bullocks were prancing – if they had not been moved out – and using a graipe [short, four-pronged fork], fill the cart with muck. Then it was off to the field – plod, plod, plod – sitting on the shaft or on the muck near the front of the cart, using an old poke to keep me reasonably dry and clean. Once into the field that was being mucked, I took the tailboard off the cart and pulled the muck out into heaps a

---

TATTIE PICKING TIME

'From midsummer into autumn was tattie picking time. A man and a pair of horses pulled the digger along each drill and the potatoes were scattered behind. Each picker had a stent [length] measured out, and if I could gather my lot quickly I could take a little rest before the digger came along again. It was backbreaking work shared by young and old alike. We were helped by German and Italian prisoners of war, who came out with an armed guard from the nearest camp, as well as DPs – displaced persons from Latvia and Estonia. The tatties were picked into pails, emptied into pokes [bags] or swills [wire baskets] and carted to big clamps [pits], where they were covered by thick bunches of straw topped by soil.

'At the end of each day potato picking I was absolutely tired out – no thoughts of getting up to mischief in those days! In any case, pleasures were few and far between then.'

---

few yards apart, using a long-shanked, bent-headed tool called a hack. Later, the heaps were spread with the graipe. Then it was plod, plod, plod back for another load.

'Shawing bagies was a hard job, bent double the whole day. This involved pulling the swedes up by the roots and using a shawing hook [a short-handled sickle] to cut off the shaws [the leafy parts of root crops], the root tips and soil. Dealing with two rows at a time, the shaws went in one heap, bagies in another, all the way up those drills which seemed to stretch on for ever. Up and down we went, making strips for the way of the horse and cart when it came to loading. That was just as back-breaking, chucking the bagies into the cart, the roots being taken off to another field for feeding to stock, or put onto the clamp for storing. Sometimes I took a load to a field of sheep where the pasture was poor, and then I had to use a cutter cart, which had a big, wooden-handled iron wheel on the side and a drum with sharp spikes in the middle. When I turned the wheel the bagies came out in thick chips into a wire basket underneath. Then I carried these to a feeding trough – if I could push my way through the milling flock of sheep without being knocked off my feet!

'When it came to threshing, the farmer had to book the travelling monster well before he needed it because all the farmers wanted it at about the same time. The man in charge of it was known as the threshman, and was generally someone who was a law unto himself! The actual threshing mill – usually a horrible orange colour – was pulled by a great steam engine belching smoke everywhere and making everything black. Its steam powered the mill's belts, which walloped around at an amazing speed and threatened to scalp anyone who forgot to duck. There were no safety regulations in those days.

'A man known as a feeder-in stood up on the mill in a small, square, sunken box, with a lethal revolving drum in front of him and a board slanting down into the gaping mouth holding the drum. If this man did not feed the mill carefully and regularly it bowked with "indigestion" and this slowed everything up. Two people called lowsers [from the Scots word "lowse", meaning to loosen] stood on either side of the feeder-in, to pass him the sheaves after cutting their bands. This they did alternately, so they faced the middle of the drum. When I did this I was frequently choked by the thick smoke and dust or chaff blowing around, so when I finally descended to earth I was like a battered, bleary-eyed sweep. Unfortunately bad weather did not seem to deter this activity: if the mill was in you just got on with your job regardless of the elements.

'After two hours on top I took my turn at the chaff – known as "caff" in Northumberland – with a partner. This was another dusty job with no chance to rest. We raked the chaff from under the mill onto a carrying sheet, which was a large, split poke, and carried it to a hemmel for feeding or bedding, depending on what corn was being threshed. Sometimes this took quite a while as we had to open and close many gates and doors, so when we got back the chaff would be overflowing. Occasionally, if the chaff was oat or wheat, nice and soft, people filled their mattresses with it.

'After the chaff I would have a shift at the huge straw bunches, which were disgorged with monotonous regularity from the rear end of the mill. We trailed these by string bands, one in each hand, to the long mow [stack] in another part of the yard, where they were stored for stock feed and bedding.

'Then I had a stint at the mouth end of the mill, where the threshed corn came out of chutes and dropped into sixteen-stone bags, which I helped the men tie and weigh. They had to carry these huge bags up the granary steps, which had no rails and were often slippery, and tip the corn out onto the floor. This was very hard work, calling for considerable strength, and was just about the only farm job which I was not allowed to do. Even though I was generally expected to do the same work as the men, I got a much smaller wage than them.

'After a day at the threshing I was very glad to get home for a good wash and rest, but there was never any hot bath or long soak indoors. Sometimes, if my brothers were out, I managed to wash in the tin bath in front of the fire, and if I was very lucky I had a bath at a friend's house. But mostly it was only a tin bath on a stone slab under a canopy of trees at the back door. And this was filled with cold water from the rain barrel, often after the ice was broken! But at least it was good for rosy cheeks. Then, after a meal, I'd maybe help make clootie mats [of rags], or do some sewing or knitting before going to bed.

'But I did have a bit of pleasure, which was a Saturday afternoon bike ride into the nearest village, to watch the pictures for 3d [1½p]. We saw all the stars of the day and, when I was about eighteen years old, I was allowed to go to village dances. I really did enjoy these and I could always get a long lie-in on the Sunday if I had no feeding to do.

'In those days we all handed our pay packets to Mother, and as well as the coupons with wartime rationing, she sorted out any pocket money. I never got anything until I was about eighteen, and then only 2s 6d [12½p] a week.

'We might have been poor, but we were a lot better off than some people who had large numbers of children as well as grandparents to keep, and were often very dirty as well as hungry. There were no pensions or handouts then, so folk often had to beg or to try and get by in other ways. One of the great local characters was Nelly the Sweep from Alnwick, who was supposed to have taken her name from her husband's job. This was often the case then, so you might have had Nelly the Joiner if her husband had been a carpenter. As far as I know she never got up any chimneys, but came by with her battered old pram selling pins, tapes and threads – and she soon got ratty if you didn't buy anything. I suppose she had some gypsy blood in her. She had a wrinkled brown face, always smoked a clay pipe, wore a long black skirt, and carried all her treasures with her in big poacher's pockets; she washed in the burns and shuffled from farm to farm, sleeping in barns or hedgerows.'

In 1950 Violet and her father went to work at North Doddington Farm, near Wooler, and the family moved into the tied cottage in which she still lives. At the age of twenty-nine she married another of the farm workers, but continued to work on the land – mostly part-time – while raising two sons. Her husband, who died in 1996, spent his entire working life on that same farm, serving three generations of the Maxwell family.

Sadly, many of North Doddington's cottages, which once housed the large workforce necessary to work on the farm and in the quarry, are now empty for much of the time, having been sold off or let as holiday homes. Now, few 'incomers' have any idea of just how hard local life was when countrywomen such as Violet Clarke were tied to the land.

Burning the Water

Poaching Tales

BURNING THE WATER

Many were the differences between the Scottish and English poacher, the former being held to be a far nobler creature. Not for him the night creeping in the woods but a mob-handed, frontal attack on the salmon river with boats, needle-sharp leisters, flaming cressets of tarred pine, wild Gaelic songs, many a dram of malt and silvery threshing of monster salmon as they were hauled over the thwarts.

Previous page: salmon fishers carry their coracles to the water

Methods of fish poaching had not the variety of those for winged or furred game, but the snatching hook, net or even leister are considered if not acceptable then at least understandable, whereas for the thugs who kill a whole stretch of river with poison for the few salmon that are in it, a blow from which it takes the water many seasons to recover, there is universal loathing among both keeper and genuine poacher.

Fish Poaching

From *The Amateur Poacher* by Richard Jefferies.

'There is a way of fishing with rod and line, but without a bait. The rod should be in one piece and stout, the line also very strong but short, the hook of large size. When a fish is discovered the hook is quietly dropped into the water and allowed to float along until close under it. The rod is jerked up and the barb enters the body of the fish and drags it out.

'This plan requires, of course, that the fish should be visible, and is more easily practised if it is stationary, but it is also effective against small fish that swim in large shoals, for if the hook misses one it strikes another. The most fatal time for fish is when they spawn; roach, jack and trout alike are then within reach, and if the poacher dares to visit the water he is certain of a haul.'

Scrope's Sneak Fisher

From *Days and Nights of Salmon Fishing* by William Scrope.
This minor classic, written in 1898, described salmon fishing on the Tweed, the strange characters who pursued that sport, and often their poaching tricks, in the days when salmon were plentiful but still jealously preserved. The throwing spear or leister was the favourite weapon, but a cunning man resorted to other tricks.

Your plausible poacher and river sneak sallies forth with apparent innocence of purpose; he switches the water with a trout rod and ambulates the shore with a small basket at his back indicative of humble pretensions but has a pocket in his jacket that extends the whole breadth of the skirts. He is trouting forsooth, but ever and anon, as he comes to a salmon cast, he changes his fly and has a go at the nobler animal. If he hooks a salmon, he looks on each side with the tail of his eye to guard against surprise and if he

sees any danger of discovery from the advance of the foeman he breaks his line, leaves the fly in the fish's mouth and substitutes the trout one — said fish swims away and does not appear in evidence.

I once came upon one of these innocents who had hold of a salmon with this trout rod in a cast a little above Melrose Bridge called the Quarry Stream. He did not see me for I was in the copsewood on the summit of the bank immediately behind him. I could have pounced on him at once, I and my fisherman. Did I do so? I tell you no. He would have broken his line as above

and lost the fish; and I wanted a salmon for, it is a delicate animal and was particularly scarce at that time.

So I desired Charlie to lie down amongst the bushes and not to stir till the fish was fairly landed and was in the capacious pocket, which was already described. Then I counselled him to give chase and harry the possessor. Judging, however, that if the man crossed the river at the ford a little below, which he was very likely to do, that he would have so much law of Charlie before he could descend the steep brae that he

might escape, I drew back cautiously, got into the road out of sight and passed over Melrose Bridge taking care to bend my body so as to keep it out of sight behind the parapet. I then lay concealed on the opposite bank.

Thus we had master sneak between us. I was at some distance from the scene of the action to be sure and somewhat in the rear, as I could advance no further under cover, but I had the upper ground and was tolerably swift of foot in those days which gave me confidence. I took out my pocket glass and eyed my man. He was no novice, but worked his fish with great skill. At length he drew him onto the shore and gave him a settler with the rap of a stone on the back of his head. He then, honest man, pried around him with great circumspection, and seeing no one he took the salmon by the tail and, full of internal contentment, deposited it in his well-contrived pocket. He then waded across to the south side of the river with the intention, as it seemed, of revisiting his household gods and having a broil.

Charlie now arose form his lair and scrambled down the steep. The alarm was given but he of the salmon had a good start with the river between him and his pursuer. So he stops for a moment on the haugh to make out what was going forward on all sides, much after the fashion of an old hare who runs a certain distance

The throwing leister

when she apprehends anything personal, she rests for a moment or two and shifts her ears in order to collect the news from all quarters of the compass.

Even so did our friend and having satisfied himself that he was a favoured object of attention he was coy and took to flight incontinently. I now sprang up from the firs for the game was fairly afoot and kept the upper ground. The pursuit came close and hot but as the fugitive like Johnny Gilpin carried weight, I soon closed with him.

'You seem in a hurry my good friend; your business must be pressing. What makes you run so?' 'Did ye no see that bogle there by the quarry stream that garred me rin this gait; haud on for our lives sir for if he overtakes us we are deid men.' 'Why, the truth is, Sandy, that I do not choose to haud on at present because I came in quest of a bonny salmon and cannot go home without one. Could you not help with me such a thing?'

At this, Sandy took a pinch of snuff from his mull and seeing my eyes fixed upon the length and protuberance of his pocket, answered quaintly enough; 'Ay, that I can, and right glad am I to do ye a favour: ye shall no want a salmon whilst I have one.'

So saying he pulled forth a ten pounder, which occupied all the lower regions of his jacket. 'How the beast got in there' said he as he extracted him gradually, 'I dinna ken, but I am thinking that he must have louped intill my pocket as I war wading the river.'

The Throwing Leister

This throwing leister is used chiefly on the upper parts of the Tweed and its tributary streams where the water is not deep. The spear has five prongs of unequal but regularly graduated length, those which are nearest the fisherman and which come to the ground first in throwing being the shortest. The entire iron frame of the spear is double the weight of that in common use. An iron hoop is then bound around the top of the pole as a counterbalancing weight and the pole itself has a slight curve, the convex part being the outermost in throwing. A rope made of goat's hair called 'the lyams' is fastened to the bar of the spear just above the shortest prong. This rope is about twelve yards long and is tied to the arm of the thrower. The spear is cast like a javelin and if thrown by a skilful hand, the top of the shaft, after it has pierced the fish, falls beyond the vertical point towards the opposite bank of the river, then the fish is pulled to land by means of the aforesaid rope or lyams so that there is little chance of him escaping in his struggles for freedom.

A Leistering Expedition

This was organised salmon poaching on a grand scale where blazing pine torches or cressets were used by a team of wild Highlanders wielding leisters in the flickering light.

All being ready a light was struck and the spark being applied to rags steeped in pitch and fragments of tar barrels, they blazed up at once amid the gloom like the sudden flash from the crater of a volcano. The ruddy light glared on the rough features and dark dresses of the leisterers in cutting flames directly met by black shadows. It reddened the shelving rocks above and glanced upon the blasted arms of the trees slowly perishing in their struggle for existence amongst the stony crevices: it glowed upon the hanging wood, on fir, birch, broom and bracken, half veiled or half revealed as they were more or less prominent.

The principals now sprang into the boats. Two men regulated the course of the craft with their leisters, the auxiliaries were stationed between them and the light was in the centre of the boat side. As the rude forms of the men rose up in their dark attire, wielding their long leisters with the streaks of light that glared partially upon them, and surrounded as they were by the shades of night, you might almost have fancied yourself in the dark and sinister realms below with Pluto and his grim associates embarked on the Stygian lake.

'Now my lads, says the master; 'Take your places. Tom stand you next to me; Sandy go on the other side of Tom and do you, Jamie, keep in the middle and take tent to cap the boats well over the rapids. Rob, do you and Tom Purdie keep good lights and fell the fish.'

Bream Poachers

In those hard times any fish, flesh or fowl could be used in the kitchen, even gulls and shelduck which they made into sausages. Coarse fish not usually eaten today were a marketable commodity in 1910 in rural Norfolk. Here one Adam Bede was on the run, or rather on the sail, in escape from the pursuing police.

He came sailing downstream with two others aboard the wherry 'plimsol down' with the weight of great whopping bream. Three police-

men were pursuing the craft alongshore on bikes. Through the Vauxhall bridge the poaching craft glided, the constables having to make a detour to the Bowling Green pub where they expected the wherry would draw up. But Adam was not going that way, you bet.

As they touched the corner of the Knowl, up went sail and they took fair wind to Breydon, and while one tended the tiller and sail, the others weighted the nets and dropped them into the water, as they thought, opposite a certain numbered post or stake, but the tide took it aslant as it

sank and they never afterwards recovered it. The fish were thrown overboard too, many to sink, but others with distended bladders floated down to the sea on the ebb. But for this mishap, the trio got off free.

The Snatching Hook

The hook is four or five inches in length. It has a shank which is hollow. The point may be barbed or it may not. In the shank there is a hole through which a strong rope is tied and the strands of the rope are bound down neatly. The rope may be five or six feet long and at its end is a loop through which a man could put his hand. The gaff is not a gaff until the poacher cuts himself a stick. As a rule the stick could be mistaken for a walking stick, a hazel rod such as any idling countryman might have in his hand when walking by the river.

A fine salmon lashes its tail and throws itself at the torrent. The leap fails and it drifts back. The man among the small stones and shingle plays with his stick. The salmon tries again and again. Now it floats back exhausted and lies in a near-at-hand pool recovering its strength, silvered and magnificent, a thing to take the breath away.

The man by the water fumbles in his pocket, draws out the hook, drives his stick into the socket, pulls the rope tight so that all is firm and looks round. In that instant he makes up his mind. The cold mountain water may swirl round his boots but he will not feel its icy bite. The rod and the hook reach out suddenly and the salmon will thresh the water as it slashes into its side. For perhaps three minutes the tug-of-war will go on. The hazel rod no longer needed will swim dizzily round the next pool and then come among the rocks. The salmon, hauled to the side and cracked on the head will cease to struggle, and the poacher will scramble to the nearest cover to hide it or pop it into a sack.

Charles St John's Highland Poacher

From *Wild Sports of the Highlands* by Charles St John

The life of a Highland poacher is a far different one from that of an Englishman following the same profession. Instead of a sneaking, night-walking ruffian, a mixture of cowardice and ferocity, as most English poachers are, and ready to commit any crime which he hopes to perpetrate with impunity, the Highlander is a bold, fearless fellow, shooting openly by daylight, taking his sport in the same manner as the laird or the Sassenach who rents the ground.

The Badenoch Leisterers

Every now and then a salmon would be seen hoisted in the air and quivering on an uplifted spear. The fish as soon as it was caught was carried ashore where it was knocked on the head and taken charge of by some man older than the rest who was deputed to this office. Thirty-seven salmon were killed that night and I must say that I entered into the fun unmindful of its not being quite in accordance with my ideas of right and wrong and I probably enjoyed it quite as much as any of the wild lads that were engaged in it. There was not much English spoken in the party as they found more expressive words in Gaelic to vent their eagerness and impatience.

What with the sale of these different kinds of game and a tolerable sum made by breaking dogs, a number of young men in the Highlands make a very good income during the shooting season which enables them to live in idleness the rest of the year and often affords them the means of emigrating to America where they settle quietly down and become extensive and steady farmers.

King of the Gamekeepers

Harry Grass: Hampshire, Durham, Suffolk and Wiltshire

KING OF THE GAMEKEEPERS

In his position as headkeeper for the late Earl Mountbatten at Broadlands, Harry Grass acquired a reputation as one of the greatest gamekeepers this century, and the popular press christened him 'King of the Gamekeepers'. This was indeed a great tribute to a man whose family has been the most famous in the entire history of gamekeeping. At their peak, there were 103 members of the Grass family working as keepers across the land at one time; they were all descended from two brothers – of surname Grasse and said to be refugees – who came over from France in about 1750 and arrived in the town then called Brandon Ferrie.

The Grasses certainly put down healthy roots in this country, and as their reputation grew many of them became associated with some of our finest and most famous shoots – Holkham, Elveden, Euston, Luton Hoo, Welbeck, Eaton, Lambton Castle, Studley, Six Mile Bottom and Windsor. Today, however, there are fewer than half-a-dozen members of the family remaining in the profession.

Harry's grandfather, father and all five uncles were gamekeepers. His father and Uncle Harry were keepers on the Earl of Durham's Lambton Castle Estate where Harry was born, at Houghton Gate, on 4 December 1908. He started work there as kennel boy at the age of fourteen, and under headkeeper Skelton his main job was to feed and exercise the fifty to sixty labradors, spaniels and flatcoats. But before that, whilst he was still at school, he used to sit in the woods with a .410, keeping watch over his father's pheasants.

One day his father said to him: 'Look here, if you're going to be a keeper always remember one thing – what you are looking after belongs to someone else.' Today, Harry says 'Too many people help themselves. In my time, if the boss said to me "Have a pheasant" I said thank you very much, but that was that.'

Harry's starting wage was 14s a week and after the first year he was given the keeper's uniform of a frocktail coat, breeches, box-cloth leggings and a trilby, though some keepers wore bowlers then.

At first, Harry was assigned as helper to beat-keeper Jim Hawkins, whose word was law. 'And in those days you only spoke to his lordship if you were spoken to first.'

As one of a team of twelve keepers, Harry stayed at Lambton for about a year and a half. Then one day his mother received word that Mr H. Wigmore of The Hermitage, Chester-le-Street was willing to take him on as underkeeper. So away he went, into lodgings with the head groom, to gain valuable experience.

The Hermitage had a good mixed pheasant and partridge shoot, but more unusual was its 1,400-acre (566ha) rookery, shot once year over about a fortnight. This provided excellent sport, much of it with shotguns as well as rifles, and Harry remembers how one evening they shot over a hundred rooks on the wing!

Then came another message from his mother, to say that headkeeper Thomas Scott of Lambton wanted to see him again. Henry Bell had taken that part of Lambton known as Penshaw and wanted Harry to be second keeper under Bob

Colpit. Thus Harry returned to the estate of his birth to become one of a team of four, including the colourful Smoker Watson – 'so called because he was never without his pipe'. Harry was to stay at Penshaw for four years, during which time there were four big coursing meetings every year, with plenty of hares to hand.

'Thomas Scott was very kind to me. Father and Uncle Harry were both killed in World War I and I always had the impression that father guessed he might not come back and asked Scott to keep an eye on me. Anyway, one day he suddenly said to me: "If you want to learn your job properly, you should go to East Anglia."'

Harry agreed and Scott eventually found him a position as one of seven beatkeepers with Lord Henniker, the eighth Baron, at Thornham Hall, Thornham Magna, near Eye, Suffolk. 'Henniker was known as "the little old man", but he was a good Shot and a well-known field trial judge. I really enjoyed my four years with him, and during that time I met and married Stella Mayes of Thornham Magna.

'At Henniker's each man was responsible for 100-150 coops. I had to walk a mile to the rearing field and be there by 6am. We had to mix all the pheasant food four times a day – at 7am, 11am, 3pm and 7pm, from when the birds were day-olds till they went to wood at six weeks. The main foods were maize, biscuit meal and sieved boiled eggs. We had to stop on the rearing field till the birds were shut up and we were lucky if we were home by 10pm. You can imagine how tired we were as we trudged back home in the dark, with the owls hooting all about and every shadow regarded with suspicion.

'We also had to feed the hens and move the coops onto fresh ground every day. And each keeper had to run 50-60 traps.'

Harry remembers his time at Thornham with great affection. 'I knew it was a caring place from the day I arrived, when the headkeeper met me at the railway station with his pony and cart. As we drove the five miles to his house, travelling down narrow country roads, I saw thatched cot-

tages with pink and cream-washed walls and I got the feeling that I had moved back in time by something like fifty years for I had not seen anything quite like it before.

'Over the next few days I met the rest of the keepers and, although we had dialect difficulties, and did so for quite some time, we all spoke "keepers' language". But I was in a completely

different world: this was true country, untouched by anything modern – craftsmen carried out their duties using methods which had long vanished in the part of the North I had known. I saw men making large farm wagons and tumbrils, and farm methods and cropping were not the same. There were no heavy Shire horses and no hills, only flat ground. Even the weather was different, and, unless my memory is at fault, all the summers seemed to be warm and dry.

'The estate was in effect a country factory and everyone in the locality was employed by it, men of all professions, including foresters, sawyers, carpenters, painters and farmworkers They even made their own bricks and field drains in moulds, The estate was self-supporting in every way and was owned and govern by a true country gentleman.

The present Lord Henniker was just a boy when Harry arrived from the North, but he vividly remembers that Grass was 'an excellent and enormously energetic keeper. Once, when walking with a senior keeper, he saw a bird he regarded as dangerous vermin – probably a magpie – and ran some two miles to his house to get a gun, then ran back and shot the bird. It was quite a feat. He was also immensely strong and regaled us with stories of his exploits at Cumbrian wrestling, at which he excelled in his youth.'

Harry turned his beat into the best on the estate and when John Palmer retired Harry took over as second keeper. Lord Henniker also said that when headkeeper John Chandler retired, Harry would take his place – but eleven years was too long for the ambitious Mr Grass to wait.

'One day a gentleman farmer came to see me and asked me to head a small two keeper shoot between Bury St Edmunds and Newmarket. So off I went and made it the best shoot of its size in Suffolk, if not in England. And when the day came for me to resign, the owner, Mr Gittus, actually cried.

'The agent of Lord Milford of Dalham Hall, near Market, came to see me and invited me to go there as headkeeper. And I am pleased to say that I made it the finest pheasant shoot in all England. One day 1,200 pheasants came out from one drive – the North Field Belt – and the seven Guns killed only sixty-eight birds, such was their quality. Lord Milford said: "Grass, you've really excelled yourself today."'

Actually, the shoot already had an excellent reputation before Harry went there. Cecil Rhodes, founder of Rhodesia, purchased Dalham in 1900 because it was 'one of the best partridge shoots in England', and the first Lord Milford bought it from the Rhodes family in 1924 for the same reason, following the expiry of his lease at Six Mile Bottom.

Lord Milford's son, Major Philipps, recalled Harry's early days at Dalham in the 1940s. 'When I came home on embarkation leave I found the Derbyshire Yeomanry, with five of the best Shots in England, living in the house and shooting all the partridges. When I returned in 1945 there were no partridges, but Harry Grass had arrived and was rearing thousands of pheasants. All the farms were let at £1 per acre provided that they grew the crops required by Harry, never cut thistles before July and never used fertilizers or pesticides.'

Harry regarded Lord Milford as 'a great man', but 'he was so different from his son, Major Philipps. Matters came to a head one day when the Major was rude to my wife; I threatened to smack him one and decided to leave'.

Another job came along quickly, taking Harry to be the head of two keepers working for Lady Janet Bailey of Lake in Wiltshire. There his reputation continued to grow and after only one year Lord Mountbatten's agent, Commander North, came to see him and asked him to 'go to Broadlands in Hampshire as headkeeper.

Harry was 'signed on' by Lady Mountbatten, who at first declared that he could not spend much money as the shoot was at rock bottom. Not surprisingly, Harry, in his typically direct way, said 'I must have sufficient funds, but most of all I want my own way of doing things'. Fortunately, Lady Mountbatten agreed and said that Harry would be answerable to no one except her, not even the agent. The five other keepers would do whatever Harry required to build the shoot up.

As a result, on their first day, less than a year later, they killed more pheasants than in the whole of the previous season. Lady Mountbatten joined the party on the last drive before lunch and said to her husband: 'How are you getting on, dear?' He replied: 'We've already discovered one thing – Grass is not going to stand any nonsense.'

Thus the shoot's big build-up began, and it wasn't long before royal guests came from all over Europe to enjoy Broadlands' much talked

THE SHOOTING PARTY

'Shooting took pride of place on the estate and dominated four days every other week. And during the Christmas period, when the boys were home from school, every day saw small parties enjoying the sport. Beaters were drawn from other departments on the estate so it really was a 'family' outing.

'In those days the shooting men gave the keepers a party in one of the 'locals' – there were two on the estate and it was held at each alternately. Those who had assisted the keepers – loaders, village policemen, head carpenter and so on – were also invited, and it was a time for everyone to let their hair down. Everyone contributed a song; the headkeeper always gave his favourite rendering of 'The Galloping Major', and when it came to the 'Bumpety bumpety bumpety bump, as though I was riding the charger' bit everyone went through the motions of doing so. We always had an extension of time so the party usually folded up at around 1am, which was considered just about the right length of time for everyone to have reached the stage when they were at least 'happy' enough to walk home safely.

'Another party was held for the entire staff in the large, rambling servants' hall at the mansion, where all the married staff went for tea and all the single staff went for the evening's entertainment – a mixture of dancing and singing helped along with fairly liberal mugfuls of what was known locally as 'owld beer', which either made you a little worse for wear or sobered you up, depending on what state you were in to begin with.

'Around midnight the family would come in and wish us all the compliments of the season. We would then all join hands to sing 'Auld Lang Syne', and we meant every word of it.'

about sport, at a time when big bags were still very much in vogue.

On Harry's best day ever, in 1968, they killed 2,139 pheasants on just four drives, and Prince Charles bagged 500! As usual, Harry blew his whistle to signal no more shooting after each drive, but after the last a single shot rang out. Harry told me 'I was so shocked, as my word was law and everyone knew it. So I marched over to the Guns to find out who the guilty party was. To my great surprise it was Prince Charles, and before I could say anything he said: "I'm sorry, but I'd killed 499 when the whistle went and I don't suppose I'll ever do that again." Still rather cross, I said to the prince: "Don't do it again, sir." "What?", he asked, "firing after the whistle?" "No, shoot 500 pheasants", I quipped, allowing a slight smile to creep across my face.'

News of the big bag travelled remarkably quickly and Harry recalls that within a few hours people were ringing up from as far away as Scotland, asking for all the details,

According to Harry, Prince Charles was then a much better Shot than the more experienced Prince Philip. When Prince Philip first went to Broadlands they shot 1,417 and he said to Harry: 'I bet you'll never do that again.' But Harry proudly recalls: 'The very next time he came we killed 1,600. There was no way I would allow standards to slip.'

Another famous guest was motoring mogul Henry Ford. One day he shot dangerously, at a partridge into the faces of the approaching beaters. Harry spun round to Lord Mountbatten and said 'Shall I go and warn him, sir?' The Earl replied: 'No, I'll get Lord Brabourne [Lord Mountbatten's son-in-law] to do it; he's a bit more diplomatic than you.'

Lord Mountbatten was 'a fair Shot', but to Harry he was 'a good employer, a good master and a real friend'. They travelled extensively together, Harry driving his master many hundreds of miles to other shoots. 'We often stopped off at his London house on the way, and we always had the same for lunch – no discrimination.'

One famous shoot which they visited frequently was Sandringham, and it was on the royal estate that Harry mentioned to Lord Mountbatten that he had his retirement papers through. The Earl looked horrified and said to Harry: 'You're not going to retire: not only are you my keeper, but you are also my friend,' So Harry stayed on.

Lord Mountbatten's death at the hands of the IRA was a bitter blow to Harry, and with his friend and employer's passing the old keeper really lost his enthusiasm for almost everything. His sadness was as deep as his roots in keepering and he still remembers vividly how he joined the estate's other three heads of department in standing guard over Lord Mountbatten's coffin at the mansion. 'When you walked in you could have heard a pin drop, and when I looked up there were ladies with tears in their eyes.'

The estate passed to Lord Romsey, the Earl's grandson, who wanted to get rid of Broadlands' reputation as a 'blunderbuss' shoot, and instead concentrate on quality birds in smaller numbers. Of course, the young lord found it extremely difficult to follow in the footsteps of such a popular and loved employer. Harry found him 'altogether a different kettle of fish, and when, after a year or so, he suggested that I might retire, I did not find the decision difficult'.

Harry was given a small cottage at Broadlands for the rest of his life, along with a small pension. Today he grows a few tomatoes and cucumbers and sometimes goes to watch on shooting days, occasionally 'waving a white flag to get the birds up a bit'. And each Thursday he still drives his old Ford the seven miles to Romsey to help out in the gunshop there.

'Yes', said Harry emphatically, when I asked him if he would follow the keeper's path if he had his time over again. And he proudly proclaims that the family tradition continues. One day at Broadlands Prince Charles turned to Harry's grandson, Ian Brown, and said: 'Are you going to be a keeper like your grandfather?' Then he turned to Harry and said: 'Grass – he'll start at Broadlands', which in due course he did.

Much of Harry's sound advice was once regularly recorded in the pages of *Shooting Times*, the editor having asked him to contribute a monthly page in the late seventies and early eighties. He always wrote in longhand and persuaded one of the ladies in the Broadlands estate office to type each piece, but his style was excellent and needed very little editing.

Harry's subject matter ranged far and wide, from rearing to roosting, from predation to tipping. The biggest tip he ever received was '£40 from a foreigner, but the average in my last few years at Broadlands was £10. And royals always tipped much in line with the other guests. As is customary, I shared the tips out with the other keepers at the end of the season, unless there was a particularly good day, when it was done immediately. In the old days at Lambton we always thought that the headkeeper kept more than his fair share when it came to pay-out time. I suppose all keepers suspect their bosses.'

But Harry is particularly renowned for his success in dealing with poachers. And he had to be specially vigilant at Broadlands, which is so easily accessible by a number of major roads and only a few miles from Southampton and other towns.

Unfortunately, a lifetime's zeal has taken its toll, and today Harry gets about only with the aid of a stick. He fell and broke his knee eighteen years ago while rushing to get his pheasants in during a thunderstorm, and this obviously still troubles him today.

While working for Sir Arthur Wood at The Hermitage a poacher stabbed him in the thigh and lower leg and he needed ten stitches. A friend advised him to learn how to wrestle and box, and this he did with a vengeance, eventually becoming one of the most feared keepers of his generation. He took lessons once or twice a week from the amateur champion of Cumberland and Westmorland style wrestling. When he could pin down and throw his tutor he went to another amateur champion to learn how to box, becoming very proficient at that, too. He was a match for anyone.

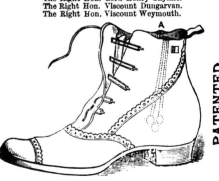

The "Viscount" Ventilating Shooting Boot
Under the patronage of
The Right Hon. the Earl of Cork and Orrery (the Master of Her Majesty's Buck Hounds).
The Right Hon. Lord Henry Thynne.
The Right Hon. Viscount Dungarvan.
The Right Hon. Viscount Weymouth.

PATENTED.

OPEN.—**A** Ventilating Air Tubes.

Harry was only eleven when he gave evidence against a poacher for the first time. He was on his way home from school when he saw one of the Lambton keepers chasing a man with a .410. Later the headkeeper was consulted and it was decided that, despite his tender years, Harry was sufficiently mature to identify the poacher in court. And afterwards, the magistrate congratulated him on the clear way he gave evidence.

As the years went by Harry became increasingly tough with the many poachers he apprehended and had no hesitation in 'giving them a good hiding'. Once a gypsy threatened Harry with a knife, but the fearless keeper had no trouble in seizing the weapon. 'I cut off the tip of his nose with it and said: "There, every time you look in the mirror you'll remember me and think twice about coming here again!"'

At Henniker's the keepers went nightwatching in groups of three, their shifts being from dusk till 1am, and 1am till dawn. Anyone caught was taken to the local police station. Harry and his colleagues never called in the police to help apprehend poachers, as is the modern, more cautious, practice.

On another occasion, at Broadlands, Harry came across a group of eight poachers, a couple of whom gave him 'a lot of lip' as they all made off. Shortly afterwards, a local farmer called Harry in to deal with two poachers, one of whom turned out to be 'the lippy one', and Harry had no hesitation in giving him a good thrashing.

At Henry Bell's, Harry once found a revolver left behind by a poacher, whom he recognised as the local Italian ice-cream seller. 'When I went in and slapped the gun down on his counter you should have seen the look on his face.'

Harry himself never carried a revolver, but he always had a home-made truncheon, two of which he still has among many shoot relics.

Despite all his fighting expertise, Harry did not go to the front in the last war. Instead, he was a sergeant in the Home Guard at Bury St Edmunds. The closest he ever came to hostilities was when two planes crashed on his shoot, 'one of ours and one of theirs, and both pilots were killed'.

However, he saw death twice in the shooting field. One accident took place at Lord Iveagh's famous Elveden shoot near Thetford, in head-keeper Turner's time, when Harry was loading for Major Philipps. The loader for a neighbouring Gun accidentally shot the second keeper in the stomach and he was dead before they reached him. Later they learned that this was the first time the careless man had acted as a loader.

While such horrific incidents often persuaded lesser men to take up safer, less adventurous occupations, Harry never wavered in his love of the keepering life. Not only was he the friend and confidant of kings and commoners, he was himself a king, the absolute ruler of fine sporting estates and the terror of those who would steal his game.

Sadly, Harry Grass died in May 1990.

The popular press nicknamed Harry Grass 'King of the Gamekeepers'. Here he is pictured outside his Broadlands cottage in 1988, with one of the old truncheons he used to keep for protection

Men of the Trees

Algy & George Lillywhite:
Timber Throwers, Sussex

MEN OF THE TREES

There is no doubt that tree felling, or timber throwing, is among the most dangerous of rural occupations, and after a lifetime in the business, brothers Algy and George Lillywhite have the scars to prove it. As soon as you shake hands with Algy you are aware of his missing thumb. 'I was taking the top out a big ash tree in a farmyard and because of a misunderstanding with the man on the ground a wire slipped and sliced my thumb right off; it could easily have been my arm. That bloody hurt and I thought I was going to faint, so as I climbed down the tree I tried to count all the moths on the bark to take my mind off it. Funny thing is it never really bled.'

On another occasion Algy nearly lost a foot. 'It was first thing in the morning and I took a big swing with the axe, which went straight through the wood – must have been a bit of tension in it – and my boot. All my toes and the front of my foot was hangin' down, but they managed to stitch it all back together again. We was strong in those days, but you 'ad to be to swing an axe all day.

'Chainsaws was really dangerous when they first came in – German Kirchners just before the war. We was about the first to have them. We had the first Danarm Tornadoe in the country, both one- and two-man, with a butterfly chain. One day we were felling an ash when the wind blew the tree back and it whipped round again in a second. The chainsaw took the lace off my left boot and went into my right leg. I had to have thirty-six stitches, but that night I managed to get down to Goodwood Club.'

George remembers the time they were working on the Goodwood estate when a branch fell out of a tree and hit another man on the back of the neck. 'It must have been stuck up there after being broken off in a storm. Anyway, it part paralysed him. That was the worst accident we ever saw.

'Yes, it's a rough and tumble job all right. I broke my ankle only three years ago, when a tree rolled on it. And Algy has broken three ribs on one occasion and four on another.' Then there was the time when Algy was using a power saw and was thrown 10ft up in the air by a branch which came up between his legs when a tree rolled round. 'It all happened in slow motion really, but fortunately I had the presence of mind to throw the saw away when I was goin' up; no way I wanted to come down again with that in my hand.

'You've really got to be on the look-out all the time. And in the old days back in the sawmill it was common for a man to lose a finger. How there weren't more people killed after the Great Storm of '87 I don't know. There was yobbos all over the place cuttin' up – and spoilin' timber through splittin' it – without any experience at all.'

Christened Algernon, Algy was born on 12 November 1926, and George was born on 26 October 1928, in a remote cottage in the woods, at Red Copse, near Boxgrove in the parish of East Dean, Sussex. Their father was a gamekeeper on the Goodwood estate. 'But 'e was also very good with his hands and became the village carpenter – makin' threshin' drums, even gunstocks – as well as a gravedigger and welldigger at East Dean. That was after he was made redundant, but they was good to him and sold him a rood [¼acre] of land on which he built a house. He was one of the men made redundant because there were a lot of death duties to pay when the Duke of Richmond died.

'Grandad had also worked around East Dean, on farms, mainly thatching. We had three sisters and a third brother who was older, but he was killed when he was 21. He came down the hill just up the road when it was dark and wet and you couldn't see much and ran straight into the back of a horse and cart on his motorbike.'

The boys went to the local school at East Dean and never had any illusions about their future employment. 'With no transport to get out the villages there was no option. It was either Green's sawmill or the farms. But they were enjoyable times and we never went hungry. One thing we do remember, though, is having to go to the isolation hospital at Chichester by horse-drawn ambulance when we had scarlet fever. One boy in the village died of it.

'After father left the duke, he 'ad the rabbit catchin' in return for lookin' after the wild game. In those days there were thousands and thousands of rabbits. Father got 9s a dozen for the largest, 6s for the next size down and 4s 6d for the smallest. In those days you usually bought the right to catch rabbits; you bid off the farmer or he would say a price. It was commonly known that rabbits would pay half the tenant farmer's rent.'

So at the age of 14 George became a full-time rabbit catcher and in his first winter he alone had

3,800 rabbits. 'Most were caught in snares but a few were ferreted. In the winter I run about three gross of wires plus gin-traps, but it was always wires in the autumn.

'We made our own entertainment then and we all had guns. There were very few deer but lots of foxes, and we used to catch them as well as badgers and stoats. We used to get penny a pair for starlings' or blackbirds' or any songbird's wings. They were dyed different colours to go on

This timber thrower worked with his crosscut saw in the same Sussex woods as the Lillywhites before they were born

the sides of ladies' hats. But we used to get 6d for a pair of jay's wings, as they're blue and colourful. A weasel fetched 1s 6d, a stoat 2s and a mole 4d or 6d, dependin' on whether it was low or high grade.

'Best of all was badgers, which fetched at least £1 each. To get 'em we used to make our own cartridges up with big lead balls and hide up a tree at night with a shotgun.'

Once George sent off two badger skins to Horace Friend, the dealer, and had a postal order for 30s each back, which was a lot of money then. So Algy thought, 'I'll have some of this and I went up next night to wait for 'em. But I lay on the ground, thinkin' it was all right as long as I

got the right way of the wind. Anyway, after a while I heard the badgers come out, rustlin' the leaves in the holes. Then I heard them all around me and I was frightened because I remembered the story of the drain man who put his rods up a den and got attacked. So I jumped up, fired two shots in the air and ran off with nothin'.

'Another thing father and us always used to do', said George, 'was put people's animals down when they wanted it. We used to get 5s or 7s 6d for this, but I always used to make 'em dig their own holes.

'The life seems hard now but we never once thought trappin' was cruel; it was a way of earning a living – survival. And as the war went on everyone was after rabbits and you got as much as 2s 3d for one, but the farmers soon put the price of the ground up. It was only seasonal work – the breeding was more to a set time then and all the rabbits lived in holes whereas so many live up top now. So come March we had to find other work.'

When Algy left school, also at the age of 14, he went timber throwing with his father for £1 a week. 'He did all the hard work and I started off with a 4½lb boy's axe, the heavier ones being 6lb and 7lb. We'd trim the bottom of a tree down straight and then cut a sink, which gave the direction to throw the tree. It was all piece-work for Green's sawmill at Chariton, near Singleton. The gang was paid three ha'pence a cube [cubic foot]. Later I went into the mill itself to help father build big sheds.

'After that I joined the gang of hauliers bringing timber into the mill. We 'ad this French lorry which ran off charcoal. It had this big furnace on one side with pipes all over it. You'd start it in the morning with a small amount of petrol and then run for the rest of the day on the gas given off by the charcoal.

'In our youth they still used horses at Goodwood. All the fields was ploughed with horses. The only mechanical thing you saw was a thrashin' machine.

'In the early days we used to bring in trees 80-100ft long. When the two dukes died within seven years there was a lot of death duties and the estate had to sell the whole of Chariton Forest and all the woods to the north. It was estimated over a million cube and at the time was the largest sale of timber ever recorded. Green's bought the lot and it worked out a real bargain – something like a farthing a cube. That was in the early Twenties and how Green's got established in the South. We came in on the throwing side towards the end of the thirty years or so it took to cut the lot down. A great deal of it was sold for Lee-Enfield rifle butts.

'After the war a lot of German beech came in and we went to do piece-work on the bandsaws in the sawmill. But after a year we were like caged animals so we went on our own loggin' firewood. A farmer gave us a wide rood of hedge, but it was full of shrapnel as it had been part of a firing range in the war. It was an awful job to

YOU SHOULDN'T LAUGH BUT...

'When the war came father was too old to join up and I was 'grade 3' – 'ad a weak stomach, but I did go in the Home Guard. And I did see some action. One day I was at the sawmill talking to a manager who was blind and partly deaf. Suddenly Gerry appeared, coming down the valley from nowhere, and the bullets was 'ittin' the ground just 2-3ft behind this manager. Well, I turned and run in the workshop and dived under the bench. Then I thought, 'This is no good, he's going to come round again', so I slid under a lorry being repaired there and in my panic fell into the inspection pit. After a while I realised that the plane had gone and went back out. To my amazement the manager was still there talkin' away, not realising that I'd gone. He didn't even know what happened, till I shook him by the shoulder. He was a lucky man.

'The plane didn't do much damage, though one shell smashed all the works of a steam crane on rails, used for lifting timber, and the operator was so frightened he never worked again. A neighbour picked up a shell and burnt her hand on it. Later her husband made a lighter out of it. After, we discovered that the German plane was shot down.

'Sometimes, when we was out rabbit shootin' we used to have a go at the doodlebugs with our 22 rifles.'

George and Algy Lillywhite in 1991: battle-scarred survivors of the dangerous tree-felling industry

sell firewood in those days. We sold most of ours to a Major Mould from London. Once he gave us a lorry because he said it was unlucky and he couldn't do any business with it. He just left the keys and took the train back to London. But we did all right with it.'

After that the brothers went loading timber for Green's, and left in 1951 to fell timber on the Goodwood estate. In one wood alone, in Singleton Forest, they worked for eight years, under contract to the Duke of Richmond. Most of the trees felled were beech up to about 180 years old and were planted by the second duke. 'Elm was almost a weed in those days, but now it is relatively rare and expensive.'

Nowadays the Lillywhites do very little timber throwing, the battle-scarred brothers admitting 'it's a young man's game'. Instead, they concentrate on the sawmill, which they took over about fifteen years ago and stands on part of Green's old site, which itself was on an earlier mill. Here they have the capacity to cut anything up to 32ft long. The biggest piece of wood they ever had to supply was oak measuring 29in square by 17ft long for a windmill, and it had to

SEASONAL CYCLE

The Lillywhites have worked in all weathers, even in the great freeze-up of early 1963, 'when the felled trees dropped out of sight in the snow. But there was always some seasonal work to do, such as rinding (taking the bark off), which had to be done just before the buds break and the sap rises. We'd chop a piece off the standin' tree and if it came away clean it was all right. After chopping around the bottom, we'd get the rinding iron in and take a ring off as high as we could comfortably reach. Then the tree would be felled and the rest taken off.

'The bark was put in stacks to dry, then bundled and sent on to the yards for tanning hides. We worked in pairs as part of a gang of eight or ten. Rinding was for about six weeks – all on oak. The bark has to be fresh for tanning to get the acid.

'Summers was spent trimming and taking the cordwood out. A cord is 4ft lengths stacked 2ft high and 16ft long. You need an oppis [Hoppus] book and a special tape for measuring the volume of the trees, but I can more or less do it in me head', says George. 'In winter we'd cut the beech.'

be very carefully chosen so that it would not crack under stress. Other monsters they've handled include a cedar of Lebanon measuring 8ft across and weighing 23 tons, which had to be felled when its top blew out in a storm. It was sold to Germans for veneer.

The brothers employ two other men at the mill, including one of Algy's sons. Now he, in turn, hears the stories which have been passed down from generation to generation A favourite goes back many years and was told to Algy by his father, who claimed that it was the most reliable account.

'In the woods above East Dean – almost at the highest point in Sussex – is a large beech called the Sergeant's Tree, which was witness to a sorry tale. In the days of the press-gangs there was a lad called Alan from Heyshott who delivered meat, and his last stop was at the bottom of Bury Hill, where he called in the pub. Inside, two soldiers asked him if he'd like a drink, so he took a pint

Above: Most country folk once relied on general carriers to bring supplies from nearby towns. T. Reeves worked the Charlton area at the turn of the century

Left: Albert Collins, cab and fly proprietor, was also an undertaker at Singleton in the late Victorian times

Foster's sawmill, which stood on the site of Green's sawmill, now run by the Lillywhite brothers

an Army officer called Sergeant, who fell by a tree. The Duke of Richmond said that tree was never to be cut down and it remains there today.

'The lad ran on to his native Graftham, where he grabbed 'andful of straw from a rick, jumped into the stream and lay in the water under a bank, breathin' through a straw. But eventually the soldiers saw him and shot him in the water. This was way before my father's time, but it's the story as 'e told me.

'One story which was from father's youth concerned some Mormons, who were great con men and baptised some local girls in a dewpond before taking 'em away to America. The local lads was so angry they harnessed the horses to the Mormons' carts the wrong way round – facing the carts – and thrashed 'em. 'Course, a horse will only go forward so they went in the pond and got stuck!'

with them. But as he drained his tankard a coin dropped in his mouth and he put it in his pocket. So the soldiers grabbed him, saying he had taken the King's shilling and had to go in the Army.

'Later the lad deserted and went into hiding. He lived in a boundary bank, which became known as Alan's Bank. His mother and sister used to leave food for him in the crook of a tree and he'd collect it at night. Then he became a highwayman with a musket and was captured on Bury Hill. When he was being chased he shot

The brothers were themselves great practical jokers in their younger days. For example, there was the time when they were 11 and, with a pal, rolled a big lorry tyre down the hill. 'It crossed the road, scared a man half to death, buckled the postmaster's bike and ploughed into an old, disused shepherd's hut.'

In the late nineteenth century a single farm needed a large staff: this team were at Charlton, where the Lillywhites live

It is not surprising that these two 'chips-off-the-old-block' are part of a close-knit family for they married two sisters. Their stories of earlier domestic life are legion.

'In the war we used to keep pigs and each year a family was allowed to keep one pig for each bacon ration given up. The biggest porker we had weighed 40 stone and took four men to carry. We used to cure our own bacon, which was normal then. The hams was rubbed with salt every other day for three weeks and then smoked for three weeks. It 'ad to be a sawdust fire of oak and beech, never softwood. One ham we had for seven years.

'But that was nothin' compared to a chunk of venison we kept. Father had this deer which was shot in the front leg and very bloody, so he decided to smoke and cook the leg for the dogs later on. But it obviously got overlooked and was still hangin' up when father died. We saw this thing in the corner all covered in dust and realised what it was. So Mum soaked it in water – it puffed right up again – and cooked it. We all had a little taste and it was perfect, but we decided to give it to the dogs, which is what it was intended for. Only difference was it was twenty-five years later and not the same dogs! And the meat had only been smoked.

'In the war we used to keep a lot of bees, but not just for the honey. You was given an extra allowance of sugar which you was supposed to feed to the bees, so we never went short of sugar. We used to make our own hives, too.'

Those days of austerity have long passed and the Lillywhites now deservedly live in comfort, in a village which has seen remarkable changes in a relatively short time. Nowadays no one needs to let rooms to visitors to Goodwood races in order to supplement their meagre income, and ham comes from the nearest hypermarket rather than from a pig kept in the backyard. And where Algy once lived next door in a thatched cottage, he now lives in a modern bungalow on a piece of land sold to him by the duke. Yet the memories remain and the countryside surrounding Chariton is as inviting as ever.

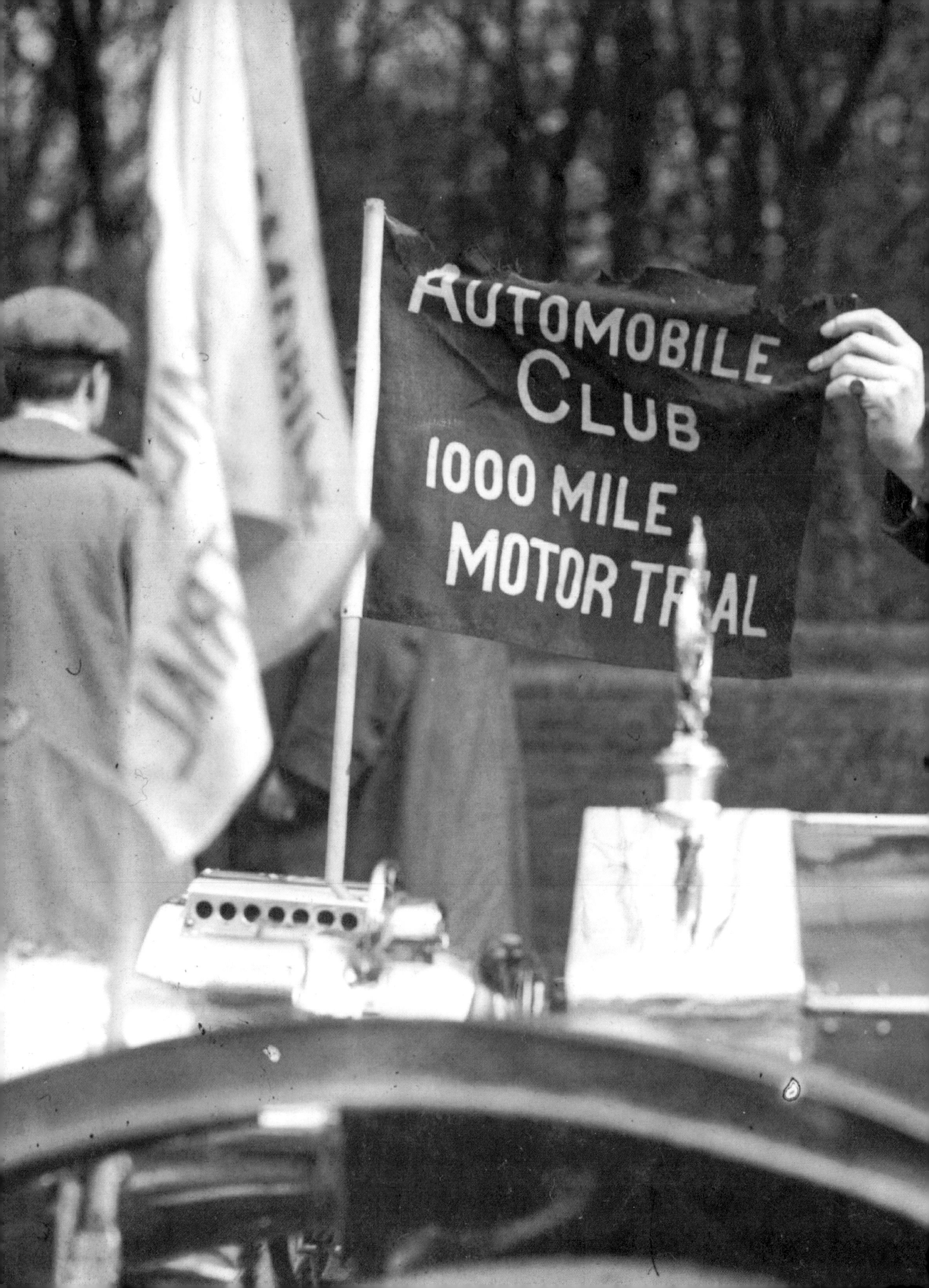
AUTOMOBILE
CLUB
1000 MILE
MOTOR TRIAL

Beaulieu

Country Estate: Hampshire

BEAULIEU

Of all the great houses, perhaps none has made such an attempt to capture the visitor as Beaulieu: although the undoubted beauty of the house, the abbey and the grounds still exists Lord Montagu has obviously set out to open his grand house to the public on a very large scale. Most notably, Beaulieu is now the home of the National Motor Museum.

(above) Fred Sheppard with his wife; (opposite) Ladies in period costume show visitors around Beaulieu; (previous page) At the tenth annual 1,000 Mile Motor Trial in 1910, Lord Montagu of Beaulieu holds the original flag, by this time somewhat nibbled by rats during storage

As Lord Montagu writes: 'Showing my home and welcoming visitors to Beaulieu since 1952 has been a great pleasure to me and their visits have ensured that Palace House, Beaulieu Abbey and other historic buildings in my care are in a better state of repair now than they have been for many decades. I hope that they will survive for many years to come, for future generations of visitors from all over the world to enjoy.'

Certainly, a tour of Palace House, historic seat of Lord Montagu's family is a delight indeed. It could well be corny – but it isn't: two lovely ladies dressed in period costume explained how the house was run back in the nineteenth century, during the Victorian period. The lady dressed as the housekeeper of that period, Mrs Chadwick, was particularly interesting. A crowd of visitors, many American, flocked around her as she guided us around the house.

It was Mrs Chadwick who had supervised all the female servants and had run the house on behalf of the present Lord Montagu's grandparents. It was her task to keep the accounts and ensure that the larders and cleaning cupboards were kept stocked, that the house was clean and the linen cupboard full. The title 'Mrs' was a courtesy for, like most housekeepers, Jane Chadwick was unmarried.

Directly under Mrs Chadwick in house hierarchy was Mrs Hale, the cook. She produced meals in accordance with Lord Montagu's grandmother's wishes, working under conditions that cooks today would find trying to impossible!

Next came the footmen and maids – Palace House had three footmen whose job included cleaning the knives and lamps which they also lit, cleaning shoes and boots and carrying coal and wood. One of their most unusual tasks was to scrub clean the small silver coins carried by the ladies of the period.

The maids were divided by areas in which they worked. The most senior was the lady's maid who, like her male equivalent, the valet, was responsible for taking care of Lord Montagu's grandmother's clothes, hair and jewellery and helping her dress in the elaborate costumes of the period. The two housemaids spent most of their time above stairs, cleaning the house, making the beds and lighting the fires, but the kitchen maid and scullery maid were confined below stairs. The former did much of the routine preparation and cooking of food for the cook, whilst the scullery maid simply washed up. Laundry maids were traditionally identified by their red hands and the laundries were found well away from the main living quarters because of the steam and smell.

Generally speaking, servants' hours were from 6am until 10.30pm or whenever the owners of the house retired. Each week they were given one evening and half a day on Sunday free, together with one free day a month.

Any of these might be stopped if work was not up to standard. They were also issued with one candle a week and a uniform, which if it wore out before the appointed time, was

replaced by stoppages from wages. These varied considerably, from the £25 to £30 a year a butler might hope to earn, to the £5 to £9 earned by the scullery maid.

As our 'modern' Mrs Chadwick made quite clear to us all that day, every servant knew the limits of his or her position and whilst conditions of service may seem unreasonable to us today, for many, in those days, the security provided by such steady employment, in such an attractive home, was immeasurably important.

Fred Sheppard, Butler

Lord Montagu quite rightly believes that Beaulieu is setting an exemplary standard when it comes to recording the history of great houses, and in the John Montagu building is housed the most impressive of archives. Susan Tomkins was the archivist at the time of my visit, and she greeted me with the hospitality for which Beaulieu is rightly recognised. She led me through endless corridors filled with tomes from the past, and certainly had a treat in store for me: many years ago, the elderly butler, a certain Fred Sheppard who had served during the 1930s, had been interviewed on two separate occasions, firstly when he was well into his eighties, and again when he was in his nineties. His most fascinating of stories begins and ends in Hampshire, but it has many interesting adventures along the way; I can do little better than to relate it as he has recorded it, in his own words:

'I was born in Salisbury in 1904, and had six brothers and sisters. My father worked on the Longford estate as a carpenter, often making fences, and we lived in an estate cottage. He was there altogether for thirty years. In those days you simply took what job you could find, and there was virtually no choice really open to anybody like us.

The beautiful Palace House at Beaulieu, viewed across the river

The most senior of the housemaids would be awarded the position of maid to the lady of the house. This was a trustworthy position often requiring tact and diplomacy

The role of the scullery maid, on the other hand, was less glamorous. This rather dramatic scene shows the debris of a grand dinner party revealed by what would have been the very early morning light. The scullery maid, not normally seen above stairs, would have to be out of sight before the house stirred for breakfast

'The house was crowded, and before the Great War, I went off to live with my grandmother. When the war broke out, boys aged thirteen or over could be engaged fulltime on the land and could leave school. I was fed up with education anyway and joined the local gardeners, and never went back; I guess they were glad to see the back of me! I certainly never regretted having a more formal education. Then, in 1917, I became a messenger around the Salisbury area and that's how, in 1919, I came across a job: a local butler at Stockbridge needed a boy to help him and I became his assistant. This is how I came to work for Sir Frederick Bathurst: I enjoyed the job, and henceforth never really left service. I was trained very well and it was fine for me. I got away from home and became myself, knowing at last what I wanted to do.

'That's how my life jogged on until the early 1930s when I came to Beaulieu. The vicar's wife told me that the Montagus were looking for a butler so I decided to apply for the job. I was called for interview by Lady Montagu at her aunt's house in Wilton Place, London. Well, I caught the train and I decided to walk there. Soon, though, being a stranger to London, I realised I was going to be late so I decided to take a taxi. I got in and put my bowler hat on the seat beside me. Well, we hadn't been going more than a mile or so when, believe it or not, we had a scrape with a van. The taxi driver and the van driver got into a violent argument – there was no separating them so I slipped out of the taxi, fearing I would be late, and ran all the way to Wilton Place. Just as I got there, all hot and sweaty and completely flustered, I realised that I'd gone and left my bowler hat back in the taxi. Now you must realise that to arrive for an interview for a butler's position in such a state of undress would at the least cramp my chances. However, I got the job, and so went on down to Beaulieu – and felt I'd never seen any building quite so lovely. You remember that phrase, "that peace which passes all understanding"? Well, for

Palace House: one of the many attractions of Beaulieu as well as the motor museum

Below: Part of the fascinating archive being put together by archivist Susan Tomkins

the first time in my life, I could appreciate it. I worked at Palace House, and in all my time there I was totally happy.

'I enjoyed life at Beaulieu right until the war broke out, when I was roped into the shipyard at Hythe. We got plenty of food in the factory and I quite enjoyed life there, air raids and all. I went back to Beaulieu after the war, but on a temporary basis; work wasn't really fulltime there any more, and so I had to help out at local hotels. It was then that I decided to go into window cleaning and had the idea of a vacuum chimney sweep! I did that for

'Even when I wasn't working I had to join the fire brigade and help with all the training. You see, it was the butler's job to be on hand if any fires broke out in the house itself. I was particularly worried about the staff because their rooms were right at the top of the house and I couldn't really see a way down safely for them if a fire should break out. Then we decided they could come down the secret stone staircase to the drawing room and go out of the door or windows there. We were fairly sure that would be safe because it was all made of stone.

'Ironically I was responsible for the only fire that ever broke out in my time there! It was Christmas and I was burning holly in one of the downstairs grates. I put on too much and the chimney set on fire. It just wouldn't go out, and the walls in the bedrooms above got absolutely baking hot. We 'phoned the fire brigade who came and put the fire-hose down the chimney and created the most dreadful mess you've ever seen. And all this at Christmas time, too!

a while even though I was still living in Palace Yard back here in Beaulieu up in the woods.

'During those years, to say my time off was a bit scanty would be the understatement of all time. My wife used to say, "If your children met you in the street, they wouldn't know you!" If the truth be known I was never home till way past dark, way past the time my two boys were in bed. Occasionally we'd go to flower shows, and sometimes we'd go to look at the ships in Buckler's Hard; we'd walk or bike, but that was about the limit of our time off.

BEING IN SERVICE IN THE 1930S

'Looking back to the 1930s, Beaulieu was a friendly place to work. We had several cooks between 1933 and 1939, but in particular I remember Mrs Percy Adams – she would cook up some wondrous stuff. Alice and Eleanor were the head housemaids, and the cook would always have two assistants. My assistant was a lad called Joe Spedding, and he really was on the lowest rung of the ladder here at Beaulieu. Times were a bit tight in those days so there was no housekeeper as such: the cook did all the ordering, and if I needed any stores she would get them for me as well. As I remember, there were two shops here locally and we'd buy from them on alternate weeks so we showed no favouritism; of course, they've long since gone, replaced by supermarkets. I remember one of them was run by a Mr Whimsey who was also head of the fire brigade here at the hall.

'Also in my time was Harold Bryant, the carpenter on the estate who would repair cottages and do any jobs in the house when needed. He was based in the estate yard, which is now the Fairweather garden centre.'

The butler often had to double as gentleman's valet

Opposite:
A photograph of Beaulieu taken in April 1948. The Montagu Arms, on the right of the picture, bears the coat of arms of the Montagu family

'One of the biggest jobs I had was helping with the preparations for any special occasions. You'd have to clean the silver till it gleamed. We had a few pieces stored in the bank, but all the usable silver had to be cleaned and polished constantly, and especially before any important guest came. Then the glassware, too, till it absolutely shone.

'There was no rest even when the Montagus were away, because then I was called on to do other jobs. In particular it was down to me to clean the windows, which was quite a job, as you can imagine; I had to clean them outside and inside, even though you might expect that to be the job of the housemaids.

'I kept record books as a butler or, rather, an extended diary of day-to-day events: all the people who came as guests, all the amusing events,

all the problems with the staff – everything was noted down. In fact, many butlers did this. Unfortunately, I don't quite know where mine have got to now.

RIGHT, SAID FRED!

'In all my time at Beaulieu I was always called Sheppard, never Fred. In actual fact my mother had called me Hector, a name which I've dropped all my adult life, preferring Fred which was made up for me. You see, back in my first job, in my footman days, I was called Frederick because that was how it was in every country house: the first footman was always called Frederick! And the second footman was always called Charles, whatever his name was. So that's how I came to be called Fred, and I've never dropped it since.'

Buckler's Hard, August 1947. By the time this photograph was taken the town had shrunk considerably in size from the days when its shipyard was responsible for building many of the ships that sailed in the Napoleonic Wars

'The staff dining room here at Beaulieu was very typical of those I've worked in in all manner of houses. However, it wasn't really very strict, and the meals were pretty informal – if you ask me, the code here wasn't strict enough. At Beaulieu we didn't stand on any sort of ceremony, and males and females all ate together, though the kitchen staff would eat in the kitchen so they could carry on with their work. Weekends were especially busy because you'd have more visitors who would come down from London to enjoy the countryside air. Christmases were absolutely hectic because the house would be full of extra guests – Lady Montagu had four nephews who always came to stay, and her stepsister also had children, so there was quite a crowd. They all brought their chauffeurs and their attendants – but I never had more staff to help me, even though I'd have liked a good few!

'In those days I always wore a black coat with a waistcoat and striped trousers in the morning.

In the evening it was a ritual that I'd put on a tailcoat, and on very special occasions I'd sometimes wear a white waistcoat with a white bow tie. These uniforms were not provided, you know, and I'd buy them at second-hand shops around the area; there were some that specialised in butlers' clothing. The cost would depend on the quality of the cloth and the overall condition. A suit of clothes could be as much as £5 which was quite a lot when you consider that when I started at Beaulieu I was only earning £90 a year. Mind you, that was considered very good at the time, though my wages stayed the same all the way through the thirties whilst I was there.

'Life at Beaulieu in my time was fairly modest, and a typical dinner party would not have a menu of any great note. We'd generally start off with soup and follow that with fish or meat. Then there'd be dessert and then fruit. The wines were particularly my job. Lady Montagu kept the cellar key and gave it to me simply when it was needed. There would certainly not be wine with every meal, and they'd often go for weeks without having any. I remember it came from London dealers, and some was laid down for years. Sherry was frequent at dinner parties, and sometimes there'd be port.

'We'd have nothing remarkable in terms of glasses, but oh, my word, getting the silver right was really something. Joe Spedding would clean it with his hands, a wash leather and then polish and polish and polish. The big thing was trying to get the scratches out. That was the art – it wasn't a question of polish, it was a case of getting the cutlery smooth. You know, I spent all my life watching the clock, and that's often been because of some damn scratch or another. As a young footman myself I could spend all day cleaning a single spoon. I suppose it's almost impossible for people to imagine in this day and age, but that's how it was then.

'A typical working day would see me on duty at around seven o'clock in the morning, and perhaps knock off around ten in the evening or sometimes later. Of course, things varied, but these were the general times, especially when the family were in residence; I might have two hours off in the afternoon, but this didn't really let me have much of a social life. I don't think I ever went to the cinema during all those years, not even once, and you've got to remember that cinema-going was the big hobby of the day!

'The House children were always having birthday parties, and I can tell you that was a devil of a job! We'd have to move all the big chairs out of the dining room, and put in small ones for them. Afterwards they would go to play in the upstairs dining room and then we'd have all the clearing up to do, once they had all gone, and that could take most of the night!

'Having said all this, I wouldn't want you to think by any means that it was a dull or unsociable place to work in – far from it! I loved my time at Beaulieu because it was a warm house and rich in stories. There was one in particular I liked,

A butler presides over an array of silverware at a party and keeps a discrete eye on the behaviour of the guests!

Lady Montagu of
Beaulieu visiting
Cowes Regatta in
July 1922. She
became the second
wife of the 2nd
Baron Montagu of
Beaulieu in 1920

that we called the venison story. Lord Montagu used to work in London and would come down for the weekends; on one particular weekend he was given a great haunch of venison which was too fresh to eat. His instructions were that the cook should prepare it for the following weekend. However, then he was ill and didn't come down for a fortnight,

'That night there was no venison, and he asked the cook where it was. She told him that they'd thrown the venison out. "Thrown it out! Where?" The cook said that she'd asked the gardener to bury it because it had gone off.

'Well, Lord Montagu leapt up and went off to see the gardener to find out where he'd dug it. The haunch of venison had been put in the dung heap – but Lord Montagu asked for a spade and he dug it out and hung it on an apple tree, then hosed it down and finally took it into the kitchens. Well, the cook simply refused to cook it. "You'll cook that venison or it will be the last thing you do in this house!" said Lord Montagu. As you can guess, it was cooked – and they said it was the best venison they'd ever tasted!

'Lady Montagu's remarriage was also a big and joyful event; we were always afraid that she wouldn't find anyone else. The catering was done by a London firm. The marriage took place in Beaulieu church and the reception was here in the house and I had to organise that. It was my job to announce the three hundred and fifty or so guests and I had them waiting by the front stairs where Lady Montagu would come down to greet them. The problem was that the happy couple decided to come down the back stairs! I'd got everybody prepared at completely the wrong end of the house! However, I managed to swop everybody round and bring them through in the right order, and the day was saved.

'There were embarrassments, too … I well remember one night I was preparing a dinner party for twelve. There were six people staying in the house and three couples were coming in from outside, two of whom I knew well but the third I'd never met at all. Everybody had arrived – all the

ones I knew, that is – and then there was a knock on the front door and a very smart man and woman were standing there. Obviously I invited them in, assuming them to be Mr and Mrs Smith, the people we were waiting for – and the ones I didn't know. I took them through to the drawing room and announced them as such – and there was total confusion! Lady Montagu looked at them and then at me and declared in surprise: "This isn't Mr and Mrs Smith!" she said. And surprised they replied, "No, we're Mr and Mrs Jones and we just came here to ask directions!" There were hoots of laughter, but I wished I could have dropped into a hole! If my memory serves me properly, Lady Montagu asked for another

Tennis parties at Beaulieu. These photographs, both taken in March 1921, show Mr E. G. Bessikir and Mrs E. H. Bethoud (top) and (below) Bunny Ryan and Gordon Lowe

Country house life between the wars: this charming family portrait, taken at Beaulieu, offers a glimpse of an idyllic world that has now changed almost beyond recognition

two chairs to be put at the table and we had fourteen for dinner that night! That, though, was typical of Lady Montagu, who was one of the kindest, most warm-hearted people I've ever worked for.

'There were other nice things about working here at Beaulieu – for instance I used to fish a lot in the river. I had a small boat which I kept moored up in the trees, though I never used to catch very much; I did far better fishing in the pond behind the house that was stocked with trout. I used to take the present Lord Montagu fishing there, when he was a child, and there would be a real hullabaloo if he got his feet wet.

'There was also seine netting on the river every year, about three or four times each summer. Of course, we didn't have nylon ropes in those days, and those old heavy hemp ones made for hard work, even for six great men. It was up to me to organise the team, and we wouldn't attempt a trip unless we'd got a full comple-

ment. The fish were generally mullet or bass, or sometimes sea trout – the mullet were given around the village, the bass and sea trout stayed in the house! We also put some crab pots out, and had those once in a while.

'After the war, as I've said, I worked a little bit more at Beaulieu, cleaning windows and doing all sorts of odds and sods. And then my life changed yet again, and on a really major scale. There was a society lady here that I knew quite well, a woman called Mrs Varley. An old friend of hers was going off to America to run the British Embassy in Washington, and evidently he was having great trouble finding a butler – and Mrs Varley, bless her, decided that she knew exactly the right person for the job: me. So she came back and I was offered the post as butler to the ambassador at the British Embassy in America!

'Links with Beaulieu were maintained whilst I was over in the States. I met Lord Montagu at the Yacht Club at Palm Beach and actually waited

The present Lord
Montagu (third
from left) with his
mother, brothers
and sisters

John Walter
Edward Douglas
Scott-Montagu,
2nd Baron
Montagu of
Beaulieu, fishing on
Sowley's Pond,
in September 1907

The nursery at
Beaulieu

on him at a dinner over in the States whilst he was on a visit. I remember it was a sweating hot day, the temperatures well up into the nineties. I had to carve the ham, and I was hot and perspiring like a fountain, but I couldn't, obviously, wipe my face; so I would drop something on the floor on purpose so I could bend to retrieve it, and would then wipe myself with a napkin, hidden under the table!

'America was certainly an interesting experience, and I met a great many important people over there – including Sir Winston Churchill, whom I found to be a terrific man. He liked his wine, his cigars and a really good joke. I remember on one occasion all the members of the embassy staff went for tea on the royal yacht when it was in the harbour. I was told the story that on the Duke of Windsor's accession to the throne he went as king to the boat. He observed that the curtains were shabby in the stateroom, and said he would like them replaced. The head steward had to go to the Ministry of Works with the request, and was asked why the king wanted new curtains; he replied: "Well, that's easy. They

were made in Queen Victoria's time. They were turned in King Edward's time. They were cleaned in King George's time and now the new king has decided he wants some fresh ones!"

'I retired, finally, when I was seventy-one, and I'd had enough of it all by then. Looking back, I can see both ups and downs as a butler in the twentieth century. It was good to be in contact with some cultured and interesting people, and I also enjoyed a really good standard of living all the way through my life, especially in America. I lived in some lovely places, too. Of course, there were downsides; in Britain especially there are some people that treat any servant like a piece of furniture – you might just as well not exist for them, and I've never liked that. You are also on call twenty-four hours a day, and this is no exaggeration! You might think that you'd knocked off late at night, but there was always the possibility of accidents or a fire, and it was your job to see that the right people were called. I don't think there's a butler's wife in existence who would choose a butler for a husband the second time around, and I've never

encouraged my children to enter the profession, or even to think about it!

'I suppose my twenty-first birthday is a pretty good example of what I'm talking about. I was a footman at the time and I remember it was a wet Sunday. The family I was working for were golf crazy and they came in from the

Above: Acker Bilk and his jazz band on stage, before an excited crowd, at the Beaulieu jazz festival in July 1960

Right: The butler in his pantry, cleaning the silver

course wet and dirty. Of course, I'd already made them tea, then I had to make them supper and then I had to clean and dry all their clothes. It was midnight exactly when I got to bed, and I didn't even have time to drink my own health because I knew I'd have to get up at six o'clock the next morning. That was my twenty-first birthday! Nor do I think I ever had a Christmas Day off for over fifty years when I was a butler – but that's just the sort of thing a butler has to put up with. It's a style of life that's like no other; but looking back over the life I've led, I guess I would say that on balance it's all been worth it.'

Below: A part of the National Motor Museum which attracts thousands of visitors to Beaulieu each year

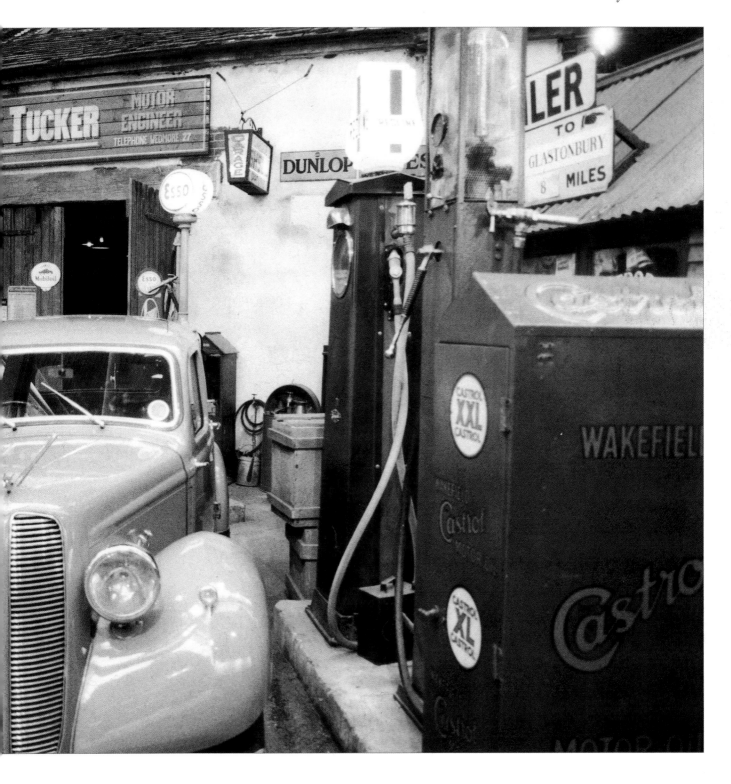

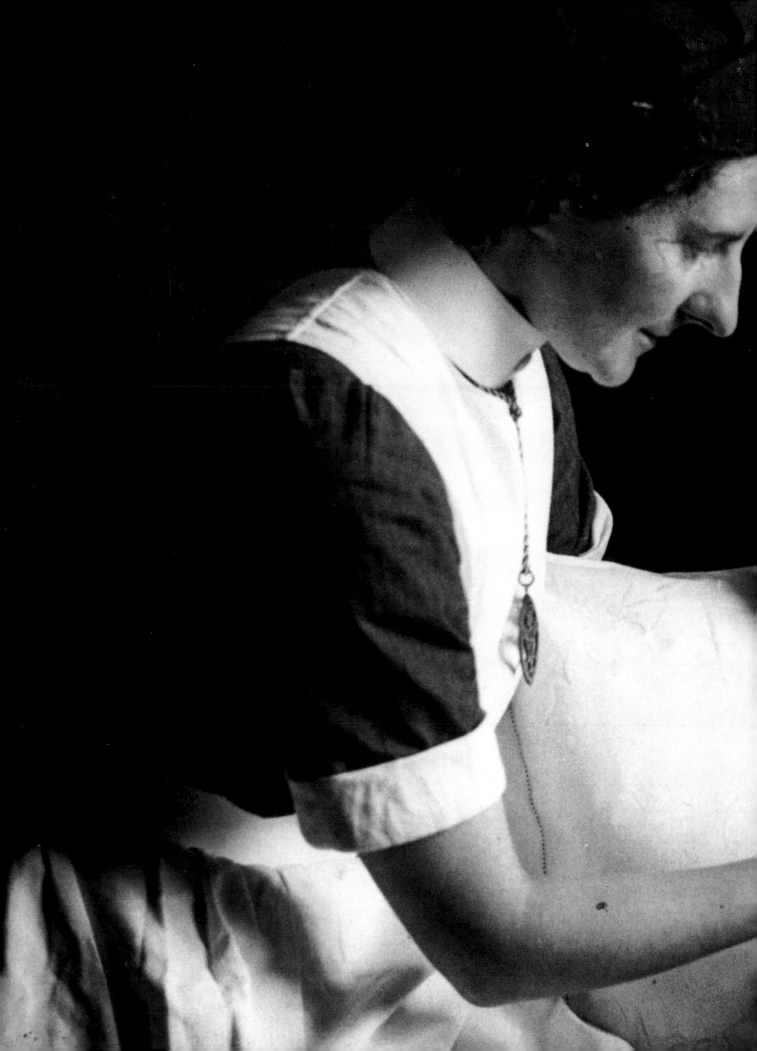

From Horseback to Helicopter

Joyce Damerell:
District Nurse and Midwife, Devon

FROM HORSEBACK TO HELICOPTER

During some thirty years as a district nurse and midwife, Joyce Damerell used many forms of transport: she started with her 'own flat feet', progressed to 'a cycle thing with a motorised back wheel', then in 1948 she was given her first car, a Humber; but much more reliable for visiting people in remote areas were her horse, her pony and trap, and the helicopter which had to be called in during the prolonged snow of early 1963, when most of the expectant mothers were evacuated.

But on one occasion in that record-breaking winter, when she was called out to Yelverton in a blizzard, Joyce had to walk to the neighbouring village of Crapstone to get a four-wheel-drive vehicle while the doctor made his own way on skis. Fortunately their mission was successful, managing to get their patient into hospital.

Joyce frequently had to abandon her car in severe weather and walk to isolated places on the moor. So whenever she changed her car she practised with the new model 'on long straights in the snow, to see how far it would slide. After all, it's no good discovering a weakness in a vehicle when you've got an emergency! Also, some of the roads were rougher in the old days, but at least that made them safer for horses.'

For most of her seventy-one years, Miss Joyce Damerell has enjoyed life at a cracking

pace. Whether galloping across the moor to deliver a baby or follow the fox, nursing sick villagers or nurturing puppies, she has had a zest for life which has left most people at the stable door. For years in the hunting field the cry 'Nurse!' was as familiar as the huntsman's horn, and Joyce's first-aid training was often welcomed by those who fell by her side.

There were many occasions on her rural round when Joyce found herself in a tricky situation; once she was even threatened with a shotgun! As she went about delivering a baby, the over-anxious mother of the young woman giving birth repeatedly warned: 'You know what you can expect if you don't do a good job,' at the same time pointing to a gun standing in the corner. Joyce recalls that fortunately the grandmother was on hand to keep everything on an even keel, and 'at least it was a very good shotgun – a Purdey!'

A farmer's daughter, an only child and self-confessed tomboy, Joyce Rose Damerell was born at Plymouth on 27 September 1925. Her greatest influence was her grand-father, a builder, with whom she lived till the age of fourteen. 'He was a great Shot and a good dog handler, and very strict too. He liked quiet, and if he wanted to attract my attention he'd soon throw a clod of earth past my ear.'

When Joyce was at St Dunstan's Abbey School, Plymouth, she wanted to be a vet, 'but lady vets weren't thought much of in those days'. So at the age of eighteen she went to the City Hospital Plymouth to become a state registered nurse. After her three-and-a-half years training she went to Paddington Hospital, London, where he sat her finals in midwifery.

Joyce was still only twenty-one when she had her first district, based at Overton, in Wiltshire. Her patch included half of Marlborough and went out to Silbury Hill. During the four years she was there the National Health Service was established (in 1948) and there was considerable conflict between the local health authority and the old nursing associa-

HORSING AROUND

The Wiltshire downs were ideal for developing an interest in horses, as Joyce recalls:

'It was a very good place for riding, up there on the Ridgeway. I got my Hunt button with the Tedworth. It was bestowed on me by the Master of Hounds, the Earl of Hardwick, and my greatest day was the first time I wore the Hunt collar, which was green on a black coat. I hired a horse from Lady Jimmy Wright, the famous showjumper, for £5 a day, which was a lot to me as I only earned about £300 a year. I was very proud, but unfortunately many of the horses then were dreadful, with no "braking system". I was given an Appaloosa which wasn't castrated till it was eight and was still very bossy. Then I bought my own horse from Oliver Dixon, the famous dealer at Chippenham, and an unkind ex-nursing association lady told me to get back into my station in life.

'Apart from sport, having a horse was a great advantage for generally getting about when petrol was restricted. It was quite something when rationing ended and I went to the garage and said: "Fill her up."'

tions, who lost their power and for whom the district nurse used to collect a few coppers from the local people. Joyce recalls the tremendous waste of money when the NHS was instituted: 'Of course, when anything's free everybody goes for it, but with my training I helped to bring a new attitude. At first there was excessive use of dressings and many people were given false teeth and supports when they'd previously done without. But the Government soon brought in stricter control.'

At Overton, Joyce was also the village school nurse, and the first thing she noticed was how bad the children's deportment was. 'The area still suffered greatly through the old serfdom system, with much tugging of forelocks, and no one paid any attention to the children.' To help rectify this, Joyce, who had many awards for competitive dancing, started to teach ballet to four girls in her drawing room. Almost overnight the class increased to about twenty, including pupils from the neighbouring village of Lockeridge, so the group had to move to the village hall.

On leaving Overton, Joyce took a post as a senior midwifery sister at Flete, the home of Lord Mildmay; he had offered the house as a maternity home for expectant Plymouth mothers away from the stress of the air raids on the town. As a result of this work, Joyce realised her calling was to district nursing and enrolled for a six-month course to become a Queen's nursing sister.

Joyce's first appointment, in 1953, was to the pretty village of Buckland Monachorum, between Tavistock and Plymouth. Her patch stretched from Postbridge and Dartmeet, in the middle of Dartmoor, to Clearbrook and Buckland Monachorum itself. She lived in a tied cottage which she later bought, and this is still her home. Apart from her work, a lifelong interest has been fieldsports; in particular the training of gundogs, at which Joyce has been

extremely successful. A person with whom Joyce shared these interests was an ex-vicar of Buckland Monachorum, whom Joyce recalls with great affection.

'He was Christopher Hughes, the parson before this one; he was also a sporting vicar and we got on famously as he established a shoot here. When he discovered my interest he said: "Ah, pointers! Well, they'll need something to point at!" and he showed me two or three hundred pheasants coming on nicely in his garden. As in other villages he also held the charity money with which I could buy prams, blankets and other things for anyone deserving. I generally bought the prams very cheaply at the local auction house, but there was little demand for them and so sometimes they were given to us. The charity money resulted from bequests but amounted to very little. One, for bread, was for only 10s a year, but this had been a substantial sum when first instituted centuries ago. In those days we had some really poor people whom we used to cook for. I tended to recommend the deserving people – mostly elderly folk or those out of work – to the Mothers' Union. There was no meals on wheels then like there is now.'

In addition to poverty, Joyce recalls some very primitive and insanitary conditions in her district, both in Wiltshire and on Dartmoor.

'Like most other fairly unspoilt areas, we had some genuine Romanies but they were always fascinating, and – through my work – some became great friends, bringing me horses to look at and giving me tea to drink. But we always went in twos to visit one family because you needed someone to keep granny under control while you did your work. She always wanted to be present at the birth of anyone in her family, but although their caravans were perfect, her hands were always dirty. The men were always sent outside, and they sat around a "witch's cauldron" boiling water for me; though before I could use it I had to skim the top off.

'But whatever the conditions, you always had to be careful not to offend people by refusing their hospitality. Generally I never had an alcoholic drink, except on Christmas Day when I was careful to start with a good, greasy breakfast to line the tummy! First stop would be at a certain old lady's by the river, where I'd be given blackberry wine. Then it was over to the old major for half a tumbler of gin, then on to someone else for port, or whatever. "Go on, it's good for you nurse," they'd say, and it was hard to resist. But what you couldn't do was take from one and refuse another, because they'd soon find out!

'Even so, there was one offer I had no hesitation in refusing. When I was at a squatters' camp on Marlborough Common this tramp asked me in for breakfast and made me look in the pot which he had hanging over an open fire. There was this chicken, not only unplucked but also undrawn! He told me he'd found it dead on the roadside.

'The camp had been a hospital during the war but was eagerly adopted by the homeless when it was abandoned. There was a great shortage of housing then and anywhere dry and warm was soon taken up. The camp people were on my patch and I had to look after them the same as anyone else.

'Also in Wiltshire, I used to visit this family who lived in the middle of a wood and were very poor. One day the mother's stew was just bacon bones and cabbage, with all this fat floating on the top. Poor woman, she could never get her words right. Once, when I was giving her a choice of immunisation dates she said: "Nurse, it's all *invenereal* to me". Another time, when I caught her on the hock and she was flustered, she said: "Nurse, I'm *prostitute*".

'Immunisation was quite an old thing, and at the mother-and-baby clinics we'd always given cod liver oil, concentrated orange juice and dried milk to combat deficiencies.

Joyce has long respected the moor people who have often had to endure very tough lives, and she has vivid memories of their fortitude.

'Over the years I've been here they've had to go out and feed their stock in some atrocious weather, and when I was out visiting it was quite a common occurrence to see one of the wives battling against a blizzard with a ewe across her shoulders, a sheep she'd dug out of the snow. But they can be cussed folk. Once I was called to the heart of the moor, but I lost my way in the dark and had to ask for directions at this remote farmhouse – and these people came to the door with a poker. A lot of moor folk had no electricity in the early days, but when it was laid on and television came in they became much more aware of a wider world. Also, better lighting helped me in my work.'

Inevitably, people who led very insular lives were particularly prone to superstition, although most of their beliefs, such as never take May blossom indoors, were harmless. However, taken to extremes by simple-minded folk, some of the old convictions led to tragedy, even as late as the 1970s. Sadly, one or two of Joyce's stories are so gruesome they must remain untold to protect the living relatives of victims.

By way of contrast, Joyce has also witnessed the good effects which strong beliefs can achieve. 'Dr Willington, an ex-general practitioner here, taught me about hypnosis, and together we trained expectant mothers in self-hypnosis; some were so successful they had no discomfort at all with their births. It's a shame that hypnosis has been so popularised on TV, because this has trivialised it and people are now afraid of making fools of themselves. Yet it's one of the best tools available. But a nurse can only use it with a doctor's permission, and they aren't all so keen.

'I've also seen animals helped with less conventional methods. One of the old healers, Mr German, was very good and did a lot with cattle, stopping bleeding and curing many ailments; I've even seen infections mysteriously disappear.

'With the introduction of the NHS the biggest change in maternity care was that the midwife could send for the doctor without asking the mother's position. This made us feel more in control. Previously mothers had resisted calling in the doctor because they had to pay. Admittedly many doctors did not charge those

---

LITTLE CREATURES

'Fleas were a common problem. One day when I went to turn the mattress of a 22-stone lady who'd been discharged from hospital after fracturing her hip, I was smothered with them; when I went home I had to take a bath with all my clothes on. So I approached the lady and told her about the old trick of using a wet bar of soap to catch them. But she was a sweet old soul and said: 'Nurse, don't 'e worry: every time I feels a bugger bite I catches 'im!' I was told that fleas didn't jump as high as Wellington boots, but that didn't help and in the end I infected my own house, as every time I returned home a few fleas would abandon ship before I reached the bathroom! There was very little help from the health authority in the control of fleas so all I could do then was suggest changing talc for DDT! Luckily, most people were very clean and would talk openly about their problems. It was always best to say: 'What are we going to do about it?' Then you had a partner rather than an enemy.

'Conditions were generally at their worst during the war, when I had scabies, impetigo and head lice repeatedly, even though you were supposed to wear a snood to keep your hair in.'

who couldn't afford it, but there was always a certain amount of pride involved.

'Also in 1948 we were given maternity boxes with sterilised pads and suchlike. Since then there has been such a change in outlook. Whereas we used to have to persuade mothers to go into hospital, with all the equipment on hand, now it is rare to have a baby at home.'

When Joyce first arrived at Buckland Monachorum, the care of the dead was quite different from today's routine. Here she describes the procedure followed in those days:

'When I first came here it was customary for the nurse not to lay people out too often as this task provided a little income for a local lady who was treated with the utmost respect in the community. And once or twice when I did it the local people were surprised when I forgot to open the windows: they believed this prevented the soul from going out, therefore leaving the body to rest in peace. Also, in the old days if you laid out a person you were off midwifery for forty-eight hours because of possible bugs. So altogether you tried not to do it. Nowadays the undertakers lay people out after you've notified the death.'

In a rural district, with relatively few people on hand to help, the ability to cope with accidents and emergencies was essential to Joyce's job, not least in midwifery. Quite a few of the hundreds of babies which she delivered on her own arrived in this world in very awkward places, including cars. Once Joyce thought she would have to deliver a baby on a mattress on the floor because the family concerned could not afford a bed, but 'something went wrong' and the mother was admitted before she actually delivered.

For some years now it has been the practice to admit to hospital all diagnosed cases of twins or other multiple births prior to delivery, but until recently 'forecasts' of such events were far less reliable. On one occasion Joyce was there 'just in time to catch the first of twins' and when the doctor arrived he said to her: 'I think you know more about it than me!'

When I asked Joyce if Christmas deliveries were special she replied: 'They may be to the mothers, but only a bit to the nurse because everybody's special and you're privileged to be there on the arrival of their baby. Also, you can't help thinking of the Christmas dinner you've left at home! Even now, after I've been retired twenty years, I get local people stopping me to say: "Don't you know what today is?" "No," I reply. Then they say something like, "Twenty-eight years ago today you delivered my son," as if they expect me to remember everything. But basically, as a district nurse you were a servant to the people, and you nursed a family right through.'

A nurse on an ABC scooter, a studio portrait taken in 1929. This was a popular and highly fashionable mode of transport before the war

At one time Joyce's kitchen was the waiting room to her surgery, and the facilities were used by the first chiropody clinic run by the Red Cross. Joyce's clinics were mainly attended by children coming home from school with cuts and bruises, as well as messages. Indeed, generations must have grown up with the idea that she was always there when needed. One of the best compliments she was paid was when a lad came to the door and said: 'Will you come now as Mother's very ill.' Without hesitation, Joyce picked up her bag and went to assist. But at the boy's house his mother was furious because she had only had a headache and had lain down on the sofa to rest! The resourceful lad had taken it upon himself to summon nurse Damerell.

Quite a few of Joyce's patients – and sometimes their relatives – had to be handled with considerable tact. Joyce remembers some of the more awkward ones:

'This old chap came to the door, his feet in a very bad way. His nails were so overgrown he'd cut holes in his shoes to let them through, so he asked me to cut them. I said: "OK, but you must soak them in soda first." This was duly done and I went back on another day to do the dressing. But when I asked the wife if she would like me to bathe her husband while I was there she screamed blue murder: "You hussy you, taking advantage of my husband; clear off!"

'Sometimes the elderly gentlemen were quite flirtatious, even in their eighties. If they were alone a lot up in their bedrooms, and you went to do things such as blanket baths, they could get a little bit wild. Some old chaps would actually say: "I'm being a naughty boy, aren't I nurse?" yet they'd still carry on. But you had to treat every patient as an individual. Some of the ninety-year-olds were very self-possessed, and you had to be a little bit careful as they were looked on with esteem!

'In the old days a lot of people were very wary – they didn't talk much to the outside world, and you had to treat them with sensitivity and consideration. You couldn't just breeze in and lay down the law. It was generally much better to bide your time and, perhaps while admiring their bullocks, casually offer to return the following day to give gran a wash and brush-up, or whatever.'

Over four decades Joyce has seen many changes in and around Buckland Monachorum. Here she describes some of the most important:

'There has been a considerable rise in the population, yet there has been a fall in the number of shops, from three grocers, a wool shop and a separate post office to just one which incorporates the post office. However, we have managed to keep our one excellent pub, The Drake Manor. There used to be a great many Nissen huts which were used for housing, but the council moved the people out onto new estates. Since then, commuters have moved in to many of the better houses, but they have really supported the village well, and taken it over to good effect.

'The hall was originally built by the WI and run by them only, with two meetings a month, but as time went by interest diminished. Now the building has a billiard hall attached; it is known as the village hall, and is mostly run by the

LAMBS' TAIL STEW

Lambs' tails were a favourite Devon dish early this century, often cooked in the open field. After scalding, the wool was pulled off, the tails soaked in salted water overnight, dried, rolled on a warm surface to remove any remaining wool, washed again, cut up, boiled until nearly tender, and cooked in a pie with chopped onion and seasoning.

commuters. Groups such as the Brownies, Guides, Scouts and youth club are all important to village spirit, too.

'I used to be a governor of the old local school, which has now been converted into two nice dwellings. The new school is only twenty years old and is well made, it takes children up to eleven and has good teachers. Also, we are lucky in that it is a church school, with the vicar's frequent contact.

'We used to have tremendous village flower shows, with the longest beans and all that, but the gardens are not the same now and people don't have the time to grow so much. But we still get good flowers and cakes displayed.

'Once there were lots of hares and partridges hereabouts, but I wouldn't know where to find even one now, and there are only a few grouse left on the high moor. The Dartmoor National Park is trying to stop us working dogs up there, but what we do is very important as we are asked by the great moors in the north of England and Scotland to help with pre-shooting season grouse counts. There was a time when I was an adviser to the national park, but not now. Overall, the decline in songbirds and flowers has

Left: During severe winters the helicopter was, and is, an important lifeline for isolated rural communities

The local health visitor weighing a newborn baby, delivered at home, in the early 1960s

Opposite: A children's clinic, where babies were weighed, assessed and treated, in operation in the 1950s

not been particularly significant round here, but the red tape has increased tremendously. There's a special orchid on the moor and nobody is allowed to pick it – but when you talk to the old people they say they used to gather it by the bunch every year, yet plenty always remained.

'I used to be on the parochial church council, and I regard a good church as the centre of a rural village. When I came here we had a Baptist chapel as well as the COE church, St Andrews, which now shares a vicar with Milton Combe. All the enthusiastic Baptists of former times have died, but the chapel remains as a Baptist hostel and hall used for general village activities.

'St Andrews is now well supported by all ages and has become something of a music centre. We have a very good group there, with instruments such as guitar, piano, flute and oboe, and some people come to church just to hear them or our excellent choir. It's all much more relaxed in church now, with less formal dress; in the old days, if two people attended with the same hat there'd be panic!

'The only real controversy at church now is over this new concept of christening. In the past I've christened sick babies which looked poorly, with no questions asked – that has always been accepted practice for nurses; then the children were christened properly afterwards. But these days it has all become much too complicated, with godparents now being obliged to attend pre-christening talks and to watch videos to make sure they know what their commitment is. This is turning many people away from church, when all should be accepted without question. It's later, with confirmation, that all the serious stuff can be addressed.'

Joyce regards Buckland Monachorum as 'a lovely, balanced village, with lots of history; a place where I can go to church, put my hand on that end pew and think of all the previous generations which have been there.' Out in the streets she enjoys speaking to everybody, and always gets a wave when people pass. But then, she did deliver many of them.

Sadly, Joyce died in 1997.

Putting the Queen Second

Gamekeeper: Berkshire, Buckinghamshire, Wiltshire and Gloucester

PUTTING THE QUEEN SECOND

When Tom Walter was presented with a long-service medal at the Game Fair in 1989 he was, of course, honoured to receive it from the Queen, but secretly he was much more excited about meeting someone else. That year the fair was held at Stratfield Saye, the home of the Duke of Wellington, enabling Tom to fulfil a very special ambition. All his life he had wanted to meet His Grace, to tell him about his great-grandfather, who had been gamekeeper to the First Duke of Wellington, the hero of Waterloo, serving Stratfield Saye for fifty-six years.

A kind friend had arranged the meeting and for Tom it could not have come quickly enough. But on the day he was last in a line of ten keepers up for awards. 'The Queen said, "That's a long wait Walter, but now you can meet the duke himself", and then he stepped forward.' It was a fitting tribute to a remarkable career.

Christened Thomas Walter ('There's no s on the end even though everyone calls me Walters') was born on 18 October 1908, at Hurst, near Reading in Berkshire. Surprisingly, neither Tom's father nor grandfather were keepers before him, but he did have a keepering uncle on the Haineshill Estate.

'Granny had four sons, all in the Scots Fusiliers in the Great War. Two came 'ome and two got killed. Father was a foreman bricklayer at only nineteen – now that's a credit! He could even show you the join where two bricklayers had worked on one house. Of course, I could never see any difference. And he was also a wonderful Shot at pigeons.'

Tom's mother did not work. 'She was too busy with me and my six brothers and four sisters. All my sisters are still going, and two of my brothers. I am the only one of the family to have been a gamekeeper.'

When Tom was at Hurst school, 'Just over the 'edge was Elijah J. Hicks, the famous rose grower who used to sweep the board at Chelsea. He was the only man ever 'ad a black rose. I saw it once, but it died with 'im. We used to see 'im in his greenhouse at night studying the plants.'

To earn a bit of pocket money while at school, Tom delivered the *Football Chronicle*, 'on Saturday nights. I got about two bob for taking thirty or forty papers. I picked 'em up from Reading Station, where each lot was rolled up in a cardboard tube. When I took 'em round all the people was waitin' at the gates for you so they could get the results.'

Tom's earliest memories of shooting are from when he was about twelve. 'We used to go beatin' different places to stand stop. At lunchtime we had lovely salt beef and cheese sandwiches, a bottle of pop and two shillings. The men had five bob.'

He also managed to make a little money from another sport. 'Three of us used to run a rat and sparrow club, when we were teenagers. We went round with clap-nets, all about the 'edges and the ivy on the buildin's. Our torch mesmerised the birds and they were soon caught. We tore their 'eads off and took 'em to the farmers, along with the rats which we used to get when we lifted up the floors on the poultry farms. The farmers had a competition to see who could get the most and the winner was announced at the flower show. We used to kill 400-500 rats a year and gettin' on for a thousand sparrows. We won all four years we entered – got about £4 for the sparrows and £4 for the rats, between the three of us. That was a lot then.

'Years ago there was sparrows everywhere – it was nothin' to get 300 or more in the edge of a wheatfield. We used to get dust shot and if you fired into 'em just right you got dozens. Everyone had sparrow pie then. They pulled the legs out and split the breasts for it. These were the only parts worth keeping. But a lot of the time sparrows were fed to the ferrets which we used to get rats.

'Sparrows are lovely sweet birds, not like a lot of 'em such as the robin and all the tits, which are bitter. With starlings you 'ave to pull their 'eads off and then they are all right. We also used to catch birds such as goldfinches and linnets in the clap-nets, but let them go.'

Tom left school at the age of fourteen to work with his father. 'I think the first thing we did together was build a sectional bungalow, mostly working on the foundations. I always remember this because they had a water diviner to set the well before placing the house.

'In 1925, headkeeper Jim Martin asked me to be his only underkeeper at Bill Hill, near Hurst. My elder brother, who worked in the garden, got twenty-five shillings a week, but I got thirty shillings as I had to work weekends. Mr Martin even arranged with the police for me to carry a gun on the road at seventeen, when it should have been eighteen. The shooting was let to Thomas Haig, the whisky man, and he was my boss – a very nice man. Shooting was much more fun in those days. Give me the old ways – crack a few jokes then on to the next drive. Each season they only shot three or four times for cocks and hens and once for cocks.'

At Bill Hill Tom had no special perks, 'but always on the last drive of the year Mr Haig called me out of the woods and gave me a new

ten-shilling note. He also said that I would get a bottle of port from Martin. But one of the best tips I ever had was in the thirties. K. V. Peppiat – the chief cashier of the Bank of England – gave me a brand new pound note. That was a lot then.

'I looked after one half of the Bill Hill shoot. There was a beautiful, steep valley, but they put the M4 right through it and there's only a little bit of my wood left now. We had a few wild partridges, but most of the work was on 500-600 reared pheasants, which was quite a few in those days. There was a lot of work, with broody hens and the coops twenty-five yards apart. We'd cut a bough off a tree and put it at the back of a coop. Then if anythin' came over the hen would go, brrr brrr, and the chicks ran for cover under the branch till she said come out again. I much preferred the old system of open-range pheasant rearing, rather than the pen rearing you get today. The broody hens really taught the chicks how to protect themselves and it made better shooting.

'Poor old Jim Martin had a sad end to his career. When he went to Haineshill he showed somebody where a 500lb bomb had dropped durin' the war. He was standing on the edge of the crater and as he turned round he tripped on some bushes and 'is gun went off and shot 'im in the thigh. People tore up shirts best they could to stop the bleeding and rushed him to Reading hospital, but the leg had to come off. Obviously, he couldn't work after that.'

After three years at Bill Hill, Tom decided it was time, 'to better meself and apply for various jobs. I could 'ave 'ad the job old Charlie South took at Windsor, but I turned it down as there were too many restrictions. You even 'ad to hand your jacket back if you left because of the buttons with the royal insignia on.

'In those days Crufts was the place to get a job. Old Cruft sold dog biscuits and was really interested in keepers. But anyway, I put an advert in the *Gamekeeper* magazine and 'ad a telegram from Parmore, near Marlow in Buckinghamshire. I went up one Friday. Tell you what, that's my lucky day: whenever I went I got the job.

'So I cycled up through Henley – about sixteen miles – and got there around 2.30 or 3pm. The Honourable Seddon Cripps, Lord Parmore's elder son, interviewed me in his office. He seemed satisfied, but I 'ad to wait for the other keeper to come back from the family's other estate. Meanwhile I went into the kitchen to 'ave tea with the maids and cooks.

'The keeper asked me to start as his second on the Monday, but on Sunday there was about three inches of snow, so I didn't get there till about 12 o'clock on me first day. It was a job even to push the bike so I left it halfway. Then I took me case to Skirmett, where the keeper had fixed me up with lodgin's in the council houses.

'The shoot was let to a lovely man – Sir Sydney Sitwell – and there were big plans for it. We 'ad the local carpenter and his son making 250 coops in a barn for us. There were stacks of wood everywhere. The carpenter also fitted out a shepherd's hut with a stove, foldin' table and gauze-fronted larder and I slept in there on the rearing field for four years. But when I was in lodgin's I 'ad to pay twenty-five shillings a week out of thirty-five shillings wages, which was above the agricultural rate in those days.

'At Parmore it always fascinated me why the pheasants stayed at home because it was all

FEEDING TIME

'Now it's all crumbs and pellets, but in my early days we cooked up our own feed for the chicks. There were three sizes of biscuit meal – fine, medium and coarse. For the first three or four weeks the chicks had the fine scalded in a pan, mixed with boiled eggs pushed through a sieve, and boiled rice – there was an art in cookin' that. If you pressed it and there was three white spots in the grain that was the time to take it off. If it was too pudding you 'ad a job to part it. You see the grains looked like maggots and that's what attracted the birds.

'For the older birds in the wood, farmers often used to bring us carcasses and we'd hang 'em up in the trees to get maggots, which would fall out. The pheasants loved scratchin' around for those. 'As the chicks got older they had Dari seed, buckwheat, hempseed, split peas and groats – that's oats with the husks off, chopped up and kibbled. Yes, there was a beautiful variety of food you could buy then.

'We used to 'ave a bit of fun with the Dari. If you covered a hen's eye and pointed the other at one of the white seeds, and then let her go, she'd stay there mesmerised for some time.'

beeches – thousands of 'em – with hardly any cover at all. Wherever you got a few stunted little bushes there'd be dozens of birds in there. But we had the land for some wonderful shooting. The M40 cuts through the estate now.

'We 'ad two hermits there. One had 'is hair right down 'is back. He used to get on the bus and people called 'im Jack Frightenem. The other one was called Luxster Jack and 'e came down to the village to get 'is ten-shilling pension and a few groceries each week. He could also catch a rabbit and anythin' to keep 'imself goin'. He made a shack on my beat and the roof was packed with bracken to keep warm. One day the police told me he was dead and they'd had to shoot 'is dog to get at 'im. He was a lovely chap – never hurt anyone.

'Near old Luxster Jack there was a whirly 'ole – one of those springs that bubbles up. If you got a bottle with a cork in and put it out in the middle it would suddenly disappear – *oooosh*. Nobody knew where it went.

'After lunch we only had one drive and would blank in all the 'angin' [hangers – steep hillside woods] for three-quarters of a mile. This took between an hour and one and a half hours and the nine Guns – five in the first line – shot 300-400 pheasants. We always had a policeman with us on shoot day – 'e was paid of course.'

With such large bags, Tom and his colleagues obviously needed a lot of feed. 'We used to get it by the lorry-load from James and Chamberlain of Hungerford, and the Polish eggs came in crates of 500. I 'ad two boilers for these out in the field.

'Then one day the headkeeper was throwing coconuts at Thame Show and twisted his knee. He told the boss he did it in a rabbit hole, and next shoot 'e sent another keeper in his place, rather than me. The boss said, "Where's Walter?" So I thought – look out for yourself here! It was time to move on. I didn't want to get involved with anyone tellin' lies. I always say tell the truth and you'll never go wrong.'

Tom then applied for a job, 'at Dashwood's place at West Wycombe. But when I saw the head

HEARSON'S
PATENT
Champion Incubators

FOR
HATCHING POULTRY,
GAME, AND OSTRICHES.

Made with adjustable drawer bottom for different sizes of eggs. Fitted with Copper Tanks.

Foster Mothers
(The " Hydrothermic ")

FOR OUTDOOR
REARING
OF CHICKENS IN
WINTER
OR SUMMER.

Show Rooms: 235, REGENT STREET, LONDON, W.
Write for Illustrated Price List to Sole Agents :

SPRATT'S PATENT LTD.,
24 & 25, FENCHURCH STREET, LONDON, E.C.

he was in hell of a stew. He'd put poison in a rabbit for vermin, just where some children walked through the wood to catch a bus. So when one girl dropped dead on the bus he thought she'd taken the rabbit home. But the verdict was heart failure.

'Anyway, the shoot moved to Ramsbury in Wiltshire and they asked me to go down there. It was run by Thomas Forbes, the insurance broker. But my wife – I married Grace in 1932 – had to stop with mother till the house was available.'

'At Ramsbury we 'ad this poacher called Monty Fox – and 'e was crafty too. Well, with the partridges my main job was finished by the end of June, so I asked if I could 'ave a few pheasants in the wood – to amuse me. So I did. But the head said, 'What shall we do about Monty?' I said,

'Just give him a couple of bob extra on beatin' day – at least if 'e's here you know where he is.'

At the time, Tom used to enjoy longnetting. 'That's the way to sweep the rabbits up. One night we had seventy-five. Only thing was you really 'ad to know your ground. Run into a patch of thistles or something and that soon snags you up. We used to go out three or four times a week. Now no one knows the trade. We could 'ave 200 yards of net pegged out in three and a half minutes. Two men would drive in – zigzaggin' – and you 'ad to guess a bit as you might be in front of each other in the dark. A chap took our rabbits to London twice a week and we always looked forward to him comin' round because he brought back lots of fruit, from the market.

'One night I heard thump, thump, thump. It was the headkeeper kickin' a fox, but 'e got out. Worst thing to 'ave in a net was an ol' hare –

'e used to thrash about an' squeal an' frighten everythin' off.

'Another time we started to put the net out when all the rabbits came runnin' by before our men came in. I thought we must be in front of another net – and we were. It was Monty's. So we gave 'im half a dozen rabbits and told 'im to go home and pack it in.

'Monty used to walk through a wood and shoot all the birds on the way back after he'd seen where they were, so that he was in and out as quickly as possible. There was this old tin bath by his gate where birds were left for collection, and one day the police was gonna catch 'im. So they got in the shed opposite and waited. Eventually the carrier came by, looked under the bath and out came the police. But there was nothin' there and off they went very disappointed. Half an hour later the carrier's son

GILBERTSON & PAGE'S
CAMLIN

We feel confident in saying that the word CAMLIN is now an absolute household word among game rearers, and that so long as gapes attack game or poultry so long will CAMLIN be used as a preventive or cure.

2/3 and 3/6 per tin postage paid.

CAMLIN CURES GAPES.

Gapes, like nearly all other diseases, is more easily prevented than cured. Camlin is not only a cure, but is of great value as a preventive, and rearers recognise that an outbreak may make vast strides and cause serious losses if Camlin is not on hand for immediate application. Camlin possesses valuable properties, for it is an excellent disinfectant, and a coop after the brood therein has been dressed with it is in a much more sweet and healthy condition. Camlin has also good effect in preventing Roup, a far more deadly disease than even Gapes, for when inhaled it acts as an antiseptic in the air-passages.

The Symptoms of Gapes, consist of a snicking or sneezing noise in the earliest stage, which soon develops into gasping, as air cannot reach the lungs down the choked passages. These sounds may be detected sooner if listened for in the morning before the brood is released from the coop, as transfer to the clear air outside often causes relief, and their consequent cessation till the disease has made further and regret- table progress.

JUST IN TIME.

I've had some!

CAMLIN CURES GAPES

2/3 and 3/6 per tin postage paid.

How to use Camlin. Place a coop of birds attacked with gapes as far from the others as possible, and then thoroughly stop up all air-holes by throwing a bag or rug over it. Fill one of our bellows with Camlin, insert the nozzle beneath the coop, and blow in sufficient of the powder to thoroughly impregnate the air within. It is not strictly necessary that the cure should be undertaken at night ; birds may be dressed at any time if they can be shut in. Be careful to thoroughly rouse the hen before blowing in the Camlin ; if this is not done, those with their heads thrust in her feathers will not inhale a sufficient quantity of Camlin. A little experiment first with an empty coop will enable one to judge the quantity of Camlin blown in.

GILBERTSON & PAGE'S
Bellows for distributing Camlin.

Metal Bellows. These Bellows hold sufficient Camlin for about 10 coops.

5/6 each. *Postage paid.*

Large Improved Camlin Bellows. Full length 24 in. Very useful for large rearers. Hold sufficient powder for about 30 broods.

18/6 each. *Postage paid.*

India-Rubber Camlin Distributors. Very popular among poultry fanciers.

No. 1, **2/9** each, *postage paid.*
No. 2, **1/3** ,,   ,,   ,,

turned up and then the birds were in place. The thing is, the police shouldn't 'ave blabbed about what they was gonna do.'

In 1936 Forbes warned Tom to start looking for another job because he expected to lose most of his money following a shipping disaster. As a result, through recommendation Tom secured his first single-handed position, for Major Huth at Wansdyke End, Inkpen, near Hungerford, Berkshire. 'He and his wife had two Wolseley cars with numbers one after the other. The shoot was 1,600 acres in one big block, with only a little wood. It was all partridges on top of the downs and a forty-foot wide sheep drove went all the way to Marlborough.'

After a year the major asked Tom if he could do anything about the moles. He replied, 'Yes, but we'll need a lot of traps.' So I got ten dozen. Well, you can only catch moles in quantity from the first week in March to mid-April, so this worked in well with my Euston system.

The major and me used to listen to this series on the wireless about a professional mole catcher. One day he said to me, "Did you hear the professional caught sixty-five moles in a 19-acre field?" I said, "I can beat that – I've caught ninety-two in four days in a 15-acre field".

'Altogether, in Wiltshire I caught about 4,000 moles in five years. One place I would catch four or five in the same trap in one day. They like a damp path best. Twice I've caught two moles in one trap going in opposite directions at the same time. Later on, in Gloucestershire, I caught twenty-two moles, one weasel and one toad in a trap that was never moved. That was in a grass garden path.

'I used to sell the skins to Friends for a penny or tuppence. Cock pheasant centre-tail feathers fetched a penny each and a lot of chaps used to slip a few out unnoticed during the big shoots. Magpie tails and pairs of wings were worth fourpence each and jays' wings about threepence a pair.'

Tom did not have to go to war. 'When it started the major said to me, "When does your

THE EUSTON SYSTEM

Ramsbury was in partridge country and Tom operated the old Euston system. 'I wish they'd do it today, we might get the grey partridges back. The idea was to find nests when the birds started to lay, pick up the eggs and put wooden ones in their place. When a clutch got to eleven I stopped putting the dummies in. I always operated in odd numbers because birds can count in twos! I always 'ad a string of eggs with me. Just cut one off and rub it off a bit. They were made by friends – mostly from beech – and were much cheaper than the bought ones.'

While the real eggs were in Tom's care they were safe from predators and sudden weather changes. 'Twenty or so would be set under a broody hen. Then, when they were chipping at twenty-two days or so I put them back in the wild nests. It was always best to get them away before they double-chipped at twenty-three days because they could hatch under your shirt as you walked round. I've carried as many as sixty chipped eggs next to me chest. I 'ad a belt round me so they couldn't drop down. People say to me didn't they die of cold, but they kept quite warm for a surprisingly long time.

'It's a wonderful thing to watch the partridges. You often 'ad to poke 'em off the nest with a stick and I've 'ad them fly up and knock me cap off before. As they were hatching off, the cock would come and sit by the hen to help dry the chicks off.

'The only thing wrong with the system was I was the only one who knew where all the nests were. So I said to the old headkeeper, "I'd better show you where they all are in case anything happens to me". He said, 'How on earth do you find all these nests?' I suppose it's a gift.'

A SIXTH SENSE

In everything he does, Tom appears to be blessed with a sixth sense. 'I suppose it's a gift. If you're out in the woods waitin' for a stoat, suddenly you know it's there even before you look round.

'One evening I was stood by this chap watchin' the pheasants go to roost when suddenly the whole lot got up and flew to the other end of the wood. He said, "There must be someone in there". But I said, "No, somethin's goin' to happen tonight". And sure enough it did – we had five inches of snow. Nature's a wonderful thing, but if you want to know it properly you've got to live with it all the time.'

Unashamedly superstitious, Tom has had quite a few unnerving experiences in foretelling events, some extremely sad. 'We 'ad a blackbird used to come out 'ere on the wire and whistle away while my wife was unwell up in the bedroom. Then one day as we were going out my daughter said, "What's that black thing on the ground by the gate? Someone must have dropped a glove". But I knew it was the blackbird and told her to go on. I would pick it up. And my wife died that evening.

'That was four years ago and people say to me, "Don't you ever get lonely?" But I say no – I've been lonely all my life in the woods. And here I've got some wonderful neighbours and friends, as well as a son and daughter who visit me. Also, there's the birds on the nuts all the time. I've had over thirty tits at once.

'But I really miss the birdlife there used to be. We don't get half the numbers now. Down in my woods there was always half a dozen chiffchaffs or willow warblers, but now there's hardly one. And back in Berkshire there were lots of nightingales.'

age group come up?" I said, "It can't be long as all my six brothers are in it already". He said, "I'll stop that – it's far too much for one family". And he did, bein' an Army man himself.

'We had a rifle range on the estate – right in the corner of Wiltshire and Berkshire – and I looked after it for the Home Guard. The Americans came there too and we used to get a few sticks of Wrigley's spearmint from them. At the same time I carried on with my Euston system. We had twenty-five old English gamebirds, so there was always plenty of hens.

'There were a lot of interesting guests on the shoot, including the Marquis of Aylesbury from Savernake Forest. He trained fox terriers to find truffles and came over to us with his headkeeper in a chain-driven Trojan car.

'In 1946 the major called me in and asked me to check over his pair of Cogswell & Harrisons, which I always looked after anyway. He told me he was too old to shoot any more and was going to sell the guns back to the makers. He said that if I see another job I should take it, but if I wanted to I could work in the woods.'

That year Tom took a job as single-handed keeper at Adbury Park, near Newbury in Berkshire. 'It was an old family shoot and they didn't care if you only got twenty or thirty a day. I left in 1952 when they was goin' to let the house as a boys' school. I thought, that's no good with boys runnin' all over the place.'

Tom's next stop was Salperton Park, in Gloucestershire, working for the Hulton family – 'the *Picture Post* people. Dr Zezi, a Harley Street man, looked after the shooting. I always remember when I went for interview, it was the day King George VI died. The master at Stroud station told me the news and when I passed it on to the people in the carriage they said rubbish!'

Life at Salperton was quite traumatic for Tom. 'Dangerous! Corrr! I remember old man (Sir Edward) Hulton shooting a pheasant on the wall and all the shot came back through me and the beaters. And we had some well-known guests too, including the authors A. G. Street and Macdonald Hastings.

'There was one time Sir Edward was determined to shoot a hare, but we walked all day and he couldn't shoot anythin'. Then I got really fed up, so when 'e fired I fired too and at last we bagged one. He never did know. I didn't want to walk no further.'

After just two years, Tom could not stand Salperton any longer. 'The farm manager didn't like 'untin' and shootin' at all and did everythin' he could to spoil it. He even got a gang of gypsies to camp right by my shoot, when they were supposed to be potato pickin'.'

In 1954 Tom's fortunes changed, when he went to work at Northleach, Gloucestershire, on Colonel Raymond Barrow's Farmington estate. 'He was a proper military man. If 'e said 'e was goin' to pick me up at six it had to be six — not quarter to or quarter past! But he was a lovely man.'

Tom has lived and worked on the Farmington Estate ever since, the first thirty-one years in one house, up to his retirement from full-time work in 1985, when he moved to his present cottage. 'I still look after a little bit of wood, helpin' Captain John Barrow's present keeper.'

Remarkably, Tom has never learned to drive or owned a vehicle, but that has never stopped him carrying out his duties efficiently. He believes that when you drive about you do not really see what is going on in the countryside. Yet, as Captain Barrow says, 'everybody knows him for miles around and he always knows what's going on before everybody else. He is a wonderful character and a real countryman.'

Tom is obviously very knowledgeable when it comes to birds and has been lucky enough to find a few rarities in his time. 'The most unusual was a pair of hoopoes — my father saw them too. Another time, in Gloucestershire, there was a foot of snow in the woods and as I walked through all these bits fell down on me. It was a flock of crossbills feeding in the trees above. And

Tom, at home,
reflecting on the
old times

I've only once found the nest of a hawfinch, It was halfway up an oak tree on a tuft. You can always tell hawfinches because as they fly along they've got a certain twitter.'

This great knowledge of birdlife has been especially useful to Tom in vermin control. 'I don't believe in traps. Only do it if you've got to. If you happen to get took bad no one but you knows where that trap is. I only used the old pole traps and ginns when they was legal and there was a very bad case, but I never used poisons.

'You can get everythin' you like if you go at the right time. Always remember that birds of a feather flock together. At one place the carrion crows come four miles to roost in a certain wood – way up in the trees. Only snag is it's a long way home in the dark. Anyway, I put this jackdaw on a fishing line and pulled it in a field where the crows used to gather before goin' up to the roost. By golly, didn't they come down to mob it I got seventeen the first night. A lot of keepers also used to attract crows with a ferret on a line.

'With magpies too the best thing is to walk about and find their roost. They like a patch of

bramble in a big wood. Then you want a good wind and shoot 'em. One place I had sixteen in an evening, and I could 'ave got more if I could see in the dark.

'Foxes have never been a big problem. I could call one up anywhere. Once I called two right through my legs! Mating time's always the best because then they've only the one thing on their mind.'

Jackdaws have given Tom a few headaches. 'At Ramsbury they used to get in the pen first thing in the morning and take the pheasants' eggs. One day I was cycling downhill on my way to deal with 'em when a rabbit ran into the spokes of me front wheel and drove the stays of the mudguard up and into my arm as I went over the top. See – I've still got the scars. Mind you, the rabbit came off worse – 'e ended up with a neck a yard long.'

On another occasion Tom was injured by a horse. 'I never liked them much anyway. We were playin' cricket and I went to get the ball when this colt lashed out, split me lip and knocked me senseless.'

But Tom's most serious injury was not at the hands of an animal. 'It was about twelve years ago on the last shoot day that year. I was runnin' through the wood when a bit of nut stick stuck in me eye and snapped off.' At the time Tom did not think too much of it but eventually it caused problems with the sight of both eyes, which he has sometimes lost despite several operations. Today he still has problems focusing and finds it very hard to read.

Fortunately, Tom has never been seriously injured by a poacher, but he has helped to nab a few. 'When I was at Inkpen, the nearby keeper at Fosbury, Ronnie Legg, used to hear a few shots before he went off in the morning. I said, "that must be one of your own people as he seems to know exactly when you're around. You want to go off and then come back unexpectedly." So 'e did, and it turned out to be the estate plumber, who was sacked a couple of days later.

'When I was at Adbury Park I knew keeper Charlie Maber of Highclere – Lord Carnarvon's castle. He said 'e 'ad someone gets a pheasant occasionally but he didn't know who. I said, "Does anyone come up to see you regularly?" He said, "Yes". Turned out it was 'im too. Whenever this man came over to see Charlie 'e stood 'is gun by a tree and bagged a bird on the way back. You've really got to try to out-think some of these people.'

Inevitably, gypsies were involved in many of the poaching incidents in Tom's day, but they also had their uses – as the providers of magical cures. Perhaps the most bizarre Tom ever encountered was during his time in Buckinghamshire. 'This man 'ad this tapeworm which all the experts just couldn't shift. Then a gypsy told 'im that the only way was to go out next time it was raining to get one of those big, black slugs. Then he had to swallow the slug after puttin' it in salt water to get rid of the slime. It worked all right because I saw the tapeworm in the yard. It must have been thirty or thirty-five feet long.'

Throughout all these adventures, Tom has encountered some very severe weather. Not surprisingly, his memories of the bitter winter of 1962–3 remain sharp as Gloucestershire was hard hit. 'One day the colonel said to me, "Let's go and see the snow." So off we went, and there was this coffin stuck in an 'earse. It was there for three weeks. Then there were stranded lorry drivers all over – goodness knows what they did for food.

'The colonel used to ride down on his white horse, Stuffy, to get the village post. And we was forever diggin' people out. Then we got a snowplough for the village. Nowadays, Derek from the farm gets out with it whenever the snow sets in. But some of these people moan, "What's Derek doin' clatterin' about at night?" So I say to them you weren't 'ere in '63. If you 'ad been you'd soon be glad of it.

'One of the worst times of all was the first year of the last war. Everythin' was froze up – even a piece of grass was wide as a board. If you could run you'd catch the hares, the ice was that thick on their backs. Loads of branches, even whole trees, came down with the weight of ice. The milkman never came for three weeks. When I managed to get my shed door open I left it open as I'd never do it again. I went to help the shepherd get 'is sheep and when 'e dropped 'is stick it shot downhill at a terrific rate. And when the sheep was down to the hay you 'ad to watch out – they'd be on top of you they was so hungry. All the rabbit holes were almost frozen right over and the rabbits lived off the chalk – their mouths and teeth were all white.'

Today these intriguing observations of wildlife form but one tiny part of the vast nature encyclopaedia in Tom Walter's memory. Few people have known the outdoors so intimately or served their masters so well. Even his great-grandfather would have been hard-pressed to match such a record.

'He was told to swallow the slug'

Much to his credit

*John Gwynne: Shopkeeper,
Talgarth, Powys*

MUCH TO HIS CREDIT

It was wholly appropriate that 'J. Gwynne & Son' was voted the 'best village store' in 1994-5, having been the runner-up in a previous year, and John Gwynne assuredly deserves this acclaim having dispensed first-class service and extremely generous credit to the citizens of Talgarth for almost three-quarters of a century. Such benevolence is partly due to the fact that many Gwynne customers are farmers who have always been used to paying on account – most on a weekly, monthly or quarterly basis, but some still half-yearly! John even used to allow twelve months' credit, but was forced to rein back on such a lenient 'slate' as inflation accelerated and credit became tight all round. He admits: 'You could never ask regulars to pay up before time for risk of offending them.'

John Hugo Gwynne was born on 20 February 1921 at the Crescent Stores, Church Road, Talgarth, where his family had been in business since 1883. But his grandfather, William H. Gwynne, first set up shop two doors away in 1881, 'in the front room of Merlin House' about half a mile from the village centre.

In those days of relatively poor transport and communications, remote towns and villages such as Talgarth had to be much more self-sufficient, so most businesses had plenty of healthy competition. However, although his enterprise has come out on top, John regrets the demise of so many others: 'In Talgarth there used to be five petrol places, whereas now there are none. The ten pubs have been reduced to three, both cobblers have gone,

William Gwynne established the family business in 1881

and all the drapers and the greengrocers have closed; also the saddler's, the ironmonger's and two blacksmiths have gone; there is only one of three newsagents and one of three butchers left, and I'm the only grocer. Even the police station and court has closed.'

Yet John has never wanted to live anywhere else, and indeed he never did except during his wartime service in the RAF. Best of all, he likes the situation of Talgarth, which remains largely unspoilt in spite of the march of man and machines. Way back in Norman times the village was regarded as the capital of Breconshire; it was eloquently, but rather archaically described as follows in the Talgarth Official Guide issued just after World War II under the auspices of an enterprising Chamber of Trade:

'Population 2,000. Market day (farm produce): Fridays. Stock auctions: Mondays. Talgarth lies to the north-west of Crickhowell, from which place it is 12 miles distant, and 9½ miles from Brecon. It is situated at the foot of Parc Hill, a spur of the Black Mountains, at an altitude of 500 feet above sea-level. Nearby is the grand range of the Brecknock Beacons, with the rolling uplands of Mynydd Eppynt on the other side. Its scenic charms, its healthfulness and the varied beauties and interests of its surroundings make it an ideal centre for a quiet holiday.

'Let not the term "Black Mountains" give the reader a wrong impression. Black, after all, is useful as a foil and a background, and the range which shows to such advantage from Talgarth only looks black under certain atmospheric conditions, and from certain angles. On a clear summer day, and from a distance, the range is rather purple than black. Although for the most part built of stone, and of considerable antiquity, Talgarth is bright and cheerful. The air is mild but not humid, the rainfall is moderate, there are plentiful supplies of sunshine, and shelter from cold winds. Talgarth is, therefore, recommended by the medical profession for people who are run down or in need of recuperation after severe illness.

'It is also emphatically a centre for the robust and energetic, especially if they accept the challenge thrown down by the hills and mountain heights, on which, of course, the airs are very exhilarating. Matters vital to health, such as a pure and abundant water supply, efficient sewerage, and good sanitary arrangements are in the hands of a vigilant Rural District Council.'

With such a thriving, close-knit community and surrounded by largely unspoilt countryside on all sides, Talgarth was a wonderful place for John to grow up in.

'I went to Talgarth School from the age of five until I was fourteen, and there were many more children then as families were bigger and not many people moved away to work. I had five brothers and two sisters and we used to have a lot of simple fun. Sometimes we tied cotton to a doorknocker or to a button to tap a window, but when the person came to the door there was no one there because we were hiding in the churchyard! But we didn't always get away with things.

'Once when I was twelve there was some real excitement, when a London businessman staying in the Tower Hotel had a nervous breakdown. He had a gun in his room, and when the police

John's father (left) and grandfather (right) outside the old Crescent Stores, where John Gwynne was born

went to arrest him he fired at them. This went on for twelve hours, and six of us kids who stayed to watch for much longer than we should got the cane for being late for school.

'There were some real characters around in those days. One of them was "Lizzie-the-Crate" Evans, so called because she was always taking apples to market. One day when she was there, us kids blocked her front door right up with snow so she couldn't get in, and then she sent the police after us.

'Another colourful person was Tom Weale, and he was always known as "Tom who roasted the cat" because one day he didn't notice that his cat had crept into the oven while the door was open and he accidentally cooked the poor creature alive!'

At the Crescent Stores, John's grandfather rapidly set about expanding the business, specialising in home-cured hams, bacon and tea-blending. He was certainly not reticent in advertising his wares; his tea-wrapper proclaimed

Left: A coal bill issued by the Gwynnes in 1918. Right: The kind of tea bag used in John's grandfather's day

'Let others boast of sparkling wines and drinks of high degree, but give to me at any time a cup of Gwynne's tea.' With such a bold approach, it was not surprising that he secured the first contract to supply the Mid-Wales Hospital with tea.

Eventually William's wife, Annie, took over the grocery business, enabling William to expand his interests in the hay, corn and coal trade. Their son Leslie started to work with them in 1904, and when Annie died, in 1916, Leslie's wife Jane took care of the shop. Leslie and Jane inherited the entire business when William died in 1934, aged 78. Leslie continued with the haulage work, his contracts including some for timber, one from the council to collect refuse, and others to deliver coal to schools. He also cut hay for local farmers, charging by the hour.

John started to work for the family at the age of twelve, while he was still at school. His first job was not with his parents, however, but with his aunt: she had a much bigger business, including a bakery, also in Talgarth. John describes those early days:

'As errand boy I delivered groceries in the carrier on my bike, but only around the village. The roads were pretty poor then as the council just used to put rough stones down, throw sand on top and roll it all in; so it wasn't surprising that I came off my bike a few times. Among the people I visited were the vicar, two doctors and the policeman, whose wife always used to give me a cup of tea. Most farmers came by horse and cart to get their own supplies, right up to the war. In those days it was nothing to see chickens and ducks in farmers' kitchens, and you still see pet lambs in some houses.

'I also helped aunty with house-to-house bread-van deliveries: she baked the bread, we took it round on a motor van and I got sixpence a week plus a meal or two.

'Another thing we used to do to earn extra money was pick hazelnuts and blackberries and sell them for a penny a pound to dealers called hucksters. These men also went round buying whinberries, mushrooms, holly, mistletoe, chickens, ducks, rabbits, hares, butter and eggs, which they took away to South Wales where they had a good market for most fresh produce in the industrial and coal-mining areas.

'I also used to blow the organ for a few bob a year. Grandad and my eldest brother were deacons in the chapel, and Grandad made us all go three times on Sunday, to 10.30am service, 2pm Sunday school and 6pm service. Many more people went to church then. In Talgarth we've always had a real mixture of denominations, including Congregationalists, Methodists and Baptists as well as the parish church, the Church of Wales. I've always been a Congregationalist, but my wife's a strong Methodist as she's from North Wales. It's common here for husbands and wives to go to different chapels.'

Following in his family's entrepreneurial spirit, John only ever wanted to work in a shop. Therefore when he left school he went straight to work full-time in the shop which had been his aunt's, but which she had just sold; her name was retained above the door, however: D. L. Edwards. John recalls memories of his three-year apprenticeship there:

'I had 2s 6d a week in the first year, 5s in the second and 7s 6d in the third. There was a manager, three of us boys, a man on the bread van and two bakers. What I found the hardest was having to learn all the prices, as very few items were marked. It's all so precise now, with bar codes and computers, but I've always worked out the prices in my head. Among those I remember from the 1930s are 11½d for twenty Player's cigarettes, 7d a pound for cheese, 8d for a 4lb loaf of bread, 7½d for a 12oz tin of corned beef, and 11½d for an 8oz tin of red salmon. May butter was very cheap at only 10d a pound because it wasn't suitable for salting for winter use. Butter from the Irish Free State was always more popular than the local produce because it was cheaper.

The shop (left) in Talgarth square, where John was apprenticed

'My first job in the morning was to sweep out, after which I had to fill the shelves. Then I'd weigh up the butter, marge, lard, currants, sultanas, raisins and that soft, moist brown sugar – I loved that! – in half-pounds and quarters. Peel and nutmegs were always whole. Salt came in blocks of 1½lb, but the farmers had much bigger blocks for salting pigs. Biscuits, flour and some tea were loose. Children used to come in after the broken biscuits because they were cheaper, and farmers' wives used to make aprons out of the flour bags. New Zealand cheese used to come in 56lb rounds – two in a crate – and we had to take the cloths off them. Grapes, too, used to come in crates, in a kind of rough sawdust, and you had to dig down with your hands and pull them out. The banana crates often had big spiders in.

'We used to make grand window displays with sultanas, dried fruits, chocolates, flour, almonds, loose mixed peel and glacé cherries, which came in 7lb boxes and was really terrible sticky stuff to weigh out. In those days you used to keep things like Christmas cakes from year to year, but you can't do that now, as everything's dated.

'There were no fridges so I had to carry everything down to the cellar to keep it cool. There was a railway station here then, and every

day we used to meet the train from Hereford at 10.30am to collect the sausages from Marsh & Baxters of Birmingham. They came on the passenger train, although less perishable items were quite all right on the goods train.

Today, John regrets the decline in Talgarth's community spirit:

'Things have changed for the worse, mainly due to people having cars. A lot of people have moved into Talgarth and quite a few commute long distances daily. Some have second homes and smallholdings in and around Talgarth, and only come here from London at the weekends for peace and quiet and the beautiful surroundings; but most are easy to get on with. At one time there were many more people on the land, and most stayed in the village so that everybody knew each other really well; but now there is so much machinery they are not needed. The main employers here were Bronllys Hospital and the Mid-Wales Mental Hospital, though the latter closed in 1998.

'There used to be many more local activities. For example, the harvest festivals used to be packed out, and we always used to have a good football team, and every year one of the farms held a "tea fight" and sports. The August show was always very popular, with horses, cattle, sheep and pigs penned on the football field. Before Talgarth's stock market was built all the stock was sold on the street. There also used to be a horse fair every May and November, which always attracted quite a few gypsies. They would come round the shop asking for dry [waste] cheese, and fat bacon to go with a rabbit.'

Rabbit was also a popular dish with the Talgarth residents, often being stewed. John recalls: 'There used to be many more roasts, and it was all joints, but now it's all stewing meat and chops sold. One of our favourite meals was a big roly-poly pudding with apples, sultanas and fruit in and boiled in a towel. Also popular were traditional Welsh cakes cooked on a hot plate.'

In the 1950s John rented a greengrocer's shop in Bell Street, which his mother ran and

WARTIME MEMORIES

'In 1942 John was called up and became an LAC despatch rider in the RAF, serving all over Europe. He admits: 'It was a great change for me and nearly broke my heart at first, until I paired up. Once I lost my way in Belgium and ended up at the front. I very soon made my way back! Another occasion I remember was when I was going into the Churchill Club in Berlin and bumped into my brother, an Army corporal in the stores. We were so surprised to see each other!'

John's father died in 1945 aged forty-seven, having been wounded in World War I. Soon after that John returned home to help his mother with the shop, and in 1946 he bought the Crescent Stores from her. He recalls:

'I had to buy the shop from Mum as we had a big family and there couldn't be any favouritism. Fortunately none of the local buildings had been damaged during hostilities and there were only a couple of bomb craters on the mountain; in fact Talgarth seemed almost unchanged after the war. There had been a lot of evacuees in the village, however, and some still call here. Homecoming parties were held in the town hall, and each serviceman returning was given a cheque from a special fund raised locally. When Father returned from World War I he was given a gold pendant, inscribed 'Talgarth 1914–18'. Nowadays my wife wears it on a chain.'

soon established as one of the best florist shops in the area. Both businesses flourished, and John began to look for larger premises. Then, in April 1957, John fulfilled a lifetime ambition when he bought – 'for about £2,500' – the shop in which he had been apprenticed, D. L. Edwards. The new premises were much better placed, being close to Talgarth Square, although only two doors away from the largest grocery outlet in the village. But John was quite undeterred by the competition and was able to devote much of his energy to the new shop while his wife, Eunice, looked after Crescent Stores. When the Bell Street shop was closed in 1961 the fruit and vegetable trade was transferred to the new store, where John now

employed three full-time staff. Eunice continued to run Crescent Stores.

But not everything went smoothly throughout this period. One day in 1954 when John was out delivering on his bike, poor Eunice sliced off two fingers in the bacon cutter. She remembers it well: 'It was the longest day of the year and they were cutting the grass in the churchyard. We called the doctor in and I was taken by car to Brecon hospital. The doctor joked: "Didn't you have enough bacon for the customers?" but it was the worst pain I ever had.' Sadly, at the time there was no chance of having the fingers sewn back on.

While most customers appreciated the Gwynnes' first-class service and remained loyal after a change of premises, there were always a few awkward ones. John himself has never actually been attacked, although one day he did have to part two men who were fighting in the shop itself. 'They'd been drinking, and were using

The village shop in the 1930s: a real Aladdin's cave

ORDERING THE STOCK

'We ordered most things from all the commercial travellers who came round. Nowadays very few reps call, and those who do only come infrequently. Everything's done by phone, which is a shame, because you lose that personal touch. In the old days if you were a good customer a rep would look after you, and each company had its own man; but now each rep has to deal with huge conglomerates and most have too much to think about.

'As boys we always asked the travellers for samples of sweets. I liked Radiance toffees best, and those slabs of sharp's toffee, which we broke up and sold by the quarter.

'During the 1920s a very good produce market was held every Friday in Talgarth Market Hall, which was always full, with six or seven hucksters present. John remembers: 'Most of them came from Merthyr; they would buy all they could get, and then use the GWR and LMS railways to take it all home. In the 1930s the market went down to just three hucksters and they used road transport. After the war the market closed, and now the hall is empty; but we hope to start a youth club there.'

supplementary clothing and ration books which the Gwynnes handled

filthy language. One woman used to have fits in the shop, and then there was the old lady who always came in just fifteen minutes before late closing, at a quarter to seven on Saturday, and I had to stay on late to take her order up on my bike. I used to curse her all right! We still get some customers who are always moanin' and groanin', but you just have to grin and bear it.'

During 1967 John chose to join the voluntary symbol group known as Mace. In the same year his son Leslie, who used to help out in the shop after school, started training for the business, enrolling at the College for the Distributive Trades in London. Twelve months later he returned with many new ideas; he became a partner in the business and in 1969 persuaded his father to buy an ailing shop in Talgarth Square, the site of the present store. John paid only £2,000 for this large and prominent building, 'because I was a Talgarth boy and an ex-serviceman. The first thing I did was change the name from "Evans The Stores"!' Their wholesalers helped with the launch, providing special offers which included butter at 2s 11d a pound, Brooke Bond tea at 1s 4d a quarter and lard at 5½d per packet. Ennig Stores was then sold and became a chemist's shop.

In 1970 many local people were alarmed when the Gwynnes revolutionised their store by turning it into a self-service shop. The older folk in particular were not at all keen on the idea, saying that it felt as if someone very important had died; but gradually they accepted it. Later the store was expanded and new lines introduced, such as pre-packed fruit and vegetables, wines and spirits and locally baked bread, these being among the most popular items. But with rapidly improving communications and transport, customers were becoming more price-conscious, so it was important to remain competitive by stocking Mace's own-brand products.

Yet further expansion into adjoining premises – first into what had been a separate bakery and confectionery, and then into a bank which had closed down – was encouraged by the growth in tourist trade, as increasingly mobile holidaymakers discovered the delights of the Brecon Beacons. Today the tourist trade remains strong, Germans and Dutch ('because of the mountains!') being the most frequent overseas customers. John does regret that being in a national park has severely restricted his development of the buildings, but in 1995 the authority did provide 50 per cent (£10,000) of the cost of restoring the shop front to more traditional style.

Previous shop fronts have seen excitement on at least two occasions. John recalls: 'One lady coming down the hill put her foot on the accelerator instead of the brake and shot through the window, and another time a chap did the same thing with an automatic.' Luckily no one was hurt on either occasion.

The only time that John was unable to continue his excellent delivery service to outlying areas – a service which has been truly appreciated by local farmers – was for two days during the great snow of 1947. Fortunately Talgarth had a local baker and a milkman who could keep people in the immediate vicinity supplied. Today the Gwynnes still offer a free delivery service to houses and farms up to about ten miles away, employing a van driver for three days a week. Such personal service, and the provision of quality products, have become even more important in retaining customer loyalty as cheap superstores have enticed many people to travel long distances to shop.

During John's lifetime little Welsh has been spoken in Talgarth, and in fact John himself cannot speak the language; but coming from North Wales, Eunice can, and she is always on hand to deal with the few older customers who prefer the native tongue.

Today the Gwynnes continue to offer quality service, yet they remain at the forefront of change. Where John once stacked soda-water syphons with a returnable 7s 6d deposit, wines from all over the world now fill the shelves. Along with chocolate, these new drinks are eagerly bought by customers calling for their National Lottery tickets.

John still works hard, but now, with the support of his family and staff, he regularly takes time off to go to the races; he has a quarter share in the horse *Treasure Again* which has had some significant wins. His fine home, beautifully situated on the outskirts of Talgarth, contains many mementoes reflecting his passion for the Turf. It's all a far cry from the early days when 'living above the shop your house was never your own, and friends were always coming in late having forgotten to buy something for supper or breakfast.'

Personal service: making up a customer's order

Calling Time on the Centuries

The Oldest Pubs in the British Isles

CALLING TIME ON THE CENTURIES

Our native ale, made without hops, was brewed in villages and settlements as early as about 5,000 years ago, but it does not appear to have been sold from alehouses until the introduction of taverns by the Romans. When ale started to be brewed with hops (to improve flavour and keeping qualities), from the fourteenth century, it became known as beer and was sold in beerhouses. Over the ensuing centuries the terms alehouse and beerhouse became interchangeable.

Previous page: Come hell or high water the village pub is expected to keep serving, the Elephant & Castle in Bampton was no exception during the floods of May 1932

None of Britain's earliest taverns and alehouses has survived, but there is some archaeological evidence, including drinking vessels found in London dating from about CE300. Being of pint and quart size, they suggest trade in ale or cider rather than wine. Most early alehouses were simply extensions to existing buildings, but some of the first inns were probably purpose built to provide accommodation as well as food and drink along established routes. As early journeys were often linked with pilgrimages, many early inns were built by the church.

By the end of the Anglo-Saxon period alehouses had already proliferated to such an extent that King Edgar, in about CE970, tried to limit the number in any one village, and also introduced graded measures. The pegs on the insides of wooden drinking vessels marked the limit for each drinker before he passed the vessel on to his companions and this gave rise to the expression 'to take someone down a peg or two'.

Eventually taverns, alehouses and inns became known collectively as public houses, or pubs, and a move to control them was made in 1495, when Henry VII gave local magistrates the power of closure. This was reinforced by an Act of 1552, which required alehouse keepers to obtain a special licence to operate. Further legislation and a shift in society's attitude steadily reduced the number of licensed premises. In 1577 there were 17,367 alehouses, 1,991 inns and 401 taverns in England and Wales, compared with some 78,000 pubs in the UK today. Allowing for the huge increase in population, the number of people per pub has soared from only 187 to about 1,029.

No one can say for sure which of our surviving buildings has been selling alcoholic drinks for the longest. Call them what you will – inns, alehouses, taverns or public houses – many have been rebuilt on the site of earlier hostelries and very few of those still standing have survived more or less intact. There can be little doubt that the old plaster, paint and panelling within innumerable antique establishments today conceal features of even greater antiquity. Many of these old buildings have been licensed premises for only part of their lives.

For the purpose of this book, there is the added problem of defining 'countryside'. Some of the oldest pubs now in towns were originally in open, undeveloped areas. Most of the earliest were built in towns, but many are in places which have since declined and now belie their former importance. Others were established along important routes, especially at key sites such as crossroads, embarkation points and river crossings.

The Royalist Hotel, at Stow-on-the-Wold in Gloucestershire, is so sure of its ancestry that it openly advertises as 'the oldest inn in England'. Behind the Jacobean façade of what is now a smart hotel in a chocolate-box tourist

...that's worth a

Worthington

town stands the original mediaeval, oak-framed structure, which has been radiocarbon-dated back to CE947.

Built by a Cornish Saxon Duke named Aethelmar, the Royalist was a refuge along the Fosse Way and over the years it has seen many different uses. Once owned by the Knights of St John's Hospitallers, it was run as a hospice and poor house, subsequently an inn known as the Eagle and Child, as well as a porch house and holmlea, a court house, base for the Royalists during the English Civil War, and a post office. But for exactly how long it has sold drink we cannot be sure.

Many interesting discoveries have been made at the Royalist, including a pit for bear baiting beneath the coffee shop, a Royalist commander's letter, a tenth-century Saxon shoe and a tunnel that leads to the church in one direction and to Maugersbury Manor (nearly a mile away!) in the other. Still to be seen are the leper holes, the circular 'witches' marks' – to ward off evil spirits – on the huge stone fireplace in the dining

room, and some of the exposed thousand-year-old timbers.

More cautious is the Bingley Arms at Bardsey, West Yorkshire, which only claims to be *one* of England's oldest inns, even though church records date it back to CE905 and the centre part of the existing building dates back to CE953. Furthermore, it is mentioned in the Domesday Book and alongside it was England's oldest known brewhouse, with records of brewers and innkeepers there from CE953. The first recorded keeper was Samson Ellis, whose family ran it right up to 1780, when Baron Bingley gave the pub its current name. Until then it had always been called the Priest's Inn, and the massive stone inglenook still contains a priest's hiding hole built after the dissolution of the monasteries in 1539, private mass being given for the gentry at that time.

Once connected with Kirkstall Abbey, the inn was used as a rest house for monks travelling to St Mary's of York. Later it was a stop for stagecoach passengers, adjoining buildings being used as stables. Also, from CE1000 it served as the local courthouse. Among interesting features still to be seen there are two expansion and contraction branches in the first-floor flues, which are perfectly preserved despite a reputed age of 700 years. The Dutch oven in the bar dates from 1738 (when the building was subject to major renovation and extension) and is one of few English examples in its original position.

The Fighting Cocks at St Albans, in Hertfordshire, is a later structure, dating from the eleventh century, but it is on a site traced back to CE795, though it may not have been used as an alehouse until considerably later. Some 400 years ago it was known as the Round House because of its unusual shape. In Stuart times the sunken area down from the bar, with its ring of comfortable seats, was a cockpit.

Another unashamed claimant to the title 'England's oldest inn' is the Old Ferry Boat Inn, at Holywell, in Cambridgeshire. Documents record that liquor was first retailed here as early as CE560, although experts estimate that the foundations are a century older. Part of the inn's granite floor contains a slab that is larger and protrudes further than those around it, marking the grave of a 17-year-old who was buried there in CE1050. Apparently she was a beautiful girl who committed suicide for the love of a local woodcutter, and she is said to haunt the inn to this day. To have the best chance of seeing Juliette you should go there on 17 March, the anniversary of her death.

Yet another pub with a claim to being 'the oldest inn in England': Ye Olde Trip to Jerusalem in Nottingham

Grace Neill's, Donaghadee, the oldest bar in Ireland

This pub certainly had good reason to have been there for so long, as the operator of a ferry across the Great Ouse. Apparently one passenger who found time to pop in for a swift half was resistance leader Hereward the Wake, on his way to Cambridge during the Norman invasion of Britain. Although the arrival of modern roads made the ferry redundant, the pub still retains the ancient rights to take people across the river. But all this rich history nearly came to an abrupt end in March 1997, when the pub lost its entire thatch to a big fire.

Dating from 1590, the Crook Inn at Tweedsmuir, in the Borders, is said to be Scotland's oldest licensed inn, with a licence dating from 1604. Sitting by the old Edinburgh-to-Dumfries road, the inn was originally built to accommodate drovers. Once the kitchen, the bar has a huge central fireplace which you can walk all around. The famous poet Robbie Burns knew the inn through his work as an exciseman and he wrote his poem 'Willie Wastle's Wife' while staying there.

Although an inn has stood on the site of Dublin's Brazen Head Inn since the twelfth century, the present building dates from 1668. Ireland's oldest surviving pub is Grace Neill's Inn built at the fishing port of Donaghadee in 1611, just three years after the establishment of the world's oldest whiskey distillery at Bushmills. With only twelve people in, the small original bar is packed, so a tourist extension was tacked on the back in 1993. However, the Russell family (who have owned the pub since 1973) have ensured that the place retains its great character. Most of the beams in the old bar are believed to be timbers from ships wrecked on County Down shores. The pub remains lively, too, with the locals often singing from the Irish folk song books or playing the tin whistles kept behind the bar. Originally called the King's Arms, the pub was renamed early this century after landlady Grace Neill, who died in 1916, aged 98. Some customers say that she haunts the place, being cross that her beloved inn has been altered.

Over the centuries, the pub has had quite a few famous customers, including the composer Franz Liszt, Thackeray, Dan O'Connell (the uncrowned King of Ireland), author Daniel Defoe (of Robinson Crusoe and Moll Flanders fame), poet John Keats and Irish author and playwright Brendan Behan, who apparently spent more time in the pub than he did painting Donaghadee lighthouse, for which purpose he had been sent north. Tsar Peter the Great of Russia stayed there, too, when on his way to Warren Point to study shipbuilding, the upstairs 'Emperor's Room' commemorating his visit.

One of the old customs at the King's Arms was for the landlady and her maids to kiss visitors on their arrival, which in the case of Peter the Great must have been both difficult and pleasurable as he was 6ft 7in tall and very handsome.

There have been less savoury associations, the County Down pub's pictures of guns reflecting long links with smuggling and horse thieving, in the days when Donaghadee was the main sea port to the Isle of Man and Galloway. Apparently a tunnel once led from the pub to the harbour, about 160 yards away, so that contraband could be moved without being intercepted. However, the inn's main trade was with passengers embarking on the short sea passage to Portpatrick, often in escape from the terrible poverty and oppression.

The ubiquitous pub dog, ever the entertainer

Men of the Woods

George & Dick Quinnell: Sussex

MEN OF THE WOODS

On a crisp and sunny afternoon, the rapid chunter of an ageing tractor could be heard rumbling merrily along the lane. Warm and clear above it came the cheerful, rumbustious singing of a happy man whose spirits had been gently lifted at the Rising Sun. A minute later the battered tractor was bouncing up the rough track that passes my farm cottage and its driver waved in greeting, his jaunty round face lit by that familiar, heart-lifting smile as he shouted hello in mid-song. George Quinnell was heading for the chestnut coppice up on the slope above the meadows. It was a good half hour before the smoke of his brashfire drifted into the sky.

The Quinnell family at Woolbeding

George is always cheerful, though more subdued in recent months. After 53 years of marriage he had lost his beloved wife, Florrie, the previous year and he misses her. His various health problems have increasingly sapped his old energy so that he rarely feels fit enough to work all day as he did. He has lost some of the sparkle, too, since the death of his younger brother, Dick, a highly skilled chestnut cleaver whose quiet, sardonic humour was in contrast to George's extrovert optimism.

Dick's death was a shock to many. He had recovered well from heart bypass surgery a few years earlier, and had been working in the copse with his usual steady vigour and care until he succumbed to cancer. He had become the third of George's brothers to die of that cruel disease.

The Quinnells were not as numerous as many country families in the 1920s. George was born in April 1917 ('I just missed being an April Fool!') up on the hill at the Old House, Woolbeding. He was fifth in the family after Bill, Charlie, Martha and Leonard. Dick was George's youngest surviving brother – there had been another, little Joey.

George's nickname at school was Mincemeat: he was a good fighter. He remembers one occasion, though – a fight with a boy who usually ran away. This would be an easy one, thought George, but the lad came at him 'like a haymaker' in an unending flurry of blows.

The family moved up to Swallows Bottom, Redford, when George was two years old. There, he used to play in the woods and watched men making hoops for barrels. 'You got four foot, you got firkins – barrel what the beer's inside – and fillikin's another barrel. They used to do twelve foot and all, you know. They split it very thin: you could bend them, like that, so they could bend round the barrel. They call them toopers, don't they? Sometimes you can get six, eight, out of one pole – all lengths. I think I'm right in saying twelve foot. And when he's shaving them, like that, they *bend like that* and I used to think as a nipper watching, I used to think, good God, that's going to break! But it never did. My uncle, he could make hoops, my uncle Albert, used to live up Titty Hill. My dad never did. My dad used to cut the poles out that the hoop shavers used.

But when you are trimming them out, you didn't dare to nick the bark, else the pole would have snapped when they were splitting out, see, then you'd spoilt it. If it didn't snap *too* short, you

H. J. Puttick, hoop-shaver, at Balls Cross, Petworth, 1939

BOXALL THE BROOMSQUIRE

William Boxall of Hammer Vale, on the borders of Sussex, Surrey and Hampshire, died at the age of ninety-one in the early 1920s, when he was one of four broomsquires living in the village. His broom-shops were rough, open-fronted sheds on the common and he made his brooms from either birch or heather. His nephew, Ernest W. Boxall, looking back in the early 1950s, remembered helping with the heather harvest towards the end of August as a boy. 'For me, that meant a day on Bramshott Common and I usually spent it hunting for mushrooms; the flavour of the heather-grown mushroom is far superior to that of the meadow variety.'

The birch would he cut from local copses 'when the catkins were still on them' and the long, feathery twigs would be stored until winter. They were trimmed with a curved knife by an expert woman, who sliced them to just over a yard long. She judged the length by eye, consistently within an eighth of an inch.

The raw material, whether birch or heather, was bundled into broomheads, tightened by a leather thong and then bound with two withies cut from willows growing by the garden stream – a stream in which the bundles would then be soaked for several days. Then they were trimmed with a sharp axe and fitted with handles made from pointed birch or hazel saplings, which had been shaved with a two-handled tool. The handles were fixed in place with a wooden peg.

The finished brooms were gathered into dozens (thirteen to the dozen) and piled high in an enormous wain hired from a local farmer in the early spring. For the next few weeks Uncle William would be on the road, selling his bundles of brooms to country houses, stables and stores as far away as Kent and Wiltshire. When stocks were low he would send a telegram to his mother, who dispatched fresh supplies from Liphook station. 'A telegram sent at ten o'clock in the morning brought a new supply within twenty-four hours without fail,' Ernest remembered. Oh, the good old days!

Précis of an article in Countryman

Dick Quinnell

could cut it for a shorter one. They used to work from seven to five – well, seven to when it gets dark in winter. They might have a lot they would do in late spring; they would have a tidy bit and then, you see, they used to go thatching when they had nothing else to do. With the shavings of the hoops – used to get it for sixpence a bundle in my day. And faggots, when we used to make what we called cottager's faggots for lighting fires, they used to be six shillings a hundred. You got to work like hell to make a hundred, you know! Not much money, was it?

'And the big poles – like that photo of old Uncle Perce rining there (*opposite*) – I forgets what we used to get for ordinary poles like that small one there but it wasn't very much, something like tuppence for twenty-five. They used to pay different for different lengths, you see, and you didn't want it too big for that sort of work: it was too heavy to handle, You got some you cut eight and ten hoops out of. It was a good trade in hoops then, and they used to make girls' hoops, too. There was an 'oop bender at Plaistow and a walking-stick factory there – they used to steam the walking-sticks to get the handle round and they used to steam the hoops too, though I never did see it.

'Well, that was one industrial; the other was pales, like Dick was making, and that's been going on for years. If you was a good bloke, like Uncle Perce Heath there, he could do everything – he was master of most things, hoop-making, pale-making, thatching like in that photograph. It's not straw he's using, it's chestnut. When they peeled the hoops, they used the peelings for the thatch-ing. Must be over seventy year ago, that picture.'

There is a Percy Heath in the area today, but he is a mere youngster in his late forties. He, too, saw the photographs. 'Great-uncle Perce was a woodman. A thatcher. Used to coppice chestnut – palings, things like that. He did a lot of chest-nut thatching and he thatched with the old wheat as well – wheat cut with a binder. He lived down on the corner, Standwater Cottage. He'd thatched a barn down a stone's throw from home, and that shed's not far from the barn. I remember when I was very small he used to buy a bit of chestnut up by the Sanatorium and he used to walk over there. I think he probably made hurdles as well. He always worked on his own, Perce. They all did – old Fred Petter, he used to cut patches of chestnut along the hill by our old place, cut in strips you know, and then the next year the next strip, and the next year the next and that. And there was a man from Midhurst used to come on his motorbike with his wife – they were Boxalls, that was when I was still at the village school. She used to rine the posts. They'd fell it all with an axe and she used to trim the poles out, put them in their piles, burn up the rubbish and then when they were pale-making she would cut the lengths off with a bow saw, push 'em back and rine them, and he would split them and tie 'em up. She did her fair share! And we used to have a bucket that stood out by our old house; we had a tap out on the corner there, and he used to stop there and fill

Below left: Uncle Perce Heath, thatching with chestnut shavings Below right: Appleton, broomsquire, of Baughurst, Hampshire, 1945. There was also a rake-maker's yard (Ernest Sims and his sons) at nearby Pamber End

the kettle up every morning on their way to the woods.'

The photographs of Uncle Perce are in a collection of old pictures from all over the valley but, frustratingly, with no captions giving clues to names, dates or places, though many are from the 1920s and 1930s. They show other local woodmen – hoop-makers, chestnut cleavers, hurdle-makers and charcoal burners among them – and George Quinnell's memory is jogged by them all.

'And they used to make hazel or chestnut spars to hold on the thatch; they could twist and bend them, push them in – like you were going to make a fork of it and push it to hold the thatch, then you give it a twist and then you can bend it, it'd bend itself then, so you could push it straight in to hold your thatch on.

MILKING TIME

Dad taught George how to milk the three or four family cows, which the boy did more willingly than his brothers. It was a skill which would come in handy in later farmwork, when he could milk eleven cows in an hour. 'One cow we had used to kick and knock me over! I must tell you this: one Sunday Dad had gone down to the Rising Sun and he come back very much the wear for drink and he says, "We'll go and milk the cow," he says, "I'll stand up side of her and she won't kick you." So we gets in there and I gets a stool and sits down and milks about half a bucket of milk out, and I felt her going to kick (you gets your head in there and you can feel her). And I grabbed the bucket, like that, and the stool, and her foot come round like that and knocked me back in the gutter. And as I went back the bucket come up with me and all the milk went down Dad. He got in a real temper – he put a rope round her horns and lifted her front legs off the ground and said to me, "Now you milk her, she's only got two legs to stand on." He never thought about me, was I hurt and that! That's how he was. When we went indoors and Mother saw the state I was in, I said the cow kicked me and she said, "I knew it would, 'cos he'd had some drink." The cows knew about that, see. Oh yeah!'

'And we used to make withs to tie up the bundle – used to wind that out of hazel, mostly, though you could use birch or anything. There was a lot of hazel around then. Trouble is, you see, as soon as thatch and hoops went out of business the hazel was let go. You had to cut it when it was about five, six, seven years old else it got too big. You cut it and it come up again in another seven years or so, like the chestnut. There's still chestnut around here but no hazel now. It's awful to think that has gone, you know, and the chestnut's going too. The council used to use a lot of that chestnut paling for partitions between the houses and their gardens but now they use wire, that horrible chainlink stuff. They used to use a lot of that chestnut fencing, like Dick made, down by the sea for sea defences. But they don't do that now.'

George thinks back to his childhood again. When he was eleven the family moved down to a smallholding, Moorhouse Farm, where they stayed for the next twenty-five years. Nobody had lived there for some time, and the grass was 'up to here'. Tucked down a muddy woodland track up a little combe along the hammerpond stream, the holding had nineteen acres of ground – mainly in long strips of meadow, with wooded slopes on either side – along with a cow pen and pig sties. They rented it all, says George in amazement, for fifteen shillings a week. 'That was cheap, wasn't it! Bloomin' great house, seven walnut trees …' Dad sold walnuts at a shilling a hundred and the children's fingers would be blackened by the juice from the husks they removed. 'It was better when you had a frawst, 'cos it used to open the husk.'

'We had the loveliest spring water down there to drink – my brother Len used to fetch it for my mum down the meadow. There was two wells: one up in the garden, the newest one, we never did drink from that – it was dirty old stuff. But the other one down by the back door, we used that. Then one day we were winding the old windlass to bring the water up and there was a bloody dead *rat* in the bucket! That stopped us

having that! Mother said, "I ain't going to drink no more of *that* water!" Mind you, where we used to dig the water out of the spring you sometimes found a mouse in it, but that's different to a rat, isn't it?'

Local people all remember Mrs Quinnell as a very sweet and gentle woman, but old Joe could be rough. 'My mother was a lovely person but my dad was the other way, worse luck, when he'd had a drink, When he was sober you wouldn't wish for a better chap, you know.'

Old Joe had joined up in 1916 and went in the heavy artillery. 'Then he went up the line and then he got made cook. He was a damn good cook. At home he'd do all the cooking of a Sunday – best dinner you ever ate!'

Old Joe also dealt with the pigmeat, pickling the belly pork in brine, smoking bacon and so on. 'Oh, we used to *live*!' cries George. 'We never got hungry. He used to make pork sausages: we had a line across the kitchen what Mum hung her tea cloths on, and the old man would hang his sausages up there – they'd be up there about two months and they used to shrivel up, you know. And he'd reach up and cut them off, put them straight in the pan – never used to wipe

them or anything. Then he'd take the ham down from the chimney, take off the muslin, and put the ham straight in the pan – he'd never wash it. And we've lived to tell the tale! Cor, what we used to do, I tell you, children don't know now what it is to have a good breakfast. Dad used to say, "Right, go on, have your breakfast – breakfast is better and if you've had a good breakfast it don't matter if you don't get no dinner." We used to have the cottage loaf, with a lump on it, and the old man used to cut up the bread – he'd cut you about five slices *that* thick, nearly cut the loaf up for one. We had to eat it all, you know. Then when we went to work he'd get the cottage loaf, take off the knob, then he'd scoop a hole like a peg top, then he'd fill it up with dripping or butter, then he'd put the knob back on. They don't know what it is now, they don't know how to *live*!'

Now the old memories are really stirring as George thinks of home cooking in his childhood. 'We did have some good times. Blackberrying – used to get buckets of blackberries. My mother used to make jam, good blackberry and apple, and damson and greengage and plum, and blackberry jelly, heaps of it. Whenever you visited,

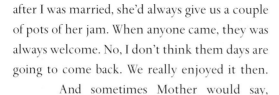

after I was married, she'd always give us a couple of pots of her jam. When anyone came, they was always welcome. No, I don't think them days are going to come back. We really enjoyed it then. And sometimes Mother would say, "Oh, we'll have a tea out today, we'll go up the field," and we'd take a cloth up and spread it out. Us boys used to take all the stuff up, and a stove thing for boiling up a kettle. That was good! We used to really enjoy our life. I know we had to work hard but … And Mother, she liked it, you know, she loved it there at Moorhouse.'

His mother Florence came from the hamlet of Henley, near Fernhurst. She had been a kitchen maid over Godalming way, some fourteen or fifteen miles distant – and she would *walk* to work there. 'I don't say she went every day. She would work, stay there and then walk back, say, for her day off. Oh, they walked in them days. She could never wait for the post cart from London to Chichester, so she walked. Didn't mind walking in the dark – there weren't the rogues about then as now.' She was only seventeen when she married Joe. How did they meet? 'I'm blowed if I know. I suppose they had a good nose! He used to get around, you know. I think Mum's relations told her she shouldn't marry him but Mother stayed with him for over sixty years. She was a *lovely* person. She never used to have a cross word for anyone. And if we upset her she'd say, "I shall tell your dad if you ain't good," and that shut us up – 'cos she knew what would happen, and *we* knew what would happen!'

Joe was typical of many of that time: he could turn his hand to most things and do them well. He ensured the family was self-sufficient, growing their own food, converting their own dairy produce and home-killed bacon, Then he took whatever work he could find and still be his own master.

'All there was round here was woods, farming and stone-digging. My dad used to do that and my uncle out at Easebourne – Lord Cowdray's place – they used to do a lot over

BEFORE LAWNMOWERS

Old Joe Quinnell was a larger-than-life character, a charming and roguish extravert, supremely self-confident and able to turn his hand to many a craft, passing on some of his skills to his several sons. George remembers being taught how to mow the grass with a scythe. 'Oh yeah, I could do it – after he'd swore at me a time or two. He used to say, "Keep your heel down on the scythe and the tip up, otherwise it goes into the ground." I done that for a time or two and once I done it and fetch it round and went and bent it – the old man got hold of it, put it on top of his head and straightened it that way! 'Now use it,' he'd say, 'and keep that bloody heel down.' You used to set them, you see: you put your foot out and if you could touch the blade you knew you weren't far out. I forget now but we used to have a bit of wood on the handle that used to go up and over so that when you cut the grass it laid the grass better. Can't think of the name for it now. You made your own handle, though I shouldn't be able to make it now if I tried. Dad used to make them straight. You got the froes, the handles that goes on, he could put them on and then you got the end of the scythe and you had a bracket went round, didn't you, and that fitted down over and you wedged it up with iron wedges – that's how you done it.

Fern-cutters exercising their commoners' rights, New Forest

there, and there was all Quinnells in one stonepit so they called it Quinnells Stonepit! My dad, he would dig and split the stone and then when he cut them up for building size he'd face them, you know, to go into a building. He used to get paid so much a yard – a yard of stone is a yard high, a yard long – well, it's a yard square. Then of course they used to dig stone for dry walls; there's a lot of that round here, anywhere in the woods and everywhere. And road stone, rubble. I used to go with Dad in the stonepit as well as in the wood work. He was so strong, he used a sixteen-pound sledge! What you did, you uncovered the stone, took all the topsoil off, then you dug down, wheeled all the topsoil away, then you cleaned that off. Then when you use your pick, you find cracks in the stone, you know, you might find a big stone, about five or ten ton – big as a room. You get down and you work right the way round it and you'd put your wedges in and use your sledge hammer to split it. Wallop! It was hard work and my dad was a masterpiece at it.

His hammer was funny: it was like *that*, and the handle go in there, and then it had a chisel end, so all the weight was on that end, so when you brought it down you had to be careful it wasn't cackhanded. I could use it when I got older. We had to laugh when we used it: the old man used to get hold of that bloody thing and get it in his hand, like that, and give it a swing and let it come down to his nose! I tried doing it but I let it slip out of my hand, didn't I – hit me *on* me nose! Yeah, it wasn't too good, that wasn't. It damn nearly knocked me out, didn't it!' George roars with laughter at the memory.

Many of the older cottages and big houses in the area are made from the local sandstone, strengthened around windows and doors and on the corners with brick quoins, and dotted in the mortar with 'witch's eyes' of ironstone, which glitter in the moonlight.

'The other thing we used to do was farming, really, because there was nothing else. Then in

'Dad sold walnuts at a shilling a hundred...'

the autumn they used to cut the bracken for bedding for the cows. All over the common. You had your commoners' rights, see. You cut the bracken, let it dry a *little*, then made wads of it – you stood on the wad, tapped it all in with your fork and left it for a day or two. Then when you went to pick it up you'd stick your fork in the wad, like that, and pick it up clean as a whistle to load on the wagon. The wagons were up so high – by the time you got halfway up you wanted a longer pitchfork! Then you'd put it in a stack – like the faggot stacks people used to have for

lighting the fires: you built them in the shape of a house with a roof on – stack them up and then lay some over to keep the weather off.'

When George left school at the age of fourteen his working life began in earnest, but it would be an immensely varied one. 'See, I went all over the place, I done nearly anything! Jack-of-all-trades, master of none. I had to. I mean, I didn't like being tied in one place. All sorts. There ain't much I can't do, if I don't do it properly. Yeah. It don't make sense, do it, all the things I've done, and you'd never think I'd do it in the time – sixty-odd years of work, you see. Well, I've enjoyed myself! But now I ain't fit – I'm fit for nothing. I get so tired out now. It's awful when you've been used to working hard …'

George's first job was as a gardener, but that lasted only five weeks. He went back with his father digging the roadstone, and in the woods again, as well as some general farm work. But when Dad packed that in, so did George. He went to work with cattle and pigs on a butcher's farm and became his roundsman, delivering home-killed meat. He was there for two years, until his dad persuaded him back into the stonepits. 'Don't know why. I was getting very good money at Drakeley's! So I went with Dad and from there I went with my brother Bill to the Shelley yard at Barns Green, where he taught me brick-making.'

Bill was ten years older than George; he was also a builder and, like most of his brothers, often worked in the woods as well. In photographs of that time at the brickworks, George really stands out from the crowd: he had a fine shock of golden hair. 'I didn't like it at all! I didn't mind seeing ladies with blonde hair but I wanted dark hair – I always wished I had dark hair.'

He loved brick-making almost as much as working in the woods. 'A thousand for ten shillings, it was,' he remembers. But he only had one or two seasons of it. By then he was seventeen and there wasn't much work about: he went on the dole for a while at seven shillings a fortnight and then back to farming.

"PUT A JERK IN IT!"

George inherited his father's adaptability and frequently changed his mind about his work preferences. As a boy, he used to watch the blacksmith for hours when he took along Dad's tools to be mended at the village forges in Stedham and at Wardley Green, and decided that he'd like to be a blacksmith. But in practice he never tried it. Instead, he helped Dad in the woods while he was still at school, cutting poles for someone else to turn into palings. Hundred pales for six shillings, tie up faggots for five shillings, that sort of thing. Place in Liphook they used to take the pales and that – she used to buy up the standing chestnut and then you'd go and cut it for her; then she'd pay you so much for everything you cut. I loved it in the woods. I used to make the faggots. Dad could make a hundred a day, I could make about fifty – I was only a nipper. I used to have to wind his withs, a hundred for him and fifty for myself, it was a tough old life. 'Come on, you,' he'd say, 'put a jerk in it!' You've seen how quick Dick is with his work – well, Dad was even faster.

'For the faggots, you trim your pole out – you had a block to put it on – then pick up the frith, get a big enough bundle together and wind the with round: you had to straighten it first – if you got a bit sticks out, you nick it down then press it in. Like making besoms, similar to that. They used the faggots for lighting fires – baker's ovens, and down in the brickyard here they used mostly bush faggots. You had a lovely pair of long gloves up your arms 'cos you couldn't handle brushes otherwise; you put your arms right round the bundle. They never used to waste a thing.'

Before the war, George met Florrie, a girl from Kirdford who was working as a cook. They married in 1939. 'Fifty-three years we were married. I do miss her, you know.'

He probably misses his mother-in-law, too: she was an excellent wine-maker and turned everything she could lay her hands on into potent wine – potatoes, wheat, parsnips, damsons, oranges, dandelions, cowslips and elderberries featured regularly in her home-made brews. George frequently reeled his way home the six miles from Kirdford, his bike with a will of its own, but there were no cars about and he only occasionally ended up in the ditch.

The variety of jobs continued. They rented a bungalow for a while at Eastlands, near Barns Green, where his landlady kept racing grey-hounds. George, a good man with dogs, soon found himself a job looking after the animals and milking the housecows. They gave him three pounds and sixpence a week. 'That warn't bad. Then they used to take thirteen shillings back for rent, so that warn't so good!'

During World War II George was needed on the land. His first son, Michael, was born while they were at Eastlands, in the early hours of one morning. What with fetching the midwife and one thing and another, George was up all night. Then he had a puncture in his bike tyre and arrived late for milking. 'I started to milk and I got half a bucket of milk and old Colonel Cameron come out and he went for me some-thing awful! He never asked me why I was late. So I just waited until he stopped for breath, and then I got the stool and the milk and chucked them straight in the corner. Then I squared up to him, drove him out of the cowpen. I give my notice first – I told him he was nothing but a damn slave driver; I said, "You think you got a regiment of soldiers under you, don't you!" 'Course, one thing led to another and then I squared up at him – I was going to get him, see. Then he went out. And I picked up the bucket and stool; I wiped the old bucket out and started to milk again. He come back and said, "You're

leaving, then?" I said, "Yes. Fortnight's notice." When the fortnight's up I couldn't find a house and had to stay another week.'

But he did find a new home and a new job: he went down to Okehurst and worked on the farm for thirty-three shillings a week, from which they docked three shillings for his rent. They lived in a cottage 'right down the lane and across the fields, right out of sight of everybody', with no access for motor cars. He had a pushbike and his wife 'used to have to walk, because of the baby, you see'. She walked three miles to Billingshurst for her shopping. But in spite of its disadvantages, they loved that Keeper's Cottage at Okehurst. He remembers the day they moved in: the previous tenant was still moving out. He was a sculptor by the name of Kinnersley and was half-way through chiselling an immense block of stone in the form of a large woman. But he decided to abandon it and asked George to bury it. Bury it? It was a huge hunk. Fortunately, it was a long way from the house, and so George simply dug an enormous pit beside it and 'rolled her in'. Unfortunately, the pit was not deep enough, and certain parts of the woman's anatomy thrust themselves resolutely above ground. He piled a great heap of earth on top to

cover her modesty and left it. 'For all I know, she's still there,' he chuckles — and no doubt a future archaeologist will dig her up and believe her to be some kind of pagan goddess …

He did all sorts. 'First off I was horse and labour, you know, then afterwards we got a tractor and I used to drive that. Chap there just said, "Well you got to learn," so I got in and drove it.' He was also out in the woods cutting faggots, pea boughs and bean sticks for use on the farm, and cutting down oaks for fencing posts, all with axes and hand-saws. 'If I hadn't got a mate working, I used to have to saw her on me own, set him in with a axe and make a fell, then I used to get the other set. But when I had a mate I used to set several and then we used to saw them down and I could trim them out with a axe.'

The farm specialised in the production of seed and they threshed cocksfoot, linseed, bent, even mangold seeds, as well as grain. 'I used to have a fortnight threshing grain. It used to stand in the rick until March. And then if you wanted to see rats jump out of the straw, you wanted to be there! You never believe how many rats there be. Their droppings, when they used to come out in the corn sack — had to blow it off the corn. Gorblimey, I thought to myself, we don't eat bread from that, do we? Awful. Underneath the ricks — used to have them on a steddle you know, wood bundles, and then you might come across a hole underneath and perhaps there was twenty rats in one hole, You keep on fetching them out, fetching them out, kill them as you took them out. You would have two or three terriers but they couldn't deal with them all. We used to have one terrier, he'd have one grab, one chop, finished it. But if the rat struggled round, if he got hold of him wrong, the rat used to get hold of their lip and tear it, you know. The old dog would shake it, the old rat would go right up in the air and then the old dog would catch him when he come down. I used to think to myself, good God, I'm pleased that dog's biting a rat and ain't biting me!'

George has always had dogs and remembers especially a much-loved labrador which he trained himself. 'She'd bring anything for me. When I trained I'd tie my handkerchief up like my old Dad told me, let the dog sniff it, then start walking off and then drop it accidentally, and the dog might be behind, then he'd pick it up and bring it, and when he got to you you'd say, "Oh, lovely dog!" — you know. And every time you dropped it he'd bring it. And of course when he got a pheasant he'd bring it instead of eating it!

'There was a go once when Dad was up Fernhurst — he used to go in a pub and there was one or two there, old Major Jackson and that. Dad said his dog would fetch his hat if he put it down. So he put it down, and Major put his hat down too, and off they went with the dog. They went a mile and then Dad said to the dog, "Go and get it." Off went the dog but he only brought Dad's hat, he wouldn't bring Major's! Well, he wasn't really a major. Them Jacksons — they was Lordy, Squibby, Major and Jack.'

George's trained labrador came into her own when he became a woodman-gamekeeper. 'When the war finished I was still on the farm, see — well I couldn't go and get another job because I'd already been exempt from the army and so I had to stick to farming. And anyhow, the time came I moved over to Dragons Green, went in the woods there, Newbuildings it was called — the woods where Scallery Blunt was buried. The place come in trust to his granddaughter, Lady Anne Lytton. They reared Arab horses there.' Blunt had died in 1922 and his woodland grave was surrounded by wire 'to keep out the rabbits'. One of George's roles was to maintain the grave, and also to chase off the gypsies who came to steal the wild daffodils growing round about. Ironically, perhaps, there was a Romany caravan in the grounds, beautifully decorated in bright colours. It was an amazing place, Newbuildings ('though nothing new about them!'): the old man's garden was full of 'roses they used in Egypt for making scent — and they did smell special', he says appreciatively. He had to trim the enormous

George Quinnell, gardener

Dick Quinnell and his sister, Martha

yew hedges there, and the little box hedges around the rose beds, as well as his woodland work, which included keepering – on his own for a time, until someone else took over the shoot and George worked with his head keeper. He thoroughly enjoyed himself, as usual.

And so it continued – a while at this, a while at that, always a little restless, trying his hand at many things. He would help with the harvest during the summer and work in the woods in the winter; he would go back into the brickyard or try his hand at road-making. A bit of this, a bit of that, but his steadiest hours have been as a

part-time gardener (on and off for some thirty years at one particular place) and in the woods on his own account, cutting chestnut poles, pea sticks, bean poles and firewood, and thinking back to the old times, good and bad.

Again and again his thoughts return to those childhood days – memories of bowling for and winning a live pig, and carrying it home on the bus under his arm: he called it Sixer because he'd knocked out six skittles to win it. Moorhouse Farm is central to his best memories – the cellars where they could keep things cool, where Mum used to set the milk from their Jersey cows in bowls and the children could not resist sticking a finger into the rising cream, Dad's soft 'butter' cheeses hung down there too, dripping out their whey, and he kept his beer down there: the cellar was flooded once and the children vividly remember the barrels bobbing about on the water. Then there was Dad's air-raid shelter which he dug out on the slope opposite the front gate, reckoning that that would not flood. It was typical of Dad – generously big, and really quite comfortable, 'but Mum said you'd never get her using it – be dead before she could reach it over there.' Sometimes the German planes during World War II would unload spare bombs in the

area on their home runs, and sometimes the woods would suddenly be full of soldiers making their way down to the south coast ports from the army camps at Bordon. But George no longer lived at home by then.

One of his biggest satisfactions has been in planting trees and going back years later to see them so full grown that he cannot get his arms round them. He has planted all sorts – oak, larch, Douglas fir, spruce and so on, especially on the estate where he has gardened all those years. It's a good heritage, one which might one day he appreciated his own seven grandchildren and six great grandchildren.

★ ★ ★

George's younger brother, Dick, was a very different character. They were quite close and shared one or two memorable holidays at Butlins with their wives, but Dick was a much steadier man and a true craftsman. Where George was a self-confessed Jack-of-all and master of none, Dick was a master.

He began his career as a cabinet-maker at Fernhurst, but the apprenticeship money was poor and at the age of fifteen he decided to become a chestnut cleaver. His tutor was old George Boniface, who taught him how to split out the pales from the poles. He also taught the lad how to sharpen tools – the secret to all good woodland crafts – but soon discovered that Dick could do the job better than he, and so Dick became Boniface's sharpener, using a flat six-inch file on the bushman saws. The war took Dick into the army, but he returned to the woods afterwards and stayed there on and off for the rest of his life, though he also helped his Dad in the stonepits.

It was in the chestnut coppices that I first met Dick Quinnell. I was walking along the ridge, with a fine view over a valley made misty by the wispy smoke of a woodman's fire, and there was the faded green canvas set on poles he had cut nearby to form a shelter and a workshop. Inside and close by were the tools and artefacts of his craft, all of them handmade in a style which would have been familiar a century or more ago.

He stood on the high knoll; the neatly trimmed chestnut stools were behind him, while below an old beech forest tumbled down the steep slope towards the stream that had long ago powered the hammers of an iron-works. We could see over the tree tops to a further distance of tree-clad slopes on other hangers, and between them the old Roman road, part lane and part woodland track. 'I used to think,' he said quietly, 'that had I been a lad here two thousand years ago I'd have stopped them Romans easy. Just roll some of these trunks down the hill! I can see them sometimes, you know, the legions, marching through the valley there, a day's march from Chichester, they say – that's why there was a posting station here, so they could rest up for the night.' He knew of other ancient sites in the area – sites which perhaps are not generally known. He had a sharp eye, did Dick.

It was always a delight to stop and watch him work, though only one or two would find the time to do so. One day I found his audience had literally drawn up a chair: 'Young' Bill Tull, in his early seventies, was comfortably ensconced and enjoying a banter. The 'young' is a relic from Bill's youth: his father was Old Bill Tull. Young Bill rarely works in the woods now (he was mainly a farm worker, especially with horses) but enjoys a gossip with his friends in the peace of the coppice, a long way from the village. He, too, has his memories of the old days in the valley.

Dick was nervous, which was uncharacteristic, but then, he'd never been on television before and was worried about the questions they might ask, He had been spotted at work by a passing researcher for the local television company's *Country Ways* series. He didn't mind being filmed at work – he never minded an audience – but he didn't like the idea of speaking in front of the camera at all and had been rehearsing what he might say.

He tended the fire, burning waste chip-pings and frith and the bark he had peeled off with his riner.

'They want a good fire going for the camera, see,' he said, looking slightly ashamed of this ruse, but we appreciated its warmth on a cold, breezy February day.

'Good job the wind's dropped a bit,' he went on. 'Couple of days back it took my canvas right off of the poles! Poles stood up well, though – I put 'em in firm and deep enough.'

The tools under the newly secured canvas were sharp and polished bright with use over many years. This skilled craftsman's only concession to the new age was in using a chainsaw to harvest his poles, but he did so with immense care, cutting close to the ground at an angle so that the rain would run off without rotting the stumps. He had worked around the coppices hereabouts for nearly six decades and returned to each one over a regular cycle, so that he had only himself to blame if they deteriorated in the meantime. They didn't. He was in his seventies then and well aware that he would never cut this

Charcoal burners provided one of the vital ingredients in the iron-smelting process. These shadowy characters travelled around the country, often in gangs, working in remote locations

particular patch again but, like all good wood-landers, he worked for future generations as well as for himself, and it was a matter of great pride to leave the stumps in perfect condition so that they would continue to be productive for many decades yet.

Everything about Dick's work was neat and methodical. His actions were precise, economical and unhurried, but hugely productive. He wasted nothing – neither time nor material. He learned long ago that skill pays: that it is a waste of effort to rush your work and risk ruining a pole with a mistimed blow. When he was young, and learning from George Boniface, they were lucky to make a farthing a pale and considerably less than a tanner a bundle. In those days he could make perhaps ten bob a day if he stuck with it, and could earn getting on for twice as much as a general farmworker. But it was all piecework, and it paid to be productive. It also paid to be tidy, if not for their own pride then for the gratitude of the landowner.

The last time I saw Dick, he had just finished a different cant along the top lane. He had paused in his work: he remarked that he had 'a little problem' and was due to visit the doctor that afternoon. Later, hearing that he was in hospital I went to visit him. But he had died an hour or two before I arrived. I never had the chance to say goodbye.

Whenever one greeted Dick and asked, 'How's life?', he would reply, 'Oh, you know me, always complaining.' it was not true. He was not as warmly enthusiastic about life as his brother George, not as beamingly cheerful, but he liked working out there in the woods, watching the wildlife, hearing the birds, imagining how it must have all been long, long ago, and plying his craft, knowing that his was always a job well done and that he could be satisfied he had lived up to old Boniface's careful tutelage. He was at ease with the woodland ghosts of the past and, long after his own death in the spring of 1992, the coppices will remember him and bear witness to his care and his skill.

Of Farriers and Cow Doctors

*Jack and Alan Walker:
Warwickshire and Oxfordshire*

OF FARRIERS AND COW DOCTORS

Warwickshire, the home of the Royal Agricultural Society of England's permanent showground at Stoneleigh, was an appropriate county for the historical exhibition, The Making of the Vet. The exhibition looked at the work of veterinary surgeons, and of the farriers and cow doctors who preceded them, over the last 250 years within the county. Among the many intriguing items on display were a bill sent out in the 1930s by 'Mr Walker, a castrator from Long Compton', and a photograph of 'William Walker, the Cow Doctor of Long Compton, south Warwickshire'. Instruments and reference books used by Walker were also displayed.

William senior's pony and trap

William Walker's grandson, Alan Walker, is a veterinary surgeon who practises from Hook Norton, just over the border into Oxfordshire on the heavier ironstone soil. The approach to the village is a delight, past fields that seem to grow smaller and smaller, with numerous fruit trees in the hedgerow along the quiet lane. The village itself is hidden until you pass under an archway of trees, and then suddenly there it is, all honey-stone cottages, some with thatch and some with stone roofs.

The surgery, however, is in a vaguely suburban street, with a splendid yard with looseboxes and lambing quarters. Within the unpretentious but quite extensive surgery building there is much activity of veterinary nurses and office staff, but all very relaxed and friendly.

Alan Walker ambles in, a large, affable man with short brown hair, looking much younger than his actual age (he was born in 1946). As we move out of doors, however, there is a degree of stiffness to his gait that seems to suggest a

problem with his hips, though he does not admit to it. We climb into his faintly battered car, with its bootful of veterinary bits and pieces apparently thrown in at random but their whereabouts all known to him. There is a horse-head mascot on the car bonnet: Alan is a horse vet by preference.

On the long drive to a distant client near Rugby, Alan is constantly pointing out local landmarks and giving little potted local histories, both general and personal. His family has lived around here for many generations, and he can trace his ancestral 'vets' all the way back to the sixteenth century:

'They were farriers, blacksmiths, cattle doctors in those days, always in Long Compton, which was conveniently placed on the old London coaching road about half-way between Oxford and Birmingham. It was where they would have a changeover of the horses, which meant that they needed people to shoe them and deal with any problems. So my forefathers were right there. They were country people, and as well as shoeing horses, they used all sorts of herbal remedies, some of which I still use today.

'Then when the railways came and coaching went into decline, the railway companies used to bring cattle and sheep, bought cheaply from the Welsh hills, and unload them at Moreton station. They'd then be taken by drovers over to Banbury (another big railway centre) to go to the east of the country for good prices. The main drovers' route was through Long Compton, and so my family became cattle doctors as well as farriers.'

In our tour of the countryside between Hook Norton and Rugby he points out the route of the old droveways and the tollgates that the drovers did their best to avoid along the way. At intervals he points out some of the many farms within his practice, and he knows the history and characters of each one – for example, how one has developed from a couple of milch cows to a 250-cow dairy herd.

The cattle doctors seemed to spend most of their time dealing with lameness and castrations, and also de-horning the cattle – almost an insult in a region which was once dominated by the splendid Longhorn breed of the Midlands. They had no medicines other than their own remedies, and they were adept at techniques such as pumping up a milk-fever cow's udder so that the pressure would stop the flow of milk and the loss of calcium that accompanied it.

'My grandfather, William, continued the tradition – in those days they handed everything down, father to son, and he had learned everything from his own father, also William. He still did his rounds in a pony and trap, dressed in breeches and gaiters and wearing a grey bowler hat. He was known as "Dr" Walker and I still have his horse twitch. Unfortunately he was killed in a car accident, as a passenger, in 1946.'

William James Walker was sixty-nine when he was killed two days after Christmas and he was given a substantial obituary in the local paper:

'Mr Walker's expert handling of sick animals resulted in many farmers and the like seeking his aid on such occasions. His jovial and unselfish nature endeared him to many, and it will be long before people in the hills get used to the absence of that cheery, grey bowler-hatted figure. Born in Long Compton, Mr Walker had lived there all his life, and in such a sporting community, it was not surprising that he was very fond of cricket and shooting.'

'My father, Joseph John Walker (known as Jack), born in 1911, and his brother Alf, were both veterinary practitioners. Before the 1950s anybody could practise in veterinary work, but then they brought in new regulation: anybody in practice in 1953 but who had not qualified through college was invited to sign a supplementary veterinary register. They had to go to Portman Square and prove that they had earned their living mainly by veterinary means in the seven years since the war. How did they prove it? By the fact that they'd been paid! Farmers are very shrewd judges of people, especially when it involves money. So my father and uncle were both on the register as veterinary practitioners; though the ones before that didn't need to be on any register – there had been no control.

'The work then was mostly large animals and horses, and a bit with pigs and poultry, though we don't do these now because they are farmed on such a large scale that they have their own specialists. They would not have done anything with small animals, apart from perhaps a working sheep-dog now and then.

William Walker senior, in gaiters

Telephone : LONG COMPTON 6
Telegrams : LONG COMPTON.

W. J. WALKER & SONS
CASTRATORS,
LONG COMPTON, SHIPSTON-ON-STOUR.
HORSES, CALVES, LAMBS, PIGS, Etc.
HORSES AND CALVES CASTRATED WITHOUT THROWING.
Operations carefully performed. :: Ruptured Colts a Speciality.
Bulls Rung. Distance no object.
Infallible remedy for Scour in Calves.

Left: Young William with his family Right: smoking his pipe

'Father worked with William right through the war; they got on well together. But when William died in 1946, father moved from Long Compton and was denounced for it by the family: his mother thought it a heresy that there were no Walkers in Long Compton any more. Alf was in the yeomanry and as much a farmer as a practitioner, but veterinary work had been father's sole means of living; he moved to Burmington in 1949 and continued the practice there. He was very much a horse man, but did cattle and sheep as well, and would look at the old cottage pig or whatever when necessary. He did not shoe horses; nor had William, but William's father had done so.

'Father died at the age of seventy-seven; he had gone into partnership at Burmington, but it hadn't worked out very well because he had always been very much his own man. If he didn't like someone, he wouldn't go there. If he started treating something and they didn't have faith in him, he'd not go back again. He was a hard-drinking man; he had his first drink at nine in the morning, and was very temperamental. He

and I never hit it off very well until my mother died, and then I got to know him better for the last ten years of his life.'

Alan was born in July 1946; his grandfather died five months later, happy to know that Jack had a son to continue the family tradition. In due course Alan went to Cambridge, but not to study veterinary medicine: he did a degree in biology and a doctorate in biochemistry first. Naturally he had always been interested in veterinary work, but on leaving school his A-levels had not been good enough to enter veterinary college immediately. Therefore it was not until 1981 that he finally qualified as a veterinary surgeon.

'In later years father had terrible arthritis in his hips; and he'd been knocked around quite a bit. The practice was dwindling – his partner had gone on to the small animal side at Shipston, and he carried on alone, though he really wasn't physically capable of doing so. But people were loyal to him, and I still go to some of his old friends even now.

'He knew that I'd started at Cambridge, and he was hanging on until I'd finished my five-year

William the younger in middle age, with his wife and daughter

there in September 1981, living over the surgery – a garage – and paying an old boy to drive my father if the older clients wanted to see him.

'At that stage we had no more than two or three calls a day, but there was a lot of good will and I'd grown up around here so people knew me and came back to us. Three months after I joined him, father went into hospital for his first hip operation and never worked again – he had a frame and sticks, and hated people seeing him like that. From being fairly rotund, he lost weight and became gaunt, and it embarrassed him for people to see the change in him. But he still expressed his opinions!

training, expecting me to join him in the practice. I really didn't want to come straight back home, but he was so immobile that I had to – he kept asking me when I was coming back. I'd been offered a job in Newmarket, and I said I'd come back on condition that he sacked the accountant, and on condition that he worked for me, not the other way around. He didn't want that! But after three months he said, "Do what you like!" So I moved the practice to Hook Norton and started

'Within five years the practice expanded from being just myself to three of us; and now we have six vets, four nurses, three receptionists and two secretaries, and we have been computerised for the last ten years. It's a mixed practice, but there is still a lot of large animal work, perhaps 80 per cent, and the biggest single thing

Jack Walker with his family, including Alan as a boy

is horses, which I like. I don't do any small animal work myself.'

We arrive at the clients' stables near Rugby, a big old stone farmhouse with a large cobbled yard surrounded by looseboxes, assorted horses peering over every stable door. A plump, friendly yellow labrador accompanies us as Alan makes his rounds, checking over a horse for sale, sounding out a snotty-nostrilled mare with a possible heart problem, looking for a murmur and finding her 'thick in her wind'. His next task is to rasp the teeth of a very active young stallion; and another pony has an enormous wart which he treats with his own ointment, made to a family recipe more than a hundred years old.

We adjourn to the kitchen for the essential mug of tea and the equally essential local gossip that keeps country vets in touch. As we leave, a small group of young hounds play in the yard with a sheepdog pup. 'That sarcoid wart,' he says

later, 'I inherited the recipe. Father used to make it up himself. They all made up their own stuff, their powders and their drenches and so on, getting the materials from a wholesale chemist. There was a big one in Coventry. I go to Loveridges in Southampton for mine. I use a lot of herbal remedies. I recognise the need for homoeopathy, too – a lot of clients like it, but it is quite expensive. I've tried things like snake venom, but I don't think it works.

'A lot of the herbs are Indian. I use some on nervous race-horses – I did that with one neurotic horse, lovely remedy for it, and the horse finished second; they were over the moon with it. I use herbal remedies for joint-ill; I use hellebore; comfrey for wounds and for encouraging horses to eat, ivy for sheep, arsenic for conditioning horses – it really makes them shine and all the old carters used it every week. Some of the stuff I can't get any more, or not easily, but there

are two firms that can usually help, or I collect herbs from the garden, often the client's garden. The herbs that I do use, I use quite often, though my father would have used many more.

'As well as herbs and conventional drugs, I also use ultrasound and laser and Faradic machines, electromagnetic pulse machines, and a fibre-optic endoscope.'

He talks of other treatments increasingly used by some vets, including therapeutic swimming. Alan's father used to 'swim' horses years and years ago, well ahead of his time; it is the ideal exercise for a lame horse that cannot bear its own weight, or as therapy for any pulled muscles. He would swim them in the canal, above the lock gates, with a man on a rope on either towpath.

We pass through Shipston and then Burmington, the place where Jack Walker had

moved to from Long Compton; Alan points out the old coaching road and its sturdy, stonebuilt lodges. And finally we come to Long Compton itself. The area hereabouts is one of gentle hills and there is a friendly feel to the landscape. In the village we pass an old stone on which, says Alan, the old fellows used to sit and watch the horses go by.

'This is the old road. The sheep came along here with the drovers but there was a tollgate at the top – so much a head to go through – and so they found ways round. Now we're passing the Rollright Stones and the King Stone.' There are fine views from up here, and a strong sense of place. Alan relates the legend of the Stones and then returns abruptly to the present.

'Last weekend was really impossible, and you can set your clock by it. June is quite busy, July can be really good; August is the holidays and I go away for three weeks. The first week in September is quiet. And then, bang! We shall be flat out now until June again. The horses are coming in from the fields, the cattle begin to come in, the autumn calving period starts, the sheep are going to the ram so there's a lot of fertility work in rams and ewes – it all just comes together at the same time.

'My father, of course, never took holidays. It was a way of life for him: his work was his pleasure. He enjoyed country pursuits, he enjoyed taking part in them with his clients and his friends. It's different now, you don't get many single-handed practices and there are far more veterinary surgeons who are not rurally inclined, not interested in the country way of life.'

One wonders about the future of the rural practice. Certainly there can be very few left now that can boast a family connection stretching back over four hundred years. Alan's predecessors would never have dreamed that at Hook Norton there would be a formal 'veterinary hospital' dealing with everything from Shire horses to pet mice, with its own laboratory and its on-site facilities for diagnosing and treating the ailments of horses, cattle, sheep and goats.

Despite all the advances in this very modern practice, Alan Walker is proud to retain the old-fashioned image of being a caring country practice, where animal welfare is of the utmost importance and where, when modern treatments are inadequate, he can fall back on the old family herbal remedies that have proved themselves over the centuries.

On the shelf of his office in the surgery, above the computer on the desk, Alan still has countless old books, all well thumbed by his father, his grandfather and no doubt his great-grandfather as well. In amongst them is a hand-written notebook, its fly page entitled *The Recept Book for Cattle*. It contains page after page of recipes for cures, everything from coughs and indigestion to scour and strains, warts and wounds. Recipes gleaned from various sources are written on scraps of paper or old postcards stuffed between the pages, some clearly very old by the style of the writing and the fragility of the paper. It is a veritable treasure-chest, and it is Alan Walker's heritage.

INDEX

THE CONTRIBUTORS

JOHN BAILEY studied history at university and then taught the subject for several years before concentrating on a life of travel, writing and photography. He specialised in the 18th and 19th centuries, notably the social history of the countryside. he is the author of several books, is co-presenter of BBC2's *Countryside Hour*, and now lives on the 18th-century Gunton Estate in Norfolk.

LOUISE BRODIE lived abroad for many years before returning to England to bring up her children. After completing an Open University degree she worked for the Museum of London, where one of her responsibilities was to conduct over two hundred interviews with people who worked on the River Thames and in Docklands. She has also worked on a television series on this subject.

EUAN CORRIE was brought up in southern Manchester, and on leaving school worked for a ship's agent, dealing mostly with Soviet cargo ships. He was then skipper of a pair of hotel narrowboats on the canals, before joining the editorial staff of the leading inland waterway magazine *Waterways World* in 1986. Since 1997 he has been Books & Guides Editor for Waterways World Ltd, also contributing a wide variety of articles to *Waterways World*, particularly of a historical and photographic nature. Euan bought his own narrowboat in 1979 and has travelled the English inland waterway system widely.

JENNIFER DAVIES' father was a Herefordshire farmer of the old kind, who used horses until tractors became prevalent. She has worked as a television researcher and associate producer, and has written a series of books concerning the Victorian garden and kitchen. She has also written books on Gypsies and the progress off the flower shop in Britain. She lives near Ledbury and combines writing with looking after poultry, old hayfields, bees and trees.

JOHN HUMPHREYS was born and brought up in a Fenland village where the land was worked by Shire horse power and the people were close to the land. The eldest son of a parson, early exposure to the countryside and its pastimes were to shape his life. He has written the popular 'country Gun' column in *Shooting Times* for many years, and twenty books on fieldsports and country ways, including *Poachers' Tales* for David & Charles. He trains gun dogs, runs a lowlands shoot, chases grouse in Yorkshire and geese in Scotland, and fishes for trout and carp on his own little reserve in Cambridgeshire, Hunter's Fen, which won a Laurent-Perrier conservation award in 1991.

BRIAN P. MARTIN has written numerous books on country life and natural history, including seven in David & Charles 'Tales from the Countryside' series, as well as the award-winning *Sporting Birds of Britain and Ireland*. After many years as a commissioning editor for *Shooting Times* and *Country Magazine*, he has been a full-time author since 1991. He has contributed to many magazines and newspapers, and is well-known for his 'Rusticus' column in both *Shooting Times* and *The Countrymen*. When not writing, he may be found propping up the bar in his local village pub, the Dog & Pheasant, where he has been a regular for over twenty years.

TOM QUINN has worked on everything from *The Times* to *Trout and Salmon* magazine and is a former editor of *The Countryman*. He has written three books for David & Charles in the 'Tales of the Countryside' series and has also written books about sporting art, World War One, antique collecting, and a biography of the artist and writer Denys Watkins Pitchford.

VALERIE PORTER lives in a Sussex cottage next door to a vet. She edits numerous agricultural veterinary and biology books, as well as writing her own books about wildlife, livestock, pets and rural life in general, three of which have been published by David & Charles. She is also the author of the highly successful title, *Yesterday's Countryside*, also published by David & Charles.

JEAN STONE is an historic garden consultant and garden designer who has lectured for horticultural societies, garden schools and the Architectural Association. Once winner of the *Sunday Times* 'Design a Period Garden' competition, her entry a 'Victorian Rustic Garden', was built at the RHS Chelsea Flower Show, where it won a silver medal. This was followed by her book, *The Rustic Garden*. Another of her books, *Voices from the Waterways*, is an invaluable record of an almost vanished way of life as once lived on British Waterways.

PHOTOGRAPHS were supplied by the following:
Pages 8, 16, 28, 38, 58, 70, 86, 98, 110, 118, 126, 138, 150, 156, 168, 171 (Keystone); 172, 183, 192, 201, 202, 212, 223, 224, 227, 227, 229(btm) (Topical Press Agency); 216, 225 (Picture Post); 226, 232(top) (Keystone); 234, 245, 246, 258, 270, 277, 278, 294, 296, 307, 312 Hulton Getty; 18, 26 The Beeson family; 19 Tom Quinn; 22, 24 Milepost; 30(top), 31, 32(top&btm), 34, 37 The Ware Family; 30(btm), 120, 123 145, 146, 194, 200, 204, 205, 208, 209(top&btm), 210(btm), 243(top), 244, 248, 256, 268, 273, 276, Brian P Martin; 40, 41, 42 BW Archives, Gloucester; 43, 48(top), 51, 52, 53(top), 54(top), 54(ctre), 55(top&btm) Sam Horne; 44, 45, 47 Sam & Gladys Horne; 48(btm), 53(btm), 54(btm) Gladys Horne; 50 The Boat Museum; 56 Alan Faulkner; 60(top), 62, 68 The Wood Family; 61, 63, 64, 175, 178, 281, 283(rt) The Museum of Rural Life, University of Reading; 7 (top&btm), 75, 76, 77, 82 Arthur Showell; 81 Charles Martell; 83 Mike Roberts; 100, 101, 103, 107, 108 GS McCann; 104 Associated Photo Services; 105 Bertram Unne; 112, 113, 114, 117 The Sharp Family; 121, The Clark family; 128, 129 Jean Stone & Louise Brodie; 130, 132, 134, 137 Hillier Nurseries; 140(top), 148 Crown Copyright; 140(btm) The Williams Family; 144 The Post Office; 152(top&btm), 153, 154 (top&ctre), 155 The Hardacre Family; 161, 168 AA Photo Library; 158(btm), 167(illus GC Wilmhurst, *The London Magazine* Dec 1903) Mary Evans Picture Library; 159, 164, 166, 169 John Bailey; 158(top), 160, 162 Geoff Hall; 174, 180 The Clarke Family; 210(top) the Lillywhite Family; 214, 215, 218, 219, 220, 221, 222, 230, 231, 232(btm) John Bailey; 228, 229, 233 Beaulieu House; 236, 243(btm) Western Morning News; 241, 266, 272, 274 Beaford Archive; 260, 261, 262, 263, 268 The Gwynne Family; 275 *The Countryman* magazine; 280(top&btm), 285, 291(top&btm), George Quinnell; 282, 283(lft) Valerie Porter; 287 New Forest Ninth Centenary Trust; 298(top&btm), 299, 300, 301(rt&lft), 302(top&btm) The Walker Family.